A History of Women and Ordination

Volume 1: The Ordination of Women in a Medieval Context, by John Hilary Martin, O.P., edited by Bernard Cooke and Gary Macy.

Volume 2: The Exclusion of Women from the Priesthood, by Ida Raming, edited by Bernard Cooke and Gary Macy.

A History of Women and Ordination

Volume 1:
The Ordination of Women in Medieval Context

Edited by Bernard Cooke and Gary Macy

The Scarecrow Press, Inc.
Lanham, Maryland, and London
2002

SCARECROW PRESS, INC.

Published in the United States of America
by Scarecrow Press, Inc.
A Member of the Rowman & Littlefield Publishing Group
4720 Boston Way, Lanham, Maryland 20706
www.scarecrowpress.com

4 Pleydell Gardens, Folkestone
Kent CT20 2DN, England

British Library Cataloguing in Publication Information Available

Library of Congress Cataloging-in-Publication Data

A history of women and ordination.
     p. cm.
   Includes bibliographical references and index.
   Contents: v. 1. The ordination of women in medieval context / edited by Gary Macy
and Bernard Cooke.
     ISBN 0-8108-4327-7 (alk. paper)
     1. Ordination of women—History. I. Macy, Gary. II. Cooke, Bernard J.

   BV676 .H57 2002
   262'. 14'08209—dc21   2002020090

♾™ The paper used in this publication meets the minimum requirements of
American National Standard for Information Sciences—Permanence of
Paper for Printed Library Materials, ANSI/NISO Z39.48-1992.
Manufactured in the United States of America.

Contents

Acknowledgments   v

Introduction to the Series   vii

Introduction to Volume 1   xi

1   The Ordination of Women in the Early Middle Ages   1
Gary Macy

2   The Ordination of Women
and the Theologians in the Middle Ages   31
John Hilary Martin

Bibliography   161

Index   177

About the Authors and Editors   183

Acknowledgments

First and foremost the editors would like to thank Fr. John Hilary Martin who graciously allowed us to edit his excellent article and to translate the extensive references in that article. His enthusiasm, helpful critiques and prompt replies to our numerous requests made the project a joy.

We would also like to thank the editors of *Escitos del Vedat* and of *Theological Studies* for granting us permission to reprint the two articles which appear in this volume. Without their cooperation this project would have been impossible. We would also like to thank the University of San Diego for the generous grants that allowed the editors to finish this work. Our grateful thanks as well to Vivian Holland who prepared our manuscript for camera ready copy and caught many errors in the process.

We would be remiss as well if we did not acknowledge the many feminist scholars who over the years encouraged us to pursue the history of women in Christianity. To name a just a few of the most important, Dr. Evelyn Kirkley who first suggested to us that a study of women's ordination would be valuable, Dr. Pauline Turner who kept us focused on the value of a feminist approach, Dr. Joann Wolski Conn, Sr. Vera Chester, and Dr. Jane Via, who for so many years provided invaluable insights and correctives to our inevitable male approach.

Finally, we wish to thank all those who encouraged us again and again to make the sources on women's ordination available to as wide an audience as possible. Members of Call to Action and of WomenChurch in particular wished to have easier access to the history and sources of the continuing historical debate on women's ordination.

Introduction to the Series

During the past half century, few issues have been more prominent and disputed in religious circles than has the ordination of women. This has been most acutely felt in the Roman Catholic, Orthodox and Anglican Churches, but other Christian groups as well as Judaism have not been completely exempt. Beginning with 1975 and the first national conference on women's ordination in Detroit, a meeting that drew national attention and eventuated in formation of the Women's Ordination Conference, there has been a continuing and vocal demand by increasing numbers of Catholics that there be a reconsideration and reform of women's status in the Church. Basically this has been a demand for full equality for women, but ordination to both diaconate and presbyterate has consistently been seen as the key symbolic recognition of such equality.

The Detroit conference drew more than national attention. Within a few months the Vatican responded with a letter on the non-ordination of women, a document that was widely criticized but did much to frame debate on the topic. Without detailing its line of argument, one of its principal points was that the long-standing tradition of the Church has always seen women as incapable of ordination. Ordination today would be contrary to this tradition and so, while Church officials appreciated the important role of women in the Church, their equality as members, and the depth of their faith and commitment, extending this to ministerial ordination lay outside the authority and power of Church officials. Change was not only inadvisable; it was impossible. For the moment, debate centered on the question of whether such a long-standing tradition should prove an obstacle; and in the absence of accurate historical knowledge, the impression in many circles was that the question of women's ordination was a very recent phenomenon, an outgrowth of the contemporary "feminist movement."

Careful top-level theological, historical, and biblical examination of the Papal argumentation disagreed with it and concluded that there did not appear to be any intrinsic block to the ordination of women. But that did not alter the Papal position nor close off the discussion. The Women's Ordination Conference has continued in existence; several other women's organizations have emerged to further urge the issue, an attempt of the U.S. bishops to skirt the question by a pastoral letter on women's role in the church foundered on women's organized objection, and support for women's ordination has gradually grown in most parts of the worldwide Church.

Meanwhile the Anglican Churches throughout the world have confronted the question and despite strong objections from some quarters have officially moved to ordination. In the United States this was triggered by the extra-legal ordination of some women in 1974, a move that was first declared "invalid" but then accepted within a year as "illicit" by the Episcopalian House of Bishops. But the deed was done. Since then Anglican ordination of women has become common; a few women have even been ordained as bishops; and some members, including clergy, have left the Anglican Church and "gone to Rome" in protest.

In Roman Catholic circles as well as in the Eastern Orthodox Churches the official position remains firmly in opposition to women's ordination. Attempting to quell growing popular support and ongoing pressure from women's groups, the Vatican attempted to suppress discussion of the issue. In 1998 a document was promulgated that forbade further debate of the question, since presumably it had been definitively decided by Papal decree. Not surprisingly, this statement proved counter-productive: to deny responsible dissent from Papal teaching on the topic was widely recognized as unenforceable and discussion was probably intensified by this move.

While all this was happening as a high-profile and rather acrimonious event, another question that was inseparably bound up with women's ordination was emerging almost unnoticed. This was the question regarding ordination itself: What was the intrinsic character of ordination in the Christian Churches? What was the actual historical origin of episcopal and presbyteral ordination in Christianity? And what did ordination effect; how did it change those who were ordained?

In Roman Catholicism, these questions were affected by the stance of Vatican II. Above all, the council's recognition of the ministerial responsibility and empowerment of all members of the Church, the people of God, raised questions about the role and power of the ordained. If the faithful were empowered by baptism to undertake most of what had come to be a clerical monopoly of ministry, what was left to the ordained as distinctively theirs? The response seemed clear: only the ordained were empowered to perform the sacramental actions, most importantly as celebrants of the Eucharist; but that was not as clear as it looked.

Implicit in both debates—about women's ordination and about the role of the ordained clergy—was the same assumption, that "ordination" had always meant what it has come to mean in recent centuries and means for people today. Scholarly research, above all by Yves Congar, had uncovered evidence that only in the twelfth-century had "ordination" come to indicate an action that produced in the ordinand two intrinsic powers, the power to absolve sins and the power to change bread and wine in the Eucharist. Prior to that time, "ordinare" had quite a different meaning: to "ordain" a person was a matter of assigning that individual a social/ ecclesiastical status and role.

How accurate are the "new" understandings mentioned here? Is there responsible scholarly study that supports them? The answer is that for some decades there has been such study, but it has been largely unrecognized, sometimes arrogantly rejected as "marginal" by mainstream academe, and scarcely known by those engaged in the debates we have mentioned. It is to remedy this lack, to bring to public attention, to help clarify the truth about historical development in the thinking of Christianity that this series is published. Bringing again to people's notice the evidences of what actually was thought and done regarding ministerial ordination of both men and women will, we hope, help to make discussion of these issues more fruitful.

Introduction to Volume One

As explained in the introduction to the series, *A History of Women and Ordination*, the purpose of these volumes is to provide the non-specialist reader with the best scholarly research on the role of women in Christian ministry and on the changing shape of ministry in Christian history. This first volume contains two such papers. The first, by Dr. Gary Macy one of the editors of this series, presents the evidence for the ordination of women in the early Middle Ages. This evidence, however, is set in the larger context of the changing definition of ordination which took place in the twelfth-century.

Up until the twelfth-century, the Latin terms, *ordo* (order), *ordinatio* (ordination), and *ordinare* (to ordain) indicated one's role in the church or the society at large and the ritual which celebrated and effected the installment of a person into such a role. Since women as well as men fulfilled important roles in church and society, they were considered be "ordained" into these positions as much as were men. Thus, a king was said to be "ordained" when he was crowned king and so was a queen. An abbot was "ordained" when he was installed as abbot and so was an abbess. A deacon was "ordained" into the diaconate and so was a deaconess.

This changed in the twelfth-century when theologians and canonists began to insist that the only "true" ordination was an ordination to those roles which served at the altar, that is, the subdiaconate, the diaconate and the presbyterate. Further, only men could serve in these roles. In order to explain the many ancient sources that referred to the ordination of kings, queens, abbots, abbesses and deaconesses, the canonists held that these were merely blessings and not true ordinations. The ancient sources had been sadly inexact in their terminology. These arguments so completely won the day that scholars, such as Fr. Martin, could state that "there were, of course, no ordinations of women to Holy Orders during this period." Fr. Martin is referring, as the readers of his paper would certainly understand, to ordination in the sense that it has been used since the twelfth-century. In this sense, true sacramental ordination can only take place when a person is accepted into the orders of subdeacon, deacon, or priest; roles limited from the twelfth-century to males.

Dr. Macy's article, which originally appeared in *Theological Studies*, 61 (September, 2000): 481-507, gives the background to the earlier understanding of ordination and discusses some of the controversy surrounding the change in the definition of ordination which occurred in the twelfth-century. Dr. Macy further makes the point that merely establishing that the church once considered women to be properly and sacramentally ordained in the past does not immediately argue for or against ordaining women in the present. The Christian church has done many things in the past which Christians now would be loath to imitate, for instance, the Crusades or the inquisitions. Of course, Christians in the past have also done many admirable things present Christians might do well to revive. The question of which practices from the past we in the present ought to imitate (and which practices in the present should be abandoned) must be examined carefully and conscientiously and prayerfully based on the best discernment of the Spirit for present circumstances. Dr. Macy's article, then, is included to provide a general introduction to the history of ordination in Christian history that is essential for understanding of the changing role of women's status in Christian ministry and the relationship of such a history for the modern question of the ordination of women.

Fr. Martin's learned and detailed study takes up the question of the ordination of women after women had already been excluded from the ordained ministry. Originally published in the Spanish Dominican journal of theology, Fr. Martin's impressive study has until now been extremely difficult for audiences to obtain, particularly in the United States. Fr. Martin presents here an amazing array of sources, proving that there was a continuous interest in the question of why women could not be ordained. In fact, the question was a reoccurring concern of theologians from the thirteenth through the sixteenth-centuries, precisely at a time when women had already been excluded from sacramental ordination. The many authors discussed by Fr. Martin were concerned with giving a reasonable explanation as to why women were so excluded from the ordained ministry since there seemed to be no obvious reason why this should be done. The problem was compounded by the fact that these authors were aware of sources which referred to women as ordained.

As Fr. Martin demonstrates, there seems to have been no one consistent reason given for the exclusion of women from ordination and that many of the reasons given by modern Christians for not ordaining women differ from those of the later Middle Ages. Perhaps, the several reasons offered never quite justified the current practice and so had to be constantly refined and reasserted by each new generation of scholars. In any case, Fr. Martin's article provides an invaluable guide to the social, political, and theological background to the centuries-old Christian practice of excluding women from sacramental ordination.

In order to make the material in these studies more accessible to a wide range of readers, the Latin notes in both articles have been translated into English. Every translator is also a traitor as the old saying goes and this translation is no exception. Several editorial decisions needed to be made which affect the kind of English that appears in the translations. First, Fr. Martin, of course, had the final say in how he wished the Latin to be translated in his article, and while the editors take full responsibility for the translation, one working principle had to be respect for the intention of the author. Secondly, the academic Latin of the Middle Ages consisted mostly of class notes of one kind or another. They are not polished prose, and so neither is the English translation. The decision was made to stick as closely to the original structure and presentation of the Latin as decent (or at least acceptable) English would allow. The editors decided to err on the side of literal accuracy at the expense of literary elegance.

In a few cases, specific Latin words offered difficulties in translation. The clearest example of this is the Latin word *sacramentum*. In general, the word can be translated as "symbol," but in certain circumstances, *sacramentum* more clearly means "ritual" or "sacrament" in the English sense of the word. In order to aid the reader in following this ambiguity, the editors have placed the Latin word *sacramentum* in parentheses following the English translation of the word as "symbol," "ritual," or "sacrament." The medieval authors would have, of course, understood the word as having the overtones of all three of the English words, probably not distinguishing as carefully between the three as modern English speakers would do.

Finally, the editors have attempted in all cases to provide clear and precise references to the original Latin sources for those readers who wish to read the original for themselves. The editors certainly encourage readers to do so; another language creates another world that even the best translation cannot capture.

Chapter 1

The Ordination of Women in the Early Middle Ages

Gary Macy, University of San Diego

In her provocative work *The Lady Was a Bishop*, Joan Morris argued that the great mitered abbesses of the Middle Ages were treated as equivalent to bishops. In partial support of her contention, she quoted *a capitula* from the Mozarabic *Liber Ordinum*, which contains the chapter heading "Ritual (*Ordo*) for the Ordaining of an Abbess."[1] Despite this intriguing find, there seems to be no further research into the ordination of women in the early Middle Ages. A survey of early medieval documents demonstrates, however, how widespread the use of the terms *ordinatio, ordinare,* and *ordo* was in regard to the commissioning of women's ministries during these years. It appears not only to describe the installation of abbesses, as already noted by Ms. Morris, but also to deaconesses and to holy women, that is, virgins, widows, nuns, or canonesses (*monacha,* or *sanctimonialis*).

References to the Ordination of Women

Several medieval ordinals refer to the commissioning rites for women as ordinations. There is, of course, the Mozarabic ordinal mentioned by Morris. Here the entire rite for ordination follows the title, "*Ordo ad ordinandam abbatissam.*"[2] The editor of this rite, Marius Férotin, noted that he had found a second manuscript containing a rite "*De ordinatione et electione abbatisse*" in the Royal Academy of Science in Madrid. The rite seems to date from the eighth or ninth-century.[3] A romano-germanic Pontifical from the tenth-century offers two references to "*ordinatio abbatissae canonicam regulam profitentis.*"[4] A twelfth-century romano-germanic Pontifical in the library of Bamberg includes the section on the ordination of religious women "*Ordinatio sanctimonialium. Consecratio sacrae virginis quae in epiphania . . . celebratur.*" William of Durand's famous thirteenth-century pontifical contains both the title "*De ordinatione diaconissae*" and one later copy of that work adds as well as the title "*De ordinatione et consecratione virginum.*" William did add that although deaconesses once were ordained in the Church, this no longer took place.[5]

Popes and bishops, too, referred to the commissioning of deaconesses, abbesses and nuns as ordination. In 1018 Benedict VIII conferred on the Cardinal Bishop of Porto the right to ordain bishops, priests, deacons, deaconesses, subdeacons, churches, and altars.[6] Calixtus II, in a privilege of 1123 to the convent of the Holy Savior and St. Julia in Brescia, reminded the abbess that the bishop has the right to ordain abbesses, nuns, and all other clerics moved to take sacred orders.[7] Bishop Gilbert of Limerick included in his *De usu ecclesiae* the injunction "The bishop ordains abbots, abbesses, priests and the six other grades."[8] The Chronicle of Thietmar, Bishop of Merseburg (d. 1018), recorded that "the same woman who at that time was twelve years old was veiled on Sunday, the kalends of May and on the next day ordained abbess."[9] A tenth-century letter of Atto Bishop of Vercelli described the initiation of deaconesses in the early Church as an ordination, "Therefore for the aid of men, devout women were ordained leaders of worship in the holy Church."[10]

Other sources from this period speak of the ordination of women as well. The editors of the *Annales Camaldulenses* recorded a charter from the year 867 granting lands to establish a convent of twenty nuns. The donors, Count Winigris and his wife Richild, insisted that the selection and ordination of the abbess remain firmly in their hands and the hands of their successors.[11] A charter of the emperor Otto II dated 961 described how Bishop Bernhard of Halberstadt desired that a monastery for religious women be constructed and his niece, Gundradam, be ordained abbess in that place.[12] A charter dated 1043 from the convent of Saint-Geniès in Maguelone described how a young woman, Albergis, was elected and accepted by acclamation of her fellow nuns. "And in this same year the bishop ordained and blessed the aforementioned young woman."[13]

Finally, in an interesting but ambiguous passage from the *Rule for Virgins*, the seventh-century missionary Waldebert warned "None of the nuns should presume, however, either to receive confession or to give penance *sine ordinatione abbatissae*."[14] The phrase could either mean that confession and penance cannot be done without the permission of the abbess or confession and penance cannot be done without ordination to the state of abbess. Since the Rule does make provision for confession to be heard by the abbess' designate, the first meaning seems most likely.[15]

"Ordination" in the Early Middle Ages

This is by no means an exhaustive list of references to the ordination of women from the early Middle Ages. A thorough and determined search of the sources, I am certain, would be able to add considerably to this list. However, even this sampling demonstrates that neither liturgies nor popes nor bishops had a problem referring to particularly deaconesses and abbesses, but also nuns, as entering into an ecclesiastical order through a ritual ordination.[16] None of these sources distinguished the ordination of deaconesses, abbesses or nuns from that of priests or deacons. In fact, two of the sources include the ordination of women along with other forms of male clerical ordination. It should be noted as well that the sources quoted cover the fifth through the twelfth centuries, some seven hundred years, not an insignificant period of Christian history.

Did that mean, however, that abbesses or deaconesses or nuns were "ordained" in the sense that term would have in the later Middle Ages or after the Council of Trent? Was their ordination considered one of the seven sacraments? Did it impart an indelible and irreversible metaphysical mark as might ordination to the diaconate and to the presbyterate? The obvious historical answer is of course not.

While the understanding of ordination operative in these early centuries certainly underlie the later concept, there are significant differences. Ordination, for example, was not seen as irreversible until the thirteenth-century. Before that time, deposed clergy were considered laity and even reordained when recanting from heresy.[17] According to Nathan Mitchell, "Not until the fifteenth and sixteenth centuries did the Church's official teaching, expressed in ecumenical councils, directly affirm the view that order is a sacrament which is permanently effective and 'imprints character.'"[18]

Historically, the words *ordo*, *ordinatio*, and *ordinare* had a far different meaning in the early Middle Ages than they would come to have in later centuries. The problem with references to ordination in the Middle Ages, in fact, lies precisely in the lack of precision with which that term was used. Yves Congar, in a brilliant exploration into the words *ordinare* and *ordinatio,* suggests that particularly in the period before the thirteenth-century, considerable diversity existed both over what constitutes an *ordinatio* and which states or *ordines* should be considered "clerical."[19]

Pierre van Beneden has argued that early Christians appropriated the language of "ordination" for use in their communities not so much from Roman law as from everyday usage.[20] This "everyday" use of the terms *ordo* and *ordinare* continued throughout the Middle Ages, as even a cursory glance at any thesaurus of medieval Latin will show.[21] *Ordo* could refer simply to one's state of life and *ordinare* would still be used in its original sense of providing order either in a political or metaphoric sense.[22] It is no wonder that canonists and theologians had difficulty in clearly differentiating which of the many appointments to posts both civil and ecclesiastic actually counted as a true sacramental ordination as well as which aspects of those ordinations were sacramentally effective.

According to Pierre Marie Gy in an article on the ancient prayers of ordination, "at least in the patristic era, *ordinare* is greater than *consecrare* or *benedicere* and designates not only the prayer of ordination but all the ecclesial processes of which this was a part. As we have already seen, the term *ordinatio* had, after all, been applied in the high Middle Ages to kings, abbots, abbesses, and by imperial Christian law, to civil functionaries."[23] In fact, based on medieval examples given in the *Novum glossarium mediae latinitas*, the words *ordinatio* and *ordinare* were used to describe not only the ceremony and/or installation of bishops, priests, deacons and subdeacons but also of porters, lectors, exorcists, acolytes, canons, abbots, abbesses, kings, queens, and empresses. The terms could also apply to the consecration or establishment of a religious order or of a monastery or even to admission to the religious life.

The foundation charter from 867 mentioned above provides one striking example of the use of *ordinare* to indicate selection or election to a particular post. Even more dramatically, Orso, bishop of Olivolo near Venice in 853, appointed his sister, Romana, as the administrator of his will. He further directed her to watch his successor closely and if he should mismanage episcopal property, "she would have the most firm power to ordain the monastery [the basilica of St. Laurence] to any person she wished" after the death of the miscreant bishop.[24] So too, an *ordo* did not necessary refer to a particular clerical state. Innocent III described canon lawyers as a separate *ordo* in the early twelfth-century.[25] At least as late as the fourteenth-century, *ordo* could also be used to designate the sacrament of extreme unction and marriage would be referred to as an *ordo* as late as the fifteenth-century.[26]

Pope Leo the Great, in a letter later included in most important canon law collections, held that a valid ordination of a bishop could not occur unless the bishop had been chosen by the clergy, accepted by the Christian community and consecrated by the bishops of the province along with metropolitan bishop. Clearly "ordination" included more than just a particular sacramental ritual for Leo and those canonists who kept his ruling alive.[27]

According to Gerard Fransen in his study of ordination in medieval canon law, "For them [the medieval canonists] *ordinare, ordinatio* did not necessarily have a sacramental meaning. One calls *ordinatio* the election of a pope, the nomination of an archdeacon, the canonical establishment of a monk that he might administer a parish."[28]

Early medieval sources discussing ordination cannot be read with the assumption that they are discussing the same institution that would emerge from either Lateran IV or Trent. In fact, as interesting as the question of what ordination comprised in the early Middle Ages, is that of whom it encompassed. The Rule of Benedict used *ordinatio* frequently to refer to the installation of an abbot.[29] Abbots, monks, and others entering the religious life were referred to as ordained throughout the early Middle Ages.[30] Kings and emperors were also considered to be ordained by themselves and/or by their contemporaries. According to Congar, "To be ordained" was the official formula of the Capetians for their coronation.[31] Pope Urban II in a letter of 1089 to Rainold, archbishop of Rheims, affirmed the archbishop's power to ordain the kings and queens of France.[32] In another example of the use of *ordinatio* for a queen, the *Annales Altahenses maiores* for the year 1043 described how King Henry led his bride to Mainz and here arranged for her to be consecrated queen, and then "having completed the days of ordination (*diebus ordinationis*) in Ingelheim, the region made preparations for the marriage."[33] The coronation rite contained in a Florentine sacramentary from the second half of the tenth-century introduces the blessing of the Empress with the description "the ordination of the Empress at the entrance to the church."[34]

Kings and queens, emperors and empresses often considered themselves and were considered by their contemporaries to be validly ordained into an important *ordo* of the Church. To quote Henry Chadwick, "So Western a writer as Pope Leo the Great can tell the orthodox Greek emperor that he is invested not only with *imperium* but with a priestly office (*sacerdotium*) and that by the Holy Spirit he is preserved from all doctrinal error."[35] No doubt such claims were more impressive when backed up with an army, nevertheless, kingship (and queenship) represent an historical example of ecclesiastically supported ordination which later Roman Catholic theology would judge not to be ordination at all.

If the terms *ordo, ordinatio,* and *ordinare* did not necessarily entail "ordination" in the sense which Trent would later use the term, what exactly did it mean to "ordain" a deaconess, an abbess, or a nun during this time? If Congar is correct when he states that "the words *ordinare, ordinari, ordinatio* signified the fact of being designated and consecrated to take up a certain place, or better a certain function, *ordo*, in the community and at its service,"[36] then what functions did these women play in the lives of their communities?

The Roles of Ordained Women
Episcopae and Presbyterae

Women were commissioned for several different *ordines* in these early centuries. The vocations of widow, virgin, and deaconess were a continuation of early Christian practices.[37] The early Middle Ages also bore witness to the ministries of canonesses, abbesses, nuns, *episcopae,* and *presbyterae*. In this study, I am going to use the Latin terms, *episcopae* and *presbyterae* for the feminine form of what might be better termed simply bishops and priests. I use this terminology so that it is immediately clear that I mean women bishops and women priests. However to refer to these offices as "women bishops" or "women priests" might imply that this is a different office from simply bishop or priest. Since part of what I want to argue is that this differentiation is not all that clear for the period under discussion such terminology may not be useful. "Priestess" is also a possibility, but this title is still associated most commonly in English with non-Christian religions and can therefore be misleading. The usual titles for the ministries of deaconesses and abbesses do not present these problems and will be used throughout.[38] Although scholars disagree about both the relative importance and about relations among these different groups, they do agree that women who assumed these roles played an active part in the Church.[39]

Apart from living chastely, the form of life which *episcopae* and *presbyterae* entailed is unclear.[40] Beginning with the medieval canonists, scholars have habitually assumed that *episcopae* and *presbyterae* held no other function than that of spouse to a bishop or priest.[41] Recently, however, Ute Eisen has pointed out bishops' wives are usually referred to in sixth-century literature as *coniux*, not *episcopa*, and that *episcopa* seems to refer to a quite different role than merely that of a spouse. She summarizes her analysis of both the epigraphic and literary evidence: "We must conclude from this that as a rule the title *episcopa* was not applied to bishops' wives."[42] The ninth-century mosaic and reliquary inscriptions that mention "*Theodora episcopa*" obviously refer to a woman who was not married to a bishop, but was rather the mother of Pope Paschal I (817-824).[43]

Presbyterae present an equally controversial situation. Although the term can refer to the wives of priests, this does not always seem to be the case. A list of forbidden marriages ascribed to Pope Gregory II and included in the ninth-century Pseudo-Isidorian decretals includes injunctions against marrying *presyterae*, deaconesses, and nuns.[44] According to Michel Andrieu, these injunctions forbid *remarriage* for the wives of priests and deacons.[45] This seems somewhat odd in juxtaposition to a similar invocation against marriage for nuns and might be seen alternatively as a demand for celibacy equivalent to that ascribed to male priests and deacons.

Further, an interpolated translation of canon 11 of the Council of Laodicea (mid- to late-fourth century) included in the ninth-century Pseudo-Isidorian decretals forbade the installation of *presbyterae* in a church as if they were appointed to it (*ordinatas*).[46] Although the canon pertained originally to the fourth-century Greek Church, the interpolation indicates that a contemporary situation required the repetition and explanation of the earlier canon.[47] It described *presbyterae*, however, not as the wives of priests, but "women who are called *presbyterae* among the Greeks, but by us, however, they are called elder widows (*viduae seniores*), a once-married women (*unvira*), and little mothers (*matricularie*)."[48] The role that the bishops seek to curtail here appears to include more that just outliving a husband priest and does not, in fact, mention these women as specifically widows of priests.[49]

A letter by the tenth-century bishop, Atto of Vercelli, included a fascinating description of both *presbyterae* and deaconesses. Asked what the law says about *presbyterae* and deaconesses, Atto responded that in the early Church, because of a shortage of workers, devout women were appointed (*ordinantur*) to help men in leading the worship. Not only men, but also women, presided over the church because of the great need. Women had been long familiar with pagan cults and been educated in philosophy and so, when converted, were well suited to teach religious practice. Atto explained, basing himself on the law of the council of Laodicea discussed above, that *presbyterae* were no longer allowed by the Church. Atto described deaconesses as those who prepared other women for baptism through catechesis and then assisted at their baptism. Since most people are baptized as infants, Atto explained, this very rarely happens any more and women in any case have been forbidden to baptize. Atto's description of the former role of *presbyterae* and deaconesses is interesting, however. "As indeed those called *presbyterae* assumed their office by preaching, commanding or teaching, so deaconesses sensibly assumed their office by ministering and baptizing."[50] Atto did not completely rule out the existence of deaconesses in his own time. He alluded to some who claim that the office once called "deaconess" is now called "abbess." Atto disagreed, but only because the words "deaconess" and "abbess" come from very different roots.[51] Atto's argument would be taken up again in detail by the twelfth-century canonists.[52]

In conclusion, the roles which *episcopae* and *presbyterae* played in the early medieval Church remain unclear. A long-standing tradition asserts that these titles refer only to the spouses of male bishops and male priests. Yet, contemporary sources and modern interpretations of them suggest that both offices may have held independent clerical positions.

Deaconesses

Deaconesses present an even more detailed and interesting problem than *episcopae* and *presbyterae*. Michel Andrieu assumed that the term could refer to either the wife of a deacon or to a liturgically functioning deaconess whose exact role in the Church was unclear.[53] It does not seem necessary, as least to me, to separate these two forms of deaconess. Could it not be possible that deaconesses and *presbyterae* (and perhaps *episcopae)* at times formed a liturgical team with their spouse?[54] That would explain why according to a Roman Ordinal from c. 900, *presbyterae* and deaconesses received their commissioning at the same time and as part of the same ceremony as the priests and deacons who were their spouses. The prayers for the ordination of deaconesses in the several sacramentaries through the twelfth-century are identical, apart from the use of the feminine, to that used in the ordination of a deacon. Both deaconesses and *presbyterae* received special vestments as part of their ordination rites.[55] These rites do not seem to distinguish between those deaconesses (or *presbyterae*) who had an active ministry and those who were "merely" the spouses of priests and deacons. It seems at best questionable to assume that a wife cannot hold a ministry of her own alongside if not apart from her spouse, while at the same time assuming that a husband *is* able to so do. That women functioned as deaconesses, whether as spouses or not, does not, however, seem to be disputed in these early centuries.

Canonesses

Whether as the spouses of deacons or as unmarried deaconesses, women continued this ministry of the early Church at least into the sixth-century. Some scholars suggest that just as deaconesses were being slowly removed from the clerical state, canonesses came to the fore to continue the ministries once held by deaconesses.[56] Canonesses were religious women who lived in loose community under an abbess, but retained their own property and took no final vows of chastity. They could return to the world and marry if they so desired.[57]

Donald Hochsteller's study of religious women in this period suggests that canonesses played an important liturgical role in the Carolingian Church. His observations are worth quoting at length:

> That the involvement of consecrated women in the mass was a widespread phenomenon is confirmed by the Council of Paris of 829. The council gives us the most explicit description of what went on at services in which women assisted. It was found that in several provinces women "have of their own accord forced themselves up to the sacred altars and have impudently touched the sacred vessels and have assisted the priests with their vestments, and, what is even more indecent and more tasteless than all that, they have offered the body and blood of the Lord to the people and done other such things which are shameful even to mention."

The legislators at Paris went on to ascribe the involvement of women in the mass to the negligence and lack of attention of the bishops and to attack the priests who had so far abandoned their duties that they would let women do such a thing. From this declaration it is obvious that there was no question of women "forcing" themselves upon unwilling priests and parishioners. It is certain that women could not have gained access to the altar without the acquiescence of the officiating bishop or priest. Clearly, not all male religious leaders belonged to the reforming party. As for the people, they took the bread and wine from the hands of the women, so ordinary believers accepted the authority of certain women to administer the sacraments. There was no mention of scandal except among the reforming bishops of Paris.[58]

There do exist *ordines* for the distribution of communion which clearly were intended for use by women. As noted in my address to the CTSA,[59]

> Although described as communion services by Jean Leclercq, he admits that "nevertheless, in their ensemble they really constitute a long eucharistic prayer."[60] While modern liturgists would understand these communion services as a form of *missa sicca* (that is mass without a consecration) it is not altogether clear that they were so understood by the participants. Given that neither the moment of consecration nor the clerical state itself had yet been closely defined, these rituals may represent the last vestiges of liturgies lead by women for their own communities.[61]

In conclusion, then, whatever role they did play, either the full liturgical role envisioned by Hochsteller or the lesser role envisioned by Andrieu, women clearly were considered to form their own *ordines* during this period and were perceived to hold as much of an "ordained" position in the Church as bishops, priests, or deacons. Indeed, Benedict IX in 1033 in a letter to Peter, the bishop of Silva Candida proclaimed all clerics free of lay duties including the orders of priest, deacon, monk, hermit, cleric, religious woman, and deaconess.[62] Further, these women fulfilled an important liturgical ministry, one that was gradually reduced by some elements of the episcopacy over a period of some four hundred years. They were, for all intents and purposes, ordained clerics in the sense that many early medieval writers would understand that category.

Abbesses

The role of abbesses in this period is much clearer than that of their sister ministers.[63] Since several rules for holy women have survived from this period, a better idea of the liturgical and clerical roles of abbesses can be ascertained. Abbesses clearly exercised functions later reserved to the male diaconate and presbyterate. The best example would be the responsibility, indeed, duty of the abbess to hear her nuns' confessions.[64] This is mentioned by at least two of the Rules for nuns from the early medieval period. The writers go on at great length about the necessity of the abbess (or her designate) to hear daily confession.[65] One of the main virtues required of an abbess was a merciful yet firm use of penance to train the nuns under her care. Abbesses also preached, as indeed did other orthodox religious women in the Middle Ages.[66] Two of the Rules indicate that abbesses may have baptized children brought to the monasteries.[67] The abbesses' power to remove nuns from either table or the divine office or both is regularly termed "excommunication."[68] The abbesses of Monheim, at least, distributed the eulogia, or bread blessed during the liturgy, to the laity.[69] One of the *Regula ad virgines* includes readings from the Gospel as part of the Divine Office to be said by the nuns.[70] In fact several twelfth-century canonists argued that the reading of the gospel by abbesses was proof that they were the successors to the earlier *ordo* of deaconess.[71] Evidence also exists that abbesses gave blessings to lay people and consecrated those nuns who entered their monasteries.[72]

The Debates of the Twelfth-Century Canonists

Indeed it is precisely the functions of abbesses mentioned above that Innocent III condemned in his letter of 1210 to the Bishop of Burgos and Abbot of Morimundo: "(Abbesses) . . . bless their own nuns, hear their confessions of sin and, reading the Gospel, presume to preach publicly."[73] At least at the time of Innocent, abbesses were thought to be still performing all of the roles mentioned above and the Pope was not happy about it. Innocent's ruling, as one might imagine, did not come as a bolt from the blue. It had been preceded by a half-century of canonical debate concerning the possibility of women's ministries. Dr. Raming has presented a thorough and intriguing study of this discussion. The canonists were clearly wrestling with broad concept of ordination that they had inherited. What did it mean, for instance, when earlier laws (and even contemporary practice) spoke of women as "ordained" and, if women were once ordained, on what grounds were they now excluded from ordination? Since Dr. Raming has provided a lucid discussion of the later question, I will concentrate on the answers the canonists offered on the first of these conundrums.

The majority followed Gratian of Bologna, the collator of the massive collection of church law known as the *Decretum*, in arguing that women could not be ordained, although not all the scholars gave their reasons for doing so.[74] The influential writers Rolandus Bandinelli, [75]Stephen of Tournai,[76] and Huguccio[77] granted that women had once been ordained but the Church later disallowed the earlier practice. Rolandus and Stephen seem to hold that there is no intrinsic reason why deaconesses could not be ordained once again if church law should so dictate.[78] The possibility of this happening was real, since most canonists agreed with Atto's colloquist that the former role of deaconess had been replaced by the contemporary position of abbess.[79] The canonists, incidentally, were joined in this opinion by the twelfth-century theologian and monk, Abelard in a letter to his wife, Heloise, herself an abbess.[80]

Other canonists, starting with Rufinus, distinguished between an "ordination" which is merely a blessing, or the granting of a particular function, and an "ordination" which is sacramental. For the majority of canonists who make this distinction, the "ordination" of deaconesses, or *presbyterae*, or of abbesses are clearly of the first, non-sacramental variety.[81] A few canonists held that not only were the ordinations of deaconesses in the early Church valid, sacramental ordinations, but so too were the contemporary "ordinations" of holy women. In the words of Raming, the anonymous author of the *Summa Monacensis*, "calls the *manus impositio consecratoria religionis* given to God-dedicated virgins a sacrament, just like the *manus impositio consecratoria ordinis* for priests and deacons."[82] Since this "ordination" is a sacrament, the author contended, it cannot be repeated.[83] Cardinal Sicard of Cremona followed the *Summa* in this opinion, although he also held that women could not be validly ordained priests or deacons.[84] The *Apparatus* on the *Decretum* written by Joannes Teutonicus after the Fourth Lateran Council of 1215 recorded the opinion of some scholars who held that when nuns are ordained (*ordinetur*), they truly receive the character of orders.[85]

To hold that women could be sacramentally ordained was clearly the minority opinion, but that such an opinion was held with no obvious implication of heresy or opprobrium does demonstrate that the concept of ordination was in considerable flux in the twelfth-century. When Innocent, then, forbade the ministries undertaken by the Spanish abbesses, he was clearly taking the side of the scholarly majority in a long-debated question. Theologians would also take up the question of the ordination of women, but not until the 1240's, some hundred years after the canonist Gratian first put forth his opinion on the subject.[86] For over twelve hundred years, then, the question of the validity of women's ordination remained at least an open question. Some popes, bishops, and scholars accepted such ordinations as equal to those of men; others did not. By the end of the thirteenth-century, however, sacramental ordination was limited only to the higher orders of the clergy. As a result, all other ceremonies and appointments once called ordinations were removed from sacramental status. Along with this movement, although not necessarily because of it, women, too, were deemed incapable of true ordination.

This change in the understanding of ordination so clearly exemplified by the debates among twelfth-century canonists was part and parcel of a much larger debate on Christian rituals. Several question on the Eucharist, for instance, were open for theological debate. There was no agreement over either what or who could validly offer the sacrifice of the Mass. Theologians did not agree, for instance, that the words of Christ at the Last Supper were the formula that had always consecrated the gifts of bread and wine. Some theologians, among them the monastic teachers Honorius Augustodunensis and Rupert of Deutz, followed Pope Gregory the Great in arguing that the original words said over the oblation were limited to the Lord's Prayer.[87] Other theologians suggested that the sign of the cross made over the gifts effected the consecration.[88] A continuing debate argued whether Jesus consecrated the gifts at the Last Supper by means of His own word or a separate blessing.[89] The moment at which the change was supposed to take place was not determined until the early thirteenth-century. Most importantly for this study, some theologians, notable the well respected Parisian liturgist John Beleth held that the words of institution, on their own, transubstantiated the bread and wine regardless of who said the words. Abelard noted that he knew of two famous teachers who argued even women could so consecrate. More heated was debate about the validity of Masses offered by heretics or schismatics. In short, the important connection between ordination and ministry in the Eucharist was still under debate in the middle of the twelfth-century.

Nor were the other sacraments yet clearly connected with ordination. Confessions was still being performed by unordained religious in the beginning of the thirteenth-century, a practice which embarrassed Franciscans needed to remove from their early histories. Fierce battles raged over the right of the laity to preach, most notably, of course, in the case of the Waldensians. Nor was the number of Christian rituals which were to be considered "sacraments" fixed in the twelfth-century. Lists differed until the *Sentences* of Peter the Lombard became the standard text of a theological education and his list of seven major rituals became accepted teaching.

The twelfth-century, then, was a watershed in the understanding of Christian ministry in the West. The separation between role of laity and minister widened as the "power" of the minister became seen as absolutely necessary for the efficacy of many Christian rituals. Most importantly, ordination became intrinsically linked to the Eucharist and to ritual penance. A properly ordained minister became essential to the proper functioning of the ritual life of the community and indeed to salvation itself. The great scholastic minds of the thirteenth-century carefully laid out the reasoning behind these connections, basing themselves on Aristotelian metaphysics and Roman law concepts of *potestas*. Their arguments stuck and their conclusions passed into the definitions of the great councils, notably Trent. The sense of novelty which such debates might occasion in the twelfth and thirteenth-century transmogrified into a sense of inevitability in later centuries. This inevitability would then be read back into early centuries and sometimes even the knowledge of earlier practices, such as that of the ordination of women, was lost.

Conclusions: Historical and Theological

What conclusions can be drawn from this overview the changing attitudes towards the ministry of women in the early Middle Ages? First there is the historical conclusion that at least some medievals, including bishops and popes, considered deaconesses and abbesses to be as ordained as any other cleric at that time, given the definition of *ordinatio* used during these early centuries. As late as the twelfth-century, there were still scholars who considered women to be sacramentally ordained. Secondly, despite continued opposition to that role by some church officials, these women routinely took on liturgical roles later reserved to the male presbyterate and the diaconate. In short, the answer to the historical question whether Christians ever considered women to be ordained clergy appears to be that they indeed did, and in fact that they were so considered at least in some ecclesiastical circles for over half of Christian history.

Now, at least for Roman Catholics, the theological explanation of this historical data is much more controverted. One could judge that the use of the term "ordination" for abbesses, deaconesses, and nuns in the early Middle Ages was a mistake, a confusion of terminology which would be clarified later; in short, that the doctrine of ordination would develop into a fuller understanding in later centuries. From this perspective, the position of those church officials in the sixth, ninth, and thirteen centuries who legislated against any clerical role for women is the only valid tradition of the Church. This is precisely the position of René Metz, in an article discussing the proper term for the installation of virgins (*consecratio* or *benedictio*). Metz dismisses the occurrences of the term *ordinatio* for such an installation as unimportant, merely a transitory usage during a period in which the terminology for the sacrament of orders had not yet been developed.[90] Although his research contains several references to ordinals containing rites for the ordination of women, he argued strongly that such references cannot be to true ordinations. "Only men could belong to the clergy. Although deaconesses and widows did perform some minor duties, essentially of apostleship and charity, and mainly in the early church, women were never part of the clergy itself. During the Middle Ages some women, especially abbesses, assumed the rights to confess and to preach, but popes and councils reacted vigorously against such actions."[91] Metz is not alone in his position, of course, but his position is a good example of this approach.

The approach exemplified by Metz, I would insist however, is a theological, not a historical, judgment and, as Terrence Tilley pointed out so well in his presidential address to the College Theology Society, it is a serious methodological error to confuse historical and theological judgments.[92] Historically one can say only that there was a time when ordination was understood more as the celebration of an entry into a vocation or a station or a ministry in life, than a rite effecting a metaphysical and irreversible change in spiritual status and that, given this understanding, many if not all, church officials in the early Middle Ages accepted that women could so enter into such a vocation or station or ministry. Theologically, however, the judgment which Metz and others like him are making is that the early Middle Ages, in this regard at least, cannot be normative for Christian life and belief.

Here I believe is the crux of the matter. Metz's position is based on a particular understanding of development in Christian history and doctrine. According to this approach, certain periods and documents are understood as normative and more importantly as irreversibly normative. All other periods must then be judged more or less incomplete, faulty, flawed, or foolish in relation to those normative periods and documents and, further, the present must conform to the normative period in so far as is humanly possible. The crucial question remains, of course, of how to decide which periods (or actions) in the long history of Christianity are normative. For the Roman Catholic magisterium in the twentieth-century that answer has often been that the magisterium decides which actions, pronouncements, and periods are normative. "Definitive" statements from the past are selectively chosen as normative. In effect, doctrine "develops" until the current pope says its development has stopped and that one or the other official statement is the last word on an issue. The normative endorsement of an official statement depends on the present pope and future popes can and have removed such endorsements, thus annulling the normative statements of early popes. What is assumed here is a kind of "ecclesial Darwinism" in which the present is always seen to be an advancement on the past in so far as the present is always better able to judge what of the past must be normative.

This may seem odd, since this form of theology usually claims to resist temptations to cave into modernity. In fact, however, only the present counts in this theology, since the past depends on the present for its authorization and authentication. To give but one example, canonical legislation from the reform movements of the fifth, ninth, and thirteenth centuries which gradually excluded women from any official role in the Church are deemed to be normative, definitive, and irreversible. However, equally strong canonical legislation and practice from the first through the nineteenth centuries insisting that ordination must include the voice of the community for which one is ordained is not equally considered normative or definitive and has been reversed in recent papal appointments to episcopal office.[93] Clearly, what counts as normative and definitive constitutes a theological discernment that can vary from era to era.

Thus, the clarity and certainty which such a theology seems to offer evaporates when seen through the larger lens of centuries of Christian history. Eternally true teaching taught everywhere and always depends, all too humanly, on which magisterium is choosing which places count as "everywhere" and which times count as "always." Certainly there are theological arguments to ground such theological decisions, but they are all too rarely presented or clearly argued. When the justification for the theological choices made in using historical sources is not presented, the appearance of authoritarianism is inevitable and fiat alone can all too often be interpreted as whimsy.

There is another way, however, to interpret the past theologically. In this understanding the history of Christianity is judged as a series of ongoing attempts to live out the Christian message in differing social contexts.[94] "Tradition" then is less a straightforward and irreformable set of church pronouncements and more a wealth of differing responses to societal needs upon which the Church can draw in its continuing attempt to live out the Gospel. It is the "treasury of things new and old" that can guide in making decisions in the related, but admittedly different, contexts of the present. Using the powerful language of Susan Ross' new book on the sacraments, this form of theology would entail a recovery and a deep appreciation of the ambiguity inherent in our tradition, or better, traditions.[95]

This form of theology is no less a matter of critically choosing what is normative for present Christian behavior than is the first method discussed. Indeed, this approach takes the ambiguity involved in such choices as a strength rather a weakness. Theological justification for such choices remains just as important in this approach as it is in the first, however. To demonstrate that the Church has done something in the past does not justify its adequacy as a proper Christian response in the present. Again, an inadequate theological justification for recovering a lost tradition can equally give the impression of fad or whimsy.

Hopefully, an awareness of the unavoidable human choice at the heart of the process of recovering our traditions, whatever theological method is adopted for that recovery, will make for a more critical and judicious application of past practices to present situations.[96] Nevertheless, the point needs to be made that all theological readings of history involve a choice, or perhaps better discernment, of what can or should be normative for the present. To deny that such discernment exists, or to fail to justify the criteria for such discernment is not only dangerous but morally suspect.[97]

The historical conclusions of this paper, then, do not automatically either justify women's ordination nor do they automatically rule out such a possibility.[98] Nor do the historical conclusions automatically justify the acceptance or rejection of a broader and more communitarian understanding of ordination. Historical conclusions do not lead automatically to theological or ecclesial conclusions. What cannot be said historically is that Christianity has never officially recognized women's ministry or that that ministry had no cultic function. Nor can it be denied that the Church once did accept an understanding of ordination as a vocation or ministry to the community from which that ministry arose. To deny any of these claims would be the result of a *theological* conclusion that affirms that these practices cannot be considered normative. That choice, however, must be justified theologically in the same way and with the same rigor as the opposing claim that such practices can play a normative function in present theological and ecclesiastical judgments.

Christians can never replicate the past. Even if we do the same things our ancestors did, they are done in a new social and cultural setting and hence cannot be the same. Therefore *we must always choose to do something new* even if that is to do something old in a new setting. Fortunately, the Christians who went before us offer us many different patterns of behavior in varying cultural settings. We can learn much from them, judiciously and prayerfully discerning what will help us most. Perhaps the greatest lesson to be learned here is that our future does not have to, and indeed cannot, replicate our past. The most wonderful gift the past gives us is the freedom to do something new and to trust, as our predecessors did, that in that newness, the Spirit is still with us.

Notes

1. *The Lady Was a Bishop: The Hidden History of Women with Clerical Ordination and the Jurisdiction of Bishops* (Cambridge: Cambridge University Press, 1978), 130. See also pp. 8 and 13. I would particularly like to thank Marie Anne Mayeski, J. Frank Henderson, and William W. Bassett for all their helpful suggestions without which this article would not have been possible. Particularly helpful was Marie Anne Mayeski, "Excluded by the Logic of Control: Women in Medieval Society and Scholastic Theology," *Equal at the Creation*: Sexism, Society, and Christian Thought, edited by Joseph Martos and Pierre Hégy (Toronto: University of Toronto Press, 1998), 70-93.

2. The ordo is contained in *Le Liber ordinum en usage dans l'église Wisigothique et mozarabe d'espagne du ciquième au onzieme siècle*, Marius Férotin, ed., reprint of the 1904 edition edited by Anthony Ward and Cuthbert Johnson, Bibliotheca «Ephemeredes liturgicae» subsidia 83, Instrumenta liturgica Quarreriensia 6 (Rome: C.L.V. Edizioni liturgiche, 1996), 113-15.

3. "J'ai copié à Madrid dans un manuscrit de l'an 976, aujourd'hui à l'Académie Royale d'Histoire (codex 62, fol. 63), un document, qui me semble inédit, sur l'*ordinatio abbatissae*. Il vaut la peine d'être signalé ici, quoique sa composition ne remonte pas, d'apres toute apparence, au delá huitième siècle, peut-être même du neuviéme. Il est tiré d'un texte de la Régle de saint Benoit, adapté à usage d'une communauté de vierges. C'est ainsi qu'á la place des mots *abbas, frater*, etc., one lit: *abbatissa, soror*, etc.— . . . Voici ce passage: «*De ordinatione et electione abbatisse*." *Ibid. 115, n. 2.*

4. René Metz, "Benedictio sive consecratio virginum," *Ephemerides litur-gicae*, 80 (1966) 263-93. The discussion of the relevant texts occurs on pages 284-85. I wish to thank Marie Anne Mayeski for bringing this article to my attention.

5. "In the past, a deaconess was ordained in this way, however, not before forty years of age," quoted by Michel Andrieu, *Les Ordines Romani du Haut Moyen Age*, 4, Michel Andrieu, ed., Spicilegium sacrum Lovaniense, Études et documents 28, (Louvain: Spicilegium sacrum Lovaniense, 1956) 147. See also Andrieu, 3:411.

6. "In the same way, we grant and confirm to you and to your successors in perpetuity all episcopal ordinations, priests as well as deacons or deaconesses; or subdeacons, churches or altars; whatever might be necessary in all of Trastevere." Quoted by Andrieu, 4:144.

7. "We freely and without withholding anything already bestowed, grant from whichever catholic leader they would be requested, the consecration of chrism, holy oil, altars or basilicas; the ordinations of abbesses or nuns; or of any cleric who had been advanced to sacred orders; or whatever pertains to the sacred mysteries as Anselperga, the first abbess of this same monastery, obtained from Paul of blessed memory, pontiff of the Apostolic See, because of the weakness of her feminine gender." Epistola 380 (3 April, 1123) in *Bullaire du Pape Calixtus*

II, 1119-24: Essai de Restitution, Ulysse Robert (ed.) 2 vols. (Paris: Imprimerie nationale, 1891) 2:165. An earlier edition of Calistus' letter was included as Epistola 222 in Jacques Paul Migne, ed., 217 vols. and indexes, *Patrologiae cursus completus . . . Series latina = PL* (Paris: Garnier Fratres and J.P. Migne,1878-90), vol. 163:1284A-B. This same formula is used to remind abbots of the bishop's duty and makes clear that the leader (*praesul*) mentioned here would be the local bishop. Cf. Robert, 2:104 (*PL* 163:1264B), Robert, 2:131 (*PL* 163:1273A), Robert 2:161 (*PL* 163:1281C), Robert 2:163 (*PL* 163:1282C).

8. "The bishop ordains the abbots, the abbess, the priest and the other six grades." *PL* 159:1002D. Gilbert was a student of Anselm of Canterbury and bishop of Limerick from 1001. He died c. 1140. Cf. A. Schmitt, "Gilbert v. Limerick," *Lexicon für Theologie und Kirche*, Michael Buchberger, ed., 10 vols. and indexes and supplements, (Freiburg: Herder, 1957-68) 4:890.

9. "Later truly the high leader (archbishop), having been asked by the ceasar, his patron, veiled the same [young woman] when she was now twelve years of age on the second kalends of May and on the next day ordained her as abbess in the presence of her father, which he later exceedingly regretted." *Die Chronik des Bischofs Thietmar von Merseburg und ihre Korveier Überarbeitung*, Robert Holtmann, ed., Monumenta Germaniae historicae, Scriptores rerum germanicarum, 9 (Berlin: Werdmannsche Bundhandlung, 1935) 93. An earlier edition is printed in *PL* 139:1223C-1224A.

10. Atto of Vercelli, *Epistola ad Ambrosium sacerdotem* (8) *PL* 134:114A. The word *cultrices* (here translated as "leaders of worship") is difficult to translate. Originally it would refer to a "female laborer" but could also mean "female worshipers" or even "female priest." See *A Latin Dictionary*, ed. Charleston Lewis and Charles Short (Oxford: Clarendon Press, 1969), 488 and the *Oxford Latin Dictionary*, ed. P. G. W. Glare (Oxford: Clarendon Press, 1982), 466. On the problem of translating references to religious women in the Middle Ages, see *Sainted Women of the Dark Ages*, Jo Ann McNamara and John E. Halborg (eds.) (Durham and London: Duke University Press, 1992) ix. Atto was the second bishop of Vercelli, governing from 924 until his death in 961. For recent information on Atto, see Edward A. Synan, "Atto of Vercelli," *Dictionary of the Middle Ages*, Joseph R. Strayer, ed., (New York: Charles Scribners, 1982-89), 1:641.

11. The selection process is quite complex and repeated several times. One summary reads, "For nothing is to be settled concerning the election and ordination itself to this same monastery without the freedom and consent of our heirs and guardians." *Annales Camaldulensis ordinis Sancti Benedicti . . .* , ed. Giovanni Mittarelli and Anselmo Costadoni (Venice: Apud Jo. Baptistam Pasquali, 1755), 1, col. 23. Cf. also ibid. col. 24 "And if the case should so happen (which God not allow to happen) that there would not be found from either my offspring or that of my husband Richild some one who would able to be abbess in the above mentioned monastery, or would not wish to be abbess, then the nuns of the aforesaid monastery would have the power and permission, with the

common awareness of our heirs and guardians, to elect and ordain an abbess from among themselves to this same aforementioned nurturing place, so that the chapter fulfills and carries all the statutes, as is read above."

12. "On account of which we wish it to be noted how the venerable Bernard bishop of the church of Halberstadt attending to our mercy, requesting often and many times, desired that a monastery for holy women be built from his paternal heritage in the village which is called Hathumeresleu, and that his niece, that is, Gundradam, be ordained abbess here and that three tenths of the villages of Hathumeresleu, Hiteburn, and Delthrop be retained in such a way as to supply these same monastics." *Diplomata regum et imperatorum Germaniae*, vol. 2, part 1 *Ottonis II diplomata*, Th. Sickel, ed., Monumenta Germaniae historica inde ab anno Christi quingentesimo usque ad annum millesimum et quingentesimum. (Hannover: Hansche Buchhandlung, 1888), 11.

13. "With one soul and like agreement, the holy women here appointed a certain girl named Albergis, coming from a most famous heritage, most beautiful in appearance, remarkable in goodness, outstanding in reputation for all her conduct, the election and proclamation of whom was done in the year of the birth of our Lord 1041, the millennial age 80, the indiction 10, the third concurrence, the Christian people celebrating the sixtieth Sunday. And in this same year coming together in the aforementioned place, and Arnald, by the grace of God the most reverent pontiff of the holy seat of Maguelone, arriving here, he ordained and blessed the aforementioned young woman." Carta 221 in *Histoire générale de Languedoc avec des notes et les pièces justificatives*, Cl. Devic and J. Vaissete, eds. (Toulouse: E. Privat, 1872-92 [1893]), 5, cols. 445-46.

14. *Regula ad virgines*, c. 7 (*PL* 88:1660C). On Waldebert, see W. Böhme, "Waldebert," *Lexicon für Theologie und Kirche* 10, 932-33.

15. "The abbess or prioress or whichever of the senior sisters to whom the abbess would have commissioned in order to hear confessions, . . . " Ibid. (ibid. 1660B)

16. For a discussion of an eleventh-century ordo for the consecration of nuns, see Hermann Gräf, "Ad monachum faciendum: Die Mönchsprofess nach einem Fest-Sacramentar von Venedig aus dem 11. Jh.," *Ephemerides liturgicae* 88 (1974), 353-69.

17. Paul F. Bradshaw, "Medieval Ordination," *The Study of Liturgy*, C. Jones, G. Wainwright, and others, eds. (New York: Oxford University Press, 1992), 377-78.

18. *Mission and Ministry: History and Theology in the Sacrament of Order* (Wilmington, Del.: Michael Glazier, Inc., 1982), 254.

19. Yves Congar, "Note sur une valeur des termes «ordinare, ordinatio,»" *Revue des sciences religieuses* 58 (1984), 7-14.

20. *Aux origines d'une terminologie sacramentelle: ordo, ordinare, ordinatio dans la littérature chrétienne avant 313* (Louvain: Spicilegium sacrum Lovaniense, 1974).

21. See for example, *Glossarum mediae et infirmae latinitatis*, ed. Charles DuCange (Graz: Abakdemische Druck-U. Verlagsanstalt, 1954; reprint of the Paris, 1883-1887 edition), 6, 58-59 s.v. "ordinatio"; 60-62 s.v. "ordo," and *Novum glossarium mediae latinitas ab anno DCCC usque ad annum MCC*, vol. O, eds. Franz Blatt and Yves Lefévre (Copenhagen: Ejnar Munksgaard, 1983), cols. 696-708 s.v. "ordinatio," cols. 714-29; s.v. "ordino," and cols. 731-72 s.v. "ordo".

22. For an example from the late tenth-century, see ". . . since indeed we know there to be three grades in the holy and universal Church of both sexes of the faithful; granted that none of whom may be without sin, however, the first is good, the second is better, the third is best. And certainly the first order is the married of both sexes; the second that of continents and widows, the third of virgins or holy women. Similarly there are there are three such grades or orders of males, of which the first is that of the laity, the second that of clerics and the third that of monks." Abbo of Fleury, *Apologeticus ad Hugonem et Robertum reges Francorum* (*PL* 139, 463A-B). On Abbo, see Lawrence K. Shook, "Abbo of Fleury (Floriancensis)," *Dictionary of the Middle Ages*, 1:12-13. Cf. Mayeski, 74, "During the ninth-century, the emphasis on the superiority of virginity diminished, while the Carolingian Church promoted the idea that married people constituted a true *order* within the Church, equal to that of the celibates." (Emphasis by author)

23. "Les anciennes prières d'ordination," *Maison-Dieu* 138 (1979) 109.

24. Andrea Gloria, *Codex diplomatico padovanno dal secolo sesto a tuto l'undecimo*, Monumenti storici publicati dalla deputazione Veneta de storia patria, 2, Serie prima documenti, 2 (Venice: A spese della Società, 1877), 23.

25. See James Brundage, *Medieval Canon Law* (London and New York: Longman, 1995), 68.

26. For references to extreme unction, see *Glossarum mediae et infirmae latinitatis*, 58. For marriage, see ibid. 60 "Perrotin de Solier . . . estant plevy en fiancé à jeune fille . . . et suidant velle esouser et recevoir l'Ordre de marriage, etc."

27. "For no reason should it be allowed that there be among the bishops those who were neither chosen by the clerics nor were proposed by the people nor were consecrated by the provincial bishops with the advice of the metropolitan." Quoted and discussed by Congar, "Note sur une valeur," 8-9.

28. "Pour eux, *ordinare, ordinatio* n'ont pas nécessairement le sens sacramen-tel. On appelle *ordinatio* l'élection du pape, la nomination d'un archidiacre, l'institution canonique donné à moine pour qu'il puisse r'gir une paroisse." "La tradition des canoniste du moyen âge," *Etudes sur le sacrement de l'ordre*, (Paris: Éditions du Cerf, 1957) *Lex orandi* 22, 259.

29. For a list of such references, see *The Rule of St. Benedict in Latin and English with Notes*, Timothy Fry, ed., (Collegeville, Minn.: The Liturgical Press, 1981) 522. I want to thank Dr. J. Frank Henderson for providing this reference.

30. For references, see n. 21 above, esp. *Novum Glossarium*, vol. O, cols. 722-28.

31. Congar, "Note sur une valeur."

32. "Moreover we deliver over to you and to your successors the preeminent and primary power to consecrate the kings of France; in order that as Blessed Remigius after converting Clovis to the faith, is known to have instituted the first Christian king into his kingdom; thus you too and your successors who, taking the place of this same Saint Remigius in the Church of Rheims by the will of God, discharge the anointing and ordaining of the kings or queens; by the highest power, you discharge this." *Epistola* 27 (*PL* 151:310B-C).

33. *Annales Altahenses*, W. de Giesebrecht and E. von Oefele, eds., Monumenta germaniae historiae, Scriptores rerum Germanicarum in usum scholarum ex Monumentis Germaniae historicis recusi, 1 (Hannover: Bibliopolii Hahniani, 1891), 33-34.

34. *Die Ordines für die Weihe und Krönung des Kaisers und der Kaiseren*, Reinhard Elze, ed., Monumenta Germaniae historica, Fontes juris Germanici antiqui in usum scholarum separatim editi, 9 (Hannover: Hansche Buchhandlung, 1960; reprinted Hannover: Hansche Buchhandlung, 1995,) no. 4b, 12.

35. *The Early Church* (London: Penguin Books, 1967), 166.

36. The entire quotation reads: "But instead of signifying, as happened from the beginning of the twelfth-century, the ceremony in which an individual received a *power* henceforth possessed in such a way that it could never be lost, the words *ordinare, ordinari, ordinatio* signified the fact of being designated and consecrated to take up a certain place or better a certain function, ordo, in the community and at its service." "My Path-findings in the Theology of Laity and Ministries," *The Jurist* 32 (1977), 180. (Emphasis by author).

37. There are many studies of the roles women played in the early centuries. Essential for the New Testament period is Elisabeth Schüssler Fiorenza, *In Memory of Her: A Feminist Theological Reconstruction of Christian Origins* (New York: Crossroad, 1983). Recent studies on women in the first three centuries of Christianity include Ben Witherington, *Women in the Earliest Churches*, Society for New Testament Studies, Monograph Series, 59 (Cambridge: Cambridge University Press, 1988); Karen Jo Torjesen, *When Women Were Priests* (San Francisco: HarperSanFrancisco, 1993); Bonnie Bowman Thurston, *The Widows: A Women's Ministry in the Early Church* (Minneapolis: Fortress Press, 1989); *Essays in Women and Christian Origins,* Ross Shepard Kraemer and Mary Rose D'Angelo, eds., (New York and Oxford: Oxford University Press, 1999) and Ute Eisen, *Women Officeholders in Early Christianity: Epigraphical and Literary Studies* (Collegeville, Minn.: The Liturgical Press, 2000), who provides an exhaustive bibliography on this subject on pages 227-95. On virgins and widows in the early Middle Ages, see Suzanne Fonay Wemple, "Women from the Fifth Century to the Tenth Century," *A History of Women in the West*, George Duby and Michelle Perrot, eds., 2, *Silences of the Middle Ages*, Christine Klapisch-Zuber, ed. (Cambridge, Mass. and London: Harvard University Press, 1992), 188.

38. Although, as discussed below, it is not altogether clear that deaconesses or abbesses were always considered differently than deacons or abbots in terms of jurisdiction or liturgical function.

39. For three recent discussions of the roles women played in the early Middle Church, see Wemple, *Women in Frankish Society: Marriage and the Cloister 500 to 900,* 127-48, (Philadelphia, University of Pennsylvania Press, 1981); Wemple, "Women," 186-201, and Donald Hochstetler, *A Conflict of Traditions: Women in Religion in the Early Middle Ages: 500-840* (Lanham, Md.: University Press of America, 1992).

40. Married bishops, priests, deacons, *presbyterae,* and deaconesses were all instructed to live chastely once they were ordained. See Andrieu, 4:140-42. Wemple, *Women in Frankish Society,* 129-36, offers an extended and learned discussion of the gradual insistence on celibacy for bishops, *episcopae,* priests, *presbyterae,* deacons, and deaconesses. Like Andrieu, she reads the prohibitions against marriage by *episcopae, presbyterae,* and deaconesses as forbidding only remarriage of those women who had been married to bishops, priests or deacons.

41. The suggestion occurs in the twelfth-century *Summa Parisiensis* as well as in Guido de Baysio's *Rosarium Super Decretum* written between 1296 and 1300. For references, see Ida Raming, *The Exclusion of Women from the Priesthood: Divine Law or Sex Discrimination?* (Metuchen, N.J.: The Scarecrow Press, 1976), 57, 69.

42. Eisen, *Women Officeholders,* 200. For the a recent discussion of *episco-pae,* see Eisen, *Women Officeholders,* 199-216. See also Andrieu, 4:141, n.3; 145; and Torjesen, 9-10. Wemple, "Women," 193, notes that at least one powerful abbess of the tenth-century held the title *metropolitana.*

43. For a recent discussion of these controversial inscriptions, see Eisen, *Women Officeholders,* 200-05.

44. *Decretales Pseudo-Isidoriana,* Paul Hinschius, ed., (Leipzig: B. Tauch-nitz, 1863; reprinted Aalen: Scientia Verlag, 1963), *Decreta pape Gregorii iunioris,* cc. 14, 754. Hinschius believes these decretales may actually date back to Gregory II (p. cvii). On the dating of the *Decretales,* see Horst Fuhrmann, *Einfluß und Verbreitung der pseudoisidorischen Fälschungen,* 2 vols., Schriften der Monumenta Germaniae historica, 24 (Stuttgart: Hiersemann, 1972), 1:182-83.

45. Andrieu, 4:141.

46. I have also translated "*ordinatas*" as "*appointed*" rather than "*ordained,*" given the earlier discussion of the meaning of "*ordinare*" during this period and to avoid the suggestion that this statute was necessarily intended as a blanket prohibition of the ordination of *presbyterae.* For a similar use of *ordinare,* compare the comments by the twelfth-century canonist, Gratian, on such an appointment of a monk: "Furthermore, if monks, in dedication to their presbyterate, accept the power as other priests of preaching, of baptizing, of giving penance, of remitting sins, of duly to enjoying ecclesiastical benefices . . . nevertheless, they do not have the exercise of their power unless they have been chosen by the people and ordained by the bishop with the consent of the abbot."

Quoted and discussed by Fransen, "La tradition," 259. DuCange, *Glossarium*, 8, 489, quotes a similar gloss contained in a manuscript of this canon, "The *presbyterae* mentioned are more generically all older widows who are free to carry out sacred things in the church."

47. These injunctions also appeared earlier in a Roman synod held in 743, see Andrieu, 4:142, again indicating a contemporary concern with this issue.

48. C. 10 of the *Capitula synodi Laodicenae, Decretales Pseudo-Isidoriana*, 274. The statute, based loosely on 1 Timothy 5:2-10, is difficult to translate. *"Seniores" can refer to elders in the technical sense of an ecclesiastical post and is the word used in the Vulgate for presbyter, e.g. Ezechiel 7:26, 2 John 1, 1 Timothy 5:1. "Matricularia" is an unusual word that comes from "matrix" and can used to mean progenitress.*

49. For a detailed discussion of the interpretation of this canon, see Raming, *The Exclusion of Women* , 21-22 and Eisen, *Women Officeholders*, 121-23.

50. *Epistola 8, PL* 134:114C. For the entire passages summarized here, see ibid. *PL* 134:114A-C.

51. "There are even some who assert that those in former times called deaconesses now we name abbesses, which to us by no means seems to agree." *PL* 134:114D.

52. See the discussion of their opinions on pages 11-14.

53. "Dès les premiers temps de l'Église, parmi les pieuses femmes consacrées à Dieu par le voeu de continence, certaines formèrent une catégorie spéciale et eurent auprès du clergé un rôle d'auxiliaires. Entre autres noms, on leur donna celui de *dicona*, qui eut bientôt valeur officielle, sanctionné par une ordination. Dans les oeuvres d'assistance et pour certaines cérémonies liturgiques, ces diaconesses furent une sort d'équivalent féminin des diacres. Il n'est pas toujours facile, lorsque'apparaît dans un ancien document romain le terme *diacona*, ou *diaconissa*, de reconnaître s'il s'agit l'une diaconesse proprement dite ou seulement de l'épouse d'un diacre." Andrieu, 4:142. Cf. also "Depuis longtemps on leur avait retiré tout rôle liturgique at administratif. Elles ne pouvaient néanmoins être confondues avec les épouses des diacres, pareillement appelée diaconissae. Celle-ci, de même que les presbyterissae, ont laissé pue de traces certaines dans les documents. Vivant à l'ombre de leures maris, elles dépensaient leur activité dans les obscures besognes familiales." Andrieu, 4:143-44.

54. Wemple, *Women in Frankish Society*, 129, suggests this may have been the case in the first three centuries of the Church. See also her discussion of deaconesses and priests' wife in "Women," 195-96.

55. Andrieu, 4:140-41, 146, Wemple, *Women in Frankish Society*, 132.

56. Wemple, *Women in Frankish Society*, 136-41, argues that legislation against the diaconate for women was more or less successful by the sixth-century when women were then forced into the monastic life if they wished to follow a religious vocation. Hochstettler, 81-88, follows earlier scholars in asserting that the role of deaconesses was taken over by the canonesses.

57. For a description of canonesses, see Hochstetler, 81-83, Wemple, "Women," 190, 192, and Morris, 10-12.

58. Hochstetler, 99-100

59. "The Eucharist and Popular Devotion," *Proceedings of the Fifty-second Annual Convention of the Catholic Theological Society of America*, vol. 52, Judith A. Dwyer, ed. (Catholic Theological Society of America, 1997), 41-42; reprinted in Gary Macy, *Treasures from the Storehouse: Essays on the Medieval Eucharist* (Collegeville, Minn.: Liturgical Press of America, 1999), 174

60. Jean Leclercq, "Eucharistic Celebrations Without Priests in the Middle Ages," *Worship*, 55 (1981), 160-68. The text of the prayer reads: "Hear, I ask O Lord, my cry for your unworthy handmaidens and beseeching sinners, and, while I despair of the quality of my merits, I seek to obtain not judgment, but mercy. Through the Lord. The entire text of this *Oratio ad accipiendam eucharistiam* has been published by Jean Leclercq, "Prières médiévales pour recevoir l'eucharistie pour saluer et pour bénir la croix," *Ephemerides liturgicae* 97 (1965), 329-31.

61. Medieval theologians speculated that the Sign of the Cross, or the entire Canon, or perhaps even the Lord's Prayer, could consecrate, see Gary Macy, *Theologies of the Eucharist in the Early Scholastic Period* (Oxford: Clarendon Press, 1984), 57.

62. "Concerning these things, while doing nothing new, we know what our holy predecessors of Albi, Ostia and its port area, and of other churches have done; we establish by this our apostolic precept on the present sixth indiction and by so establishing we confirm that priests, deacons, monks, cloistered religious, clerics of whatever order or dignity they might be, religious women or deaconesses, all should be immune from lay service, judgment, and public alienation of property in Galeria whether within the castle or outside; so that if the emperor or marquis, or their legates or successors might come to us in that place, in no way should expenses be collected by public officials from the aforementioned persons, nor in any other way should injury be inflicted on them." *Italia sacra sive de episcopis italiae* . . . . Ferdinando Ughello, ed., 2nd ed., Nicolai Coleti, ed. (Venice: Apud Sebastianum Coleti, 1717), 1:303.

63. The jurisdictional power of abbesses was also considerable. For a recent discussion of their power, see Mayeski, 75-79.

64. See Morris, *The Lady Was a Bishop*, Appendix 6, *Sainted Women of the Dark Ages*, 12, and Wemple, "Women," 189. Morris also discusses information from the Rule of St. Columbanus and the Rule of St. Basil.

65. Cf. Waldebert, *Regula ad virgines*, c. 6, "Concerning the attentive giving of confession" and c. 7 "Concerning the not making known of the sister's confessions" (*PL* 88:1059A-1660C) and Donatus of Besançon, *Regula ad virgines*, c. 23 "How they ought to come to confession every day." (*PL* 87, col. 282C-D). On the Rule of Donatus, see Hochstetler, 8.

66. For recent studies on women preaching in the Middle Ages, see *Women Preachers and Prophets through Two Millennia of Christianity*, Beverly Wayne Kienzle and Pamela J. Walker, eds. (Berkeley: University of California Press,

1998), esp. the articles by Katherine Ludwig Jansen, "Maria Magdalena: *Apostolorum Apostola*," 57-96; Nicoles Bériou, "The Right of Women to Give Religious Instruction in the Thirteenth Century," 134-45; Carol Muessig, "Prophecy and Song: Teaching and Preaching by Medieval Women," 146-50; Darleen Pryds, "Proclaiming Sanctity through Proscribed Acts: The Case of Rose of Viterbo," 159-72, and Roberto Rusconi, "Women's Sermons at the End of the Middle Ages: Texts from the Blessed and Images of the Saints," 173-95. On lay preaching in general in the Middle Ages, see Rolf Zerfaß, *Der Streit zum die Laienpredigt. Eine pastoral-geschichtliche Untersuchung zum Verständnis des Predigtamtes und zuer sienen Entwicklung im 12. und 13. Jahrhundert* (Frieberg, Herder, 1974).

67. "No abbess [*nulla*] should except an infant from baptism," Aurelian of Arles, *Regula ad virgines*, c. 16 (*PL* 68, col. 402 A) and "No abbess [*nulla*] should presume to except anyone's daughter from baptism, neither rich nor poor," Donatus of Besançon, *Regula ad virgines*, c. 54 (*PL* 87, col. 290C). On the Rule of Aurelian, see Hochstetler, 8.

68. Cf. Waldebert, *Regula ad virgines*, cc. 18-20 (*PL* 88:1067B-1068C), and Donatus of Besançon, *Regula ad virgines*, cc. 69-71 (*PL* 87:294C-295D).

69. The devotion is mentioned by Janet Nelson in her article, "Les femmes et l'évangélisation au ixe siècle," *Revue du Nord*, 69 (1986), 480. See also Donat-us of Besançon, *Regula ad virgines*, c. 53: "If for the love of parents or knowledge of any one, she might wish to send some letters or the bread of the eulogia, it should be offered to the mother, and if she permits it, given through the porters, and they send in the name of that one to whomever she wished. Without the prior or porter, should presume herself to neither to give nor to accept anything from anyone. If she should presume this, she should do penance for three applications." (*PL* 87, col. 290B) and "And when they have walked around the parts which she [the abbesses] wishes, they should return directly either to the greeting room or the door where following thereafter if it had seemed proper to the abbess, from her, if she wished, they would accept the eulogia for those present or others, or the remainder that they decided to offer." Ibid. c. 56 (Ibid. col. 291A).

70. The *Regula ad virgines* of Aurelian of Arles contains an addition containing directions for the Divine Office which includes readings from the Gospel, *PL* 68:403C-460D.

71. Raming, *The Exclusion of Women*, 49-50, 54, 61, 65. According to Ramming, the abbesses of the Carthusian Order sang the Epistle or Gospel at high mass during the Middle Ages.

72. Hochstetler, 101-02. Again, this was done by the abbesses of Monheim, see Nelson, 480.

73. "News of certain things recently has reached our ears, about which we are not a little amazed, that abbesses, namely those constituted in the diocese of Burgos and Palencia, bless their own nun, and hear the confessions of sins of these same, and reading the Gospel presume to preach publicly. Since then this is equally incongruous and absurd (nor supported by you to any degree), we order

through the apostolic writing at your discernment so that, lest this be done by others, you take care by the apostolic authority firmly to prevent [these actions] because even though the most blessed virgin Mary was more worthy and more excellent than all of the apostles, yet not to her, but to them the Lord handed over the keys to the kingdom of heaven."*Corpus Iuris Canonici, Decretales* 1.5, t. 38, c. 10, E. Friedberg, ed. (Graz: Akademische Druck-U. Verlagsanstalt, 1959), 2:886-87.

74. Raming, *The Exclusion of Women*, 26-69.

75. "There is no doubt that in ancient times deaconesses, that is readers of the gospel in church, by custom had been ordained. . . ." Raming, *The Exclusion of Women*, 180, n. 52.

76. "The same thing is able to be said of certain lower orders. But concerning this, it is said, since it seems likely, for in ancient times there were deaconesses, which order today is not in the church." Raming, *The Exclusion of Women*, 185, n. 95.

77. "Others say that once upon a time a woman was ordained to the diacon-ate, but later at the time of Ambrose, this was prohibited; again later, at the time of this council (the Council of Chalcedon), they were ordained; now they are not ordained." Raming, *The Exclusion of Women*, 192, n. 157.

78. Raming, *The Exclusion of Women*, 50, 55.

79. Raming, *The Exclusion of Women*, 51, 53, 54, 61, 65, 69. Eg., Stephen of Tournai, "In ancient times, deaconesses were ordained in the churches, that is readers of the gospel; who, since they are no longer in the church in this way, we perhaps call them abbesses, and they ought not to be ordained before forty years of age." Ibid. 184, n. 89.

80. "Truly we believe seven persons among you to be necessary and to suffice for the administration of the entire monastery: namely, the porter, the cellerar, the vestiary, infirmarian, cantor, sacristan, and at last, the deaconess whom we now call abbess." *Epistola* 8 in *Petri Abailardi Opera* . . . , Victor Cousin (ed.), 2 vols. (Paris: Apud Aug. Durand, 1849) 1:164. See also Wemple, *Women in Frankish Society*, 147, n. 112 for other references to abbesses as the replacement for deaconesses. I disagree with her reading of Atto of Vercelli, however, as I do not think he agreed with those who associated abbesses with deaconesses as she suggests. See note n. 46 above.

81. Ibid. 51, 56, 61, 64, 65.

82. Ibid. 58.

83. The entire text reads "The consecratory imposition of hands is appropriate only for the bishop and is a sacrament and ought to be done at certain times. . . . As it is a sacrament, it cannot by law be repeated." Ibid. 187, n. 123.

84. Ibid. 59-60.

85. "Others say that if a nun is ordained, she truly receives the character of orders, since the question had been asked who had been ordained and how one is able to be ordained after baptism." Ibid. 67.

86. For an excellent and thorough study of the medieval discussion of women's ordination see John Hilary Martin, "The Ordination of Women and the Theologians in the Middle Ages," *Escritos del Vedat*, 36 (1986), 115-77, and 38 (1988) 88-143.

87. Cf. Honorius Augustodunensis, *Gemma animae* (*PL* 172:572B) and Ruper of Deutz, *De divinis officiis*, l. 2, c. 18 (Rhaban Haacke, ed., *Ruperti Tjuitiensis Liber de divinis officiis*, Corpus christianorum, Continuatio medievalis, 7 [Turnhout: Brepols, 1967]). The thirteenth-century Waldensians appear to have retained this custom in their liturgies. For a complete discussion of this issue, see Macy, *Theologies of the Eucharist*, 160, n. 115.

88. Cf. Macy, *Theologies*, 160 n. 116.

89. Ibid. See also Edward Kilmartin, *The Eucharist in the West: History and Theology*, Robert Daly, ed. (Collegeville, Minn.: Liturgical Press, 1998), 132-33.

90. On Metz's overall evaluation of the importance of the texts, see "Benedictio sive consecratio virginum," 267-68: "Au XIIe siècle, nous rencontrerons aussi le terme de ordinatio; mais cette expression a été utilisée de façon passagére seulement, si bien qu'elle ne mérite pas de retenir notre attention." and 285 "Les dénominations s'expliquent par l'imprécision des termes; c'est seulement à partir du XIIe siècle que l'on s'efforce d'apporter les distinctions voulues à la terminologie du sacrement de l'order."

91. *Dictionary of the Middle Ages*, Joseph R. Strayer, ed. (New York: Char les Scribners, 1982-89), 3: 443 "Clergy."

92. "The role-specific responsibility of the theologian is *not* to accept the hypotheses of historians—or sociologists, social psychologists, or ethnographers—as vetoes on faith and practice or as sufficient warrants for expressions of faith and patterns of practice. Rather the theologian must accept these hypotheses as indicators of varying reliability of how the faith has been lived, been practiced, been incarnated both 'there and then' and 'here and now.' The theologian can then make her own recommendations for reformation or restoration—*but empirical claims, even if fully warranted, are not sufficient, and may not even be necessary, to warrant theological recommendations.*" (emphasis by author) *"Practicing History, Practicing Theology,"Theology and the New Histories* (Proceedings of the Annual Convention of the College Theology Society, 1998) Gary Macy, ed. (Maryknoll, N.Y.: Orbis Press, 1999), 10. For two recent and insightful discussions of the role of tradition, see Terrence Tilley, *Inventing Catholic Tradition* (Maryknoll, N.Y.: Orbis Books, 2000), and Orlando Espín, "Toward the Construction of an Intercultural Theology of Tradition," *Journal of Hispanic/Latino Theology* (forthcoming).

93. Cardinal Congar has written extensively on the history of community involvement in election and ordination of bishops, see, for example, *Lay People in the Church: A Study for a Theology of the Laity*, 2nd rev. ed., Donald Attwater, transl. (Westminster, Md.: The Newman Press, 1967), 244-47; "Ordination invitus, coactus de l'église antique au canon 214," *Revue des sciences philosophiques et théologiques*, 50 (1966), 169-97; "My Path-Findings," 178-80. For an

excellent review of the early history of election, see Thomas F. O'Meara, "Emergence and Decline of Popular Voice in the Selection of Bishops," *The Choosing of Bishops*, William W. Bassett, ed. (Hartford, Conn.: The Canon Law Society of America, 1971), 21-32. For a insightful discussion of the novelty of the recent papal practice of appointing bishops, see Garret Sweeney, "The Wound in the Right Foot: 'Unhealed'," *Bishops and Writers: Aspects of the Evolution of Modern English Catholicism*, Adrian Hastings, ed. (Wheathampstead, Hertfordshire: Anthony Clarke, 1977), 207-34.

94. What I have in mind here has been described by Yves Congar as ". . . history understood less as continual process of "development," that is as progress achieved through a gradual unfolding of what was already implicit, and more as a series of formulations of the one content of faith diversifying and finding expression in different cultural contexts." "Church History as a Branch of Theology," *Church History in Future Perspective*, Roger Aubert, ed., *Concilium*, 57 (New York: Herder and Herder, 1970), 87. For a similar approach, see Walter Principe, "The History of Theology: Fortress or Launching Pad," John P. Boyle and George Kilcourse, eds., *The Proceedings of the Catholic Theological Society of America*, 43 (Macon, Ga.: Mercer University Press, 1988), 19-40.

95. *Extravagant Affections: A Feminist Sacramental Theology* (New York: Continuum, 1998), esp. 64-93. I wish to use "ambiguity" here in the rich sense that Dr. Ross suggests.

96. For a recent and extended discussion of the problems of discerning the Christian tradition, see the essays in Macy, *Theology and the New Histories*.

97. On the moral dimension involved in the making of church policy, see Norbert Rigali, "On the Humanae Vitae Process: Ethics of Teaching Morality," *Louvain Studies,* 23 (1998), 3-21.

98. Again, I agree here with Tilley, 11 "Whatever 'ordination' has meant—and it has meant many things—if it can be demonstrated historically that the Church 'ordained' women in the past, that is neither necessary nor sufficient warrant for 'ordaining' women today. If it could be demonstrated that the Church never 'ordained' women in the past, that would not be necessary or sufficient warrant to prohibit the ordination of women today. While theological arguments often can and should be influenced by historians' excavations, analyses, and reconstructions, normative theological claims cannot stand or fall solely on the basis of historical warrant."

Chapter 2

The Ordination of Women and the Theologians in the Middle Ages

John Hilary Martin, O.P.

There was a continuing discussion, and presumably a continuing interest, in the ordination of women throughout the Middle Ages. One hastens to add discussion about the "possibility" of such ordinations because there were, of course, no ordinations of women to Holy Orders during this period. That women were not to be ordained was clear to theologians. But was the church's policy of not ordaining them a matter of Divine law, or was it merely an ecclesiastical convention? That was not so clear to theologians. What was the justification for the church's policy? That was less clear still. Questions such as these provided the basis for the theological discussion of the problem, especially from the early thirteenth to the late fifteenth centuries, the period we will be considering.

There are, as readers of Scripture know, no categorical statements in the New Testament which say that women shall, or shall not, be ordained. It is difficult to see, in fact, how such a statement could have been framed in the context of the early Christian communities. Did "being ordained" mean that someone presided over the Eucharist, did it mean that they preached publicly and officially in the Christian assembly, did it mean that they healed the sick and forgave sins, did it mean that they baptized, or did it mean that they governed and administered the local community, or did it mean some combination of these things? From the texts of the New Testament it is not immediately clear how these questions should be sorted out. St. Paul might say, quite categorically, that "I do not permit women to teach, or to exercise authority over men"; or "it doesn't become a woman to pray to God with her head uncovered"; or "Let women keep silence in the churches for it is not permitted for them to speak, rather let them be submissive."[1] But these remarks, however sharp, do not say in so many words that a woman could never be ordained. When approaching the problem of the ordination of women, theologians had to deal with the problem obliquely without much direction from proof-texts of Scripture.

They might argue, and often did, that women could not be ordained because Paul had said that "they should not preach or assume leadership in the Christian community." To say that these words of Paul also meant that women could not be ordained at all was to draw an inference from Paul's text; it involved interpreting the Scripture in a particular way. This left room in medieval treatises for discussion. The appropriate role for women was taken up in numerous commentaries on Paul's Epistles to 1 Corinthians and 1 Timothy where Paul explicitly lay down strictures against women preaching or assuming leadership over men. Comments by theologians occasionally appear in the Epistle to the Galatians where it touches on the same issue. A more direct and systematic treatment is to be found, however, in commentaries on the *Sentences* of Peter Lombard, and it is to that work which we now turn.

Throughout the Middle Ages the *Sentences* of Peter Lombard provided the forum for ongoing discussion of many theological issues, and such was the case for the ordination of women. The *Sentences,* composed by Peter Lombard in 1157 or 1158, are a collection of texts (i.e., *sentences*) taken from the Fathers and other authoritative sources. They were arranged by Peter Lombard to form a continuous comment on the major statements of the faith as set down in the Creed. The genius of Peter Lombard consisted primarily in the arrangement and organization of materials, for he himself made little personal comment. His work was much admired in the twelfth-century and by the thirteenth had become used as a text in the schools of theology.[2] Production of a "commentary" on the *Sentences* soon became a required exercise for students who were working toward their degree of Master of Sacred Theology. As a consequence, numerous commentaries on the *Sentences* have survived from every generation of theologians between the thirteenth and fifteenth centuries. Weisheipl has pointed out quite clearly that the *Sentences* did not replace the Bible as the masterwork to be used by theologians. Commentaries on the sacred text still held pride of place in the schools and were regarded as an expression of the more mature work of a theologian.[3] Commentaries on the *Sentences* often carried about them the air of the graduate student at the beginning of his career. If these cautions are kept in mind, commentaries are invaluable for the historian and deserve study because they provide such excellent witness of the development of contemporary theological opinion in the schools.

Not all commentaries were alike, however. Some works which have come down to us bearing the title of a *Commentary on the Sentences* are little more than brief textual discussions or abridgements of what was contained in the Lombard's book. In some cases the "commentaries" are considerably shorter than Peter Lombard's original. Summaries of this type represent the work of theological students who were working toward their degrees in theology at a preliminary stage. More often than not they are the efforts of undergraduates, "unformed bachelors," as they called them, who had been set to work lecturing *cursorie* on the *Sentences* to students more junior still.[4] When cursory texts happen to contain material not found in the Lombard, it is hardly ever something propounded by the humble *cursor* on his own, but rather a report of opinions which had become generally accepted in the schools after Peter Lombard's writing. These brief summary-commentaries, as we will call them, are very different in style and spirit from the large and elaborate works left by the great masters, such as Bonaventure, Thomas Aquinas, or Ockham. The great commentaries, so familiar to students of medieval thought, represented quite a different stage of a theologian's career. They were the work of graduated Masters in Sacred Theology, the professors at the universities. Such commentaries were addressed to advanced theological students who were already familiar with the text and the problems raised by Peter Lombard because they had been presented to them in previous years of their academic program by the *cursor*. In the great, full-length commentaries Masters were expected to break new ground, either by asking questions which had never been raised before, or by answering old questions in a new and original manner, or at least giving the old answers some new theological precision or extension. A few examples of commentaries also exist which fall somewhere in between. They raise too many objections to Lombard's text, and they open up theological discussion in a way that would not be suitable for a class of beginning students who would be looking for a simple summary of Peter Lombard. On the other hand, they are not elaborate enough or sophisticated enough to reflect a series of lectures given at a university. They might best be described as "middle-commentaries," too developed to pass as cursory lectures and not large enough to cover issues with full detail. They may have been university notes written up by their authors with no particular classroom audience in mind, or they may have been composed for theology programs given at local theology *studia* that were below the university level.

Commentaries of all these types are useful for our present study, for in their different ways they are an expression of the attitude of the learned clergy of the day toward the ordination of women. Whatever else may be said about the value of the theology found in *Sentence* commentaries, whether of the humble or grander sort, they are excellent witnesses to the actual content of the current theological opinion of the schools. The summary-commentaries put together by aspiring Bachelors may not have had much to offer in the way of originality, their arguments at times may seem thin or even trivial, but they represent the content of the curriculum in use in the schools, and present a summary of the conclusions which were regarded as the standard and received Christian teaching. The brief and schematic conclusions which were presented as the appropriate summary of Christian faith and church practice were read not only by graduate students and future Masters, they were also read out to large classes of clerics who made up the undergraduate student body of the theology faculty of the universities. Many of these clerics would be ordained, leave the university and not pursue theology to any greater depth. They would become the journeymen clerics of the church who would be found at all levels of its administration. As such, they would be an important factor in passing on theological attitudes within the church.

The full-length commentaries of the great scholastic Masters are also important in this regard, but have special value for another reason. Such commentaries obviously represent the theology of their time, but they also enable us to discern the way in which theological opinion was growing and developing. This is made evident both by what is positively said in them, as well as by their omissions and "forgetfulness." It is in the full-length commentaries that the "argument from silence" can be traced effectively. Authors composing the short summary-commentaries on Peter Lombard were called upon to summarize faithfully what was written there. Theologians privileged to write full-length commentaries addressed to advanced students (who had already covered all the material once in summary fashion) would be under no such constraint. They would feel free to pick and choose, to expand and shorten their coverage to a particular question. In these *Sentence* commentaries the Master's "argument from silence" becomes significant. An omission, or even notable shortening of an argument in a full-length commentary, can hardly have been an accident. The quality of attention given to a question can often provide us with a valuable insight into the current level of interest in a problem.

The distribution of material in the *Sentence* commentaries, middle and full-length commentaries, did change to a noticeable degree, particularly as the fourteenth and fifteenth centuries advanced. The "Introductions" to the Lombard's work, and commentaries on the first book (which dealt with methodology and with our conceptualization of God) were expanded, while the material assigned to the other books was much reduced. The material to be covered in the fourth book (which dealt with the sacraments) was more and more slighted as time went on. By mid-fourteenth-century, commentaries on the fourth book formed a thin volume, one which covered only a few selected questions. We will return to this later when discussing theologians of the latter fourteenth and fifteenth centuries.

The Silence of the First Schoolmen

Although the *Sentences* of Peter Lombard provided the locus for discussion of the ordination of women from the early thirteenth-century onward, Peter makes no mention of the issue himself. He treats the sacrament of Holy orders in book four of his *Sentences,* Distinctions 24 and 25. This occurs during his general discussion of the seven sacraments.[5] Holy orders appear as the sixth sacrament, located between Extreme Unction and Matrimony, the more common position in medieval lists of the seven sacraments. His discussion is relatively brief if we compare it with what he has to say, for example, about the sacraments of Matrimony or the Eucharist. He tells us that there are seven grades of spiritual office in the Church. Order is a sacred sign whereby a spiritual power and an office are handed over to the person ordained. He lists the powers attached to each of the seven grades. He then mentions the episcopacy which in his eyes is not a separate *order*, but a *dignity*. He talks about the problem of ordinations performed by heretics and those made under the influence of simony.[6] He brings the whole discussion to a close by reporting what the ancient canons had to say about age requirements for each order.

In his *Sentences* Peter Lombard is primarily interested in giving a brief account of the seven orders and their powers. He is not much interested in the quality of training for clerics, nor the conditions of their life. Except for the mention of minimum age requirements for the various orders (which no longer seem to have been enforced in his own day), he does not establish requirements for orders in any systematic manner.[7] In such a context there was obviously no particular need for him to take up a question about the ordination of women. It did not seem to be of any theological concern.

Other treatises written about the same time, and which treat the sacrament of Holy orders, do not go into the question either. The anonymous *Summa Sententiarum* and the important and influential *On the Sacraments of the Christian Faith* of the Parisian, Hugh of St. Victor, say nothing. Hugh's treatise which was written in 1141, shortly before the *Sentences* of Peter Lombard, does go into a bit more detail in drawing up a list of requirements for ordination. No stranger, no one physically mutilated, no criminal, no public penitent, for example, can be licitly ordained. Since the masculine case is used throughout the section, it seems fair enough to infer that the author presumes that all clerics, whether high or low, will be male, although this is never explicitly stated.[8] A work of Alan of Lille, his *Four Books Against the Heretics,* written probably in the south of France in the 1170's against the Waldenses and Albigenses is also silent.[9] Since there is some evidence that these groups accepted women into their ministry, we might expect to find some words of comment about the ordination of women in Alan's work. Although he is at pains to prove that only properly ordained priests, and not pious layfolk, have the power to consecrate the Eucharist and to forgive sin, he does not speak about ordaining, or about not ordaining, women. Except for some scornful references to the Waldenses who caused women to preach in the community of the faithful, he does not mention any special ministry performed by women.[10] Another treatise of this period, the *Sentences* book of Peter of Poitiers, composed about 1160, also passes over the matter.[11] This work, divided into five books instead of Peter Lombard's four, was produced for many of the same reasons which motivated the Lombard. Like Peter Lombard, he gives a summary of doctrine supported by sentences extracted from authorities. Like the Lombard's, his work was well-known and popular. Although these treatises do not exhaust the literature of the time, they are representative. None of them makes mention of the ordination of women, leaving us with the unavoidable impression that the question was not an issue of their time among the theologians.

The matter does not seem to have interested theologians in the first part of the next century either. No reference is made, for example, in the important *Golden Summa* of William of Auxerre, a comprehensive survey of Christian doctrine composed between 1215-1220.[12] William of Auvergne, a contemporary and a future bishop of Paris, says nothing in his treatise on the sacraments, which forms a part of his lengthy *Instruction on Divinity.* Turning to a somewhat different literary genre, the liturgical treatise of Gui of Orchelles, entitled *Summa on the Rituals and Offices of the Church* we again find nothing.[13] This work, which must have been written around 1220, examines the parts of the Mass, the feasts of the church, the rubrical functions of the various ministers during worship services. Texts of this type (which have roots going back to the ninth, perhaps even to the seventh-century) drew upon elaborate allegories to explain the parts of the Mass and other liturgical rites. In the spirit of a thirteenth-century schoolman, Gui proceeded to introduce historical and theological grounds to help with these explanations. This provided him with ample opportunity for discussing the appropriateness of women clerics, but he never does so.

As the thirteenth-century advanced discussion of Holy Orders in the commentaries on the *Sentences* began to move beyond what Peter Lombard had to say. We can see this development in the *Glosses on the Sentences* by Alexander of Hales, a seminal theologian who made considerable use of the *Sentences*.[14] His *Glosses* are not a full-length commentary, and yet something more than the brief comments of a "cursor." In them Alexander gives a far more elaborate survey of requirements for ordination than the Lombard. In discussing distinction 25 of Lombard's *Sentences*, a locus that was later to become the standard place for discussing the ordination of women, he lists the factors that render a person incapable of Holy Orders. Defects can occur, he says, on the part of the body, on the part of the soul, or on the part of the "body as joined-to-the-soul" (i.e., insofar as someone is a concrete individual and not an abstraction). Defects of body, as we might expect, included physical deformities such as loss of a finger or a limb. Defects of the soul included weakness of intellect, lack of faith, a criminal or otherwise evil moral life. Defects of a personal character could include epilepsy or insanity. A condition arising from quite special circumstances such as illegitimate birth, being baptized in an heretical sect, or having been married more than once, were also mentioned.[15] Alexander's discussion amounts to a tidy arrangement of impediments to orders found in canon law. It is precisely in a list of this sort that a statement about the need for masculine sex for ordination could have easily been introduced. A statement of some sort even seems called for, if only for the sake of completeness. Perhaps Alexander felt the matter was too obvious to need mention, or perhaps he was himself uncertain of the answer. Although there is evident interest in the requirements for those to be ordained, he leaves off without making any reference to women and ordination.

Alexander wrote his *Glosses* sometime between 1222 and 1229 when he was still lecturing at Paris as a secular master. He began a much lengthier and more definitive summary of his theology later in his life which has come down to us as the *Summa of Brother Alexander*.[16] Unfortunately, this work was left unfinished at his death in 1245. His continuators did not complete the section that would have been devoted to Holy Orders.

Another commentary from this generation of theologians also can be mentioned, and that is the brief work of the prominent Dominican Cardinal, Hugh de St. Cher. This commentary is quite clearly of the "cursory" type, and so would be less likely to add to what Peter Lombard had had to say than a full-length commentary. It has been shown that Hugh's commentary was heavily dependent upon both William of Auxerre and Gui of Orchelles, which means that it was probably written after 1223 and before 1229. Hugh discusses Holy Orders very briefly and does not mention the ordination of women.[17] Hugh is not remembered, of course, for this somewhat unremarkable *Sentence* commentary, but for his monumental and influential *Postillae* on the whole of Sacred Scripture. It will be useful to refer here, parenthetically so to speak, to his Scripture commentaries. Here he has much to say about the status of women which will be reported by theologians later. In his *Postillae* on 1 Corinthians and on 1 Timothy he says that women should keep their heads veiled to show their present state of subjection, that they should keep silence in the churches and not preach about doctrine (*per modum doctrinae*) in the presence of men. Both by nature and as the result of original sin women should not command or govern men.[18] Hugh's vast work, undertaken when he was in charge of the Dominican School of San Jacques in Paris between 1230 and 1235, is obviously too large to be the work of a solitary individual but rather the work of some sort of committee working under his direction.[19] All of the strictures against women which it reports would be barriers to the ordination of a woman, to be sure, but Hugh (and his helpers) never actually get around to forbidding the ordination of women as such. The commentary on the *Sentences* and the *Postillae* on the writings of Paul are interesting because they indicate that Dominican as well as Franciscan Masters (and the attitude of seculars can perhaps be included as well since Alexander of Hales can be claimed by both) still passed over explicit discussion of the question.

Another example of the views of a Dominican Master is found in the commentary on the *Sentences* of Albert the Great. He wrote about twenty years later than the above, being a teacher at Paris from 1234 to 1245. His commentary reflects a changing interest in the theology of orders. The questions which interested Peter Lombard, who remembered the struggle over lay investitures with its concern about simoniacal and heretical ordinations, are not dropped entirely by Albert, but they are given much less attention and space.[20] Instead we find in Albert a new set of questions about the nature of the sacramental "character" imparted with Holy Orders. Like Alexander, Albert too is concerned about the qualifications of candidates. He drops the age requirements listed in Peter Lombard (which had long since become dead letters) and gives ones in current use. Like his contemporaries he is interested in intellectual preparation and holiness of life of candidates. But even in his full-blown commentary Albert does not see any necessity to raise the question of the possible ordination of women one way or the other.

The failure of theologians to discuss the ordination of women well into the thirteenth-century is puzzling. Perhaps they excused themselves for the same reason that Peter of Poitiers gave when he discussed Holy Orders in his *Sentences*. In that work he passed directly from a consideration of Extreme Unction (the fifth sacrament) to Matrimony (the seventh) without saying anything about Holy Orders. He could safely omit orders, he tells us, because treatment of that sacrament was taken up "by the canonists."[21] Unlike the theologians, the canonists of the twelfth-century had taken up the question of the possible clerical status of women. In terms of the canons at their disposal they had recorded a negative verdict on the ordination of women, both to the priesthood and to the office of deacon. The business of canon lawyers, of course, is not the same as the business of theologians. The duty of a lawyer is to expose the law, and this is what the canonists of the period did. To be sure, the ways in which laws are gathered, codified, and interpreted by canonists may deeply shape ecclesiastical institutions and modify religious practices, but this is all done through the device of "reporting" the law rather than in justifying it. Despite their undoubted influence upon theological developments in the church, canonists in their glosses and legal treaties do not lay down general theological principles. That is for theologians to do. In interpreting legislation, in explaining its application and in elucidating the meaning of the law texts, twelfth-century canonists might occasionally offer a "proof from Scripture," and they did try to show the consistency of the laws among themselves. But it was not their task to extrapolate universal principles, or to create a consistent theological picture from the mass of particular and specialized legislation. The theological work which Peter of Poitiers had thrust upon the canonists still remained to be done. When it was finally undertaken in the mid-thirteenth-century, it would bare the impress of the previous work done by canon lawyers, particularly the twelfth-century canonists.

The Canonical Position as Articulated by the Canonists of the Twelfth-Century

There were several collections of the ancient laws of the church known in the earlier Middle Ages.[22] All of them contained some canons which suggested that women should not, probably could not, function in the church in a clerical capacity. The oldest strata of this law, the *Dionysiana Collectio,* came from a collection which had been prepared in the second half of the sixth-century at Rome. This collection included canons from the Councils of Nicea, Ancyra, Neocaesaria, Gangra, Antioch Laodicea, Constantinople, Sardica, Carthage, Chalcedon, and a work called the *Canons of the Apostles.* A number of decretals from Pope Siricius were also included in some manuscripts. In the ninth-century this collection was revised slightly, and was transmitted to Charlemagne by Pope Adrian, becoming known as the *Hadriana Collectio.* In the same century this collection was joined to *Hispana Collectio,* a version attributed, at the time, to Isidore, the sixth-century bishop of Seville. This *Hadriana-Hispana Collectio,* as it is now called, existed in various local editions and versions in northern Europe. It formed the basis for several collections of *decreta* made about the time of the Gregorian Reform. Two such *decreta* (collection of laws), the *Decretum* of Burchard of Worms compiled in the eleventh-century, and the *Decretum* of Ivo, the twelfth-century bishop of Chartres, were particularly influential.[23] Finally, in the twelfth-century, the Camaldolese monk, Gratian, produced a *Decretum* which was to become "the" *Decretum,* i.e., the standard law collection in everyday use among canonists.[24] As has frequently been pointed out, and as the very title of the work suggests, *The Concordance of Discordant Canons,* Gratian's purpose was to unify the presentation of church law and to reduce to a minimum its inconsistencies and apparent disagreements. He accomplished this by rearranging the order of the canons, and by setting aside some canons which he found inauthentic or unworthy of inclusion for one reason or other. He also added a minimum of comment of his own. His personal remarks were not so much gloss or commentary on the canons themselves, but rather explanations of their placement and how they related to one another. In the course of time his own comments eventually assumed a certain legal value among the canonists, although not as much as the canons which he had codified. It was through Gratian's *Decretum* that the laws of the ancient church were transmitted to the medieval theologians. With rare exceptions it was his work which was quoted in the *Sentence* commentaries when the sacred canons were discussed.

This is not the place to enter in to a discussion of the clerical position of women in the ancient church which might be reflected in these laws.[25] Still less is it the place to discuss the authenticity of the ancient canons themselves. For our purpose it will be enough to point out that strictures against clerical status for women regularly appeared in some form or other in church law. It will also be enough to point out that the canonists and theologians who made use of these collections assumed that they reflected the church's teachings. The question of whether the supposed author of a decree was in fact its actual author was, for them, an irrelevant consideration. Whatever its origin, if a canon was subsequently promulgated by legitimate church authority, it acquired the force of church law. It was then assumed to be a law put forward by the church, and one that faithfully enshrined age-old practice and traditional values.

While the theologians of the later Middle Ages still read their Gratian, they did not as a general rule regard themselves as experts on the mass of legislation which they found in the *Decretum*. Even a cursory glance at commentaries on the *Sentences* and on scriptural texts shows that theologians relied heavily on a standard body of glosses which guided them in their interpretation of the canons. It would take us too far afield to trace the growth of all the glosses which shaped the interpretation of canon law. They would undoubtedly throw light on attitudes toward the clerical status of women. At the beginning of the thirteenth-century one such gloss established itself. That was the gloss of John Teutonicus which covered the entire *Decretum* and was to become the *Glossa Ordinaria*, the apparatus customarily used in the schools. It was published in 1216 or 1217 and was quickly adopted by the law schools of Bologna. It soon found its way into general use among theologians as well, and became the authoritative text for interpreting Gratian. Upon the publication of the *Decretales* of Gregory IX in 1234, John's *Glossa* was revised slightly by Bartholomew of Brescia and in this form they continued in use throughout the Middle Ages.[26] After the first quarter of the thirteenth-century theologians were content to view the *Decretum* with its complex legislation through the window of John's revised *Glossa*. Later books of the *Corpus Iuris Canonici* containing the canons collected after the beginning of the thirteenth-century contained virtually no new legislation pertaining to the ordination of women. As a result, when looking to the law of the church, theologians resorted to the canons of the *Decretum* as interpreted by the *Glossa Ordinaria*.

When examining the *Decretum* of Gratiam itself, the surprising discovery is not how much legislation there is to be found there about the clerical status of women, but how little. If we except a few words of comment made by Gratian, theologians interested in the problem would find in the *Decretum* perhaps half a dozen laws which actually seemed to suggest that women could be ordained at least to the diaconate. In all instances some inference, some argument, has to be drawn to apply the canon precisely to the question of ordination as such. The decrees which provide the locus for the canonical discussion, and more importantly for later theological discussion, are as follows: *Sacratas* (Dist. 23, c. 25); *Adicimus* (*Causa* 16, question 1, c. 19), along with the two forms of *Mulier quamvis* (Dist. 23, c. 29 and *De Con.,* Dist. 4, c. 20); *Mulier debet* (*Causa* 33, question 5, c. 19); *Presbiter* and *Mulieres* (Dist. 32, cc. 18 and 19); *Diaconissam* (*Causa* 27, question 1, c. 23) and *Si quis rapuerit* (*Causa* 27, question 1, c. 30). The additional words of comment made by Gratian himself can be found in a prologue to *Causa* 15 which begins with the words *Clericus quidem crimine.*[27]

Among the canons listed above the most openly restrictive is *Sacratas,* written according to its title to the Bishops of Italy by Pope Soter, who reigned from 166 to 174.[28] *Sacratas* simply says that it has come to the attention of the Holy See that consecrated women and nuns have been handling the sacred vessels and linens, and have been offering incense at the altar. This practice has to cease as soon as possible, the canon insists, so that this plague does not spread. From this, the inference can be drawn immediately that, if these somewhat minor activities in connection with the liturgy are judged to be wrong, then more important actions like offering the Eucharist or preparing the offerings and distributing communion are *a fortiori*, even more inappropriate. Later in the Middle Ages, when the action of handing over the chalice and patten (i.e., the sacred vessels) by the bishop to the those to be ordained came to be regarded as an essential part of the ordination ceremony, the stricture laid down in *Sacratas* could easily be promoted as a decisive canonical argument forbidding the ordination of women to all the higher orders where sacred vessels were used.[29]

Three other canons, *Adicimus* and *Mulier quamvis* (which is to be found in two quite similar forms), take up the question of the right of a women to preach in the church, especially in an assembly where men are present. *Adicimus,* which comes from a letter of Pope Leo to the Bishops of Cyprus, says that only ordained priests have the right to preach. It then goes on to say that monks and layman cannot do this, however learned they may be.[30] The two canons which begin *Mulier quamvis,* and which are virtually identical, are said to come from the fourth and the fifth Councils of Carthage, according to their titles.[31] They make the point that the right to teach (*docere*) in an assembly does not depend upon knowledge or sanctity, and that a woman should not presume to teach in the presence of men no matter how qualified she may be. (The fifth Council of Carthage goes on to say that a woman should not baptize anyone either.)[32] While these canons do not specifically deny that a woman can be ordained, they obviously raise a major difficulty. If a woman were ordained, she would certainly be expected to preach, and to preach to the community at large. Leadership and a corresponding degree of eminence could hardly be denied to anyone placed in such a position in the church. But this kind of activity would run counter to the words of St. Paul, who had said that he was "not giving women permission to speak or to tell a man what to do." When these words of Paul were remembered in connection with *Adicimus,* and the other canons we have just been considering, they became a locus for the discussion of ordination.

In its comments on *Adicimus* and *Mulier quamvis,* the *Glossa Ordinaria* reaffirms the right of the priest to preach and to teach, and ties this more closely to *priestly* ordination. According to the *Glossa,* deacons are said to "preach" only in the sense that they are permitted to read or chant the Gospels and say formal prayers during the liturgical services. In exceptional cases where deacons have a prelacy (as, for example, when they deputize for their bishop or metropolitan) they are said to preach by reason of their prelacy, but not by reason of their order as deacon. Laymen and even women can be given permission to "preach" by a priest in the sense that they can be allowed to *read out* material in the church, but they are never given permission to preach in the proper sense of the word.[33] Since a woman could not preach, and since preaching was attached to the priestly office, as the *Glossa Ordinaria* insisted, it was evident that a woman could never really fulfill the priestly role. While these canons about teaching and preaching do not declare against women's ordination in so many words, they do put a major stumbling block in the way. After a hesitant beginning, as we shall see, theologians began to put forward *Adicimus* as a serious, if not the most serious, objection found in church law to the ordination of women.

The canon *Mulier debet,* while somewhat to the side of the ordination question, is nonetheless cited from time to time by medieval theologians.[34] The attitude which it expresses is clearly in the background of much medieval thinking. According to this canon, "women ought" to keep their heads veiled as a sign that they are in a state of subjection. Their subjection is a result of the fact that women were responsible, initially at least, for the fall of the human race into sin. The obvious reference here is to the scriptural story of the temptation of Adam and Eve in the Garden of Eden found in Genesis. As a consequence of her role in this event, a woman should not have her head free in the churches, but veiled out of reverence. Moreover, the canon notes, women do not have the power of speaking out in church because of the deference which they should show to the bishop, who is Christ's representative. In a symbolic sense, as a result of sin, a woman does not stand in the church as the image of God, but as subject. The *Glossa Ordinaria* goes on to extend Gratian's notion of reverence to the bishop to reverence for all priests who are Christ's symbolic representatives.[35] In the light of this type of symbolism, it would be difficult for women to be ordained, for then their symbolic role would shift from that of subjection to that of eminence in the church. The notion of *eminence,* i.e., the status of being symbolically set over others for leadership in religious matters, will become a common theme in later theological literature, especially when the matter of ordination comes up.

In contrast to *Adicimus* and *Mulier debet* we find two canons, *Presbiter* and *Diaconissam*, which give religious titles to women. At first sight these canons seem to refer to the existence of deaconesses and women elders (*presbyterae*) in the ancient church, and so they were sometimes read. The canon *Diaconissam,* which carried the weight of the Council of Chalcedon, gives rules for arranging for the ordination of women deaconesses.[36] It states that they are not to be ordained before they are forty years of age, and then only after careful examination. After their "ordination," they are not to marry. *Presbiter,* which is an extract from the *Dialogues* of St. Gregory, directs priests (who are in charge of a church) from the moment of their ordination to love their priestly woman (*presbytera*) as a sister and not to continue in a more intimate relation with them.[37] Another canon of the *Decretum* (found initially in the *Novellis* of Justinian, *Si quis repuerit*) also speaks in passing of deaconesses.[38] To the uninstructed reader these texts might seem to suggest that women were in fact being ordained at one time and on a regular basis.

It was the duty of the canonists, or at least they thought that it was, to put these canons in proper context and to correct inconsistencies. If the canons were left to stand without interpretation they would appear to contradict *Sacratas.* With regard to *Presbiter* it was Gratian himself who led the way. In one of his rare personal comments he refers to the Council of Laodicea which defined the meaning of the word *presbyterae* (i.e., priestly women). Its canon, *Mulieres,* which immediately followed the canon *Presbiter* in the *Decretum,* states that those who are called *presbyterae* among the Greeks are called by us (i.e., those in Latin-speaking churches) widows, or elders, or mothers of the church. The canon *Mulieres* concludes by saying that such *presbyterae* should not be regarded as ordained.[39]

The canon *Diaconissam* poses a somewhat more difficult problem to reconcile with *Sacratas* since it is from all appearances a positive statement, backed by the authority of a General Council, which describes an existing office of the deaconeses.[40] In order to reconcile *Diaconissam* with *Sacratas* glossators had to find an authority among the early Fathers who held a different view, or else re-interpret the notion of diaconal ministry, or both. In his *Glossa* John Teutonicus presents such an authority. He argues that the content of *Diaconissam* as it stands seems to run contrary to the words of Ambrose, who wrote *before* the Council of Chalcedon. (The underlying presumption here is that a General Council would never intend to contradict anything said by a saint like Ambrose who was a Doctor of the Church.)[41] As a matter of fact, the quotation from Ambrose that John Teutonicus knew is actually not from Ambrose. It comes from the commentary on the Epistles of Paul by Ambrosiaster, something not known by John or by any of Gratian's glossators. The passage which John cites from Ambrosiaster on 1 Timothy 3:11 and reads, "Women likewise [i.e., like deacons] should be respectable . . . " Paul does not intend to say here that "women likewise are *deacons,*" Ambrosiaster insists, but rather that they likewise should be *respectable.* What Paul wants is that the people (the *plebs*) should be holy just as the clergy are (viz., the bishops and the deacons), and that this level of holiness should even be found among women who might seem to be of little importance. Seizing on the words of Paul, he continues, the Cataphrygians tried to twist them out context to imply that Paul talked about the deaconesses as well as the deacons at the church. For Ambrosiaster, it is clear that Paul should not be interpreted in this way since he had already commanded women "to keep silence in the church" in the previous passage. Besides, the Cataphrygians were tendentious in proposing their view since they knew very well that the Apostles had chosen seven male deacons even though there were holy women in their company.[42] Armed with the supposed authority of Ambrose, John Teutonicus adds his own words to the gross. "I reply that women do not receive the diaconal character by reason of the impediment of sex and the constitution of the church. Hence they cannot exercise the office of an ordained person." He confirms this by referring us back to the canon *Sacratas*.[43] In order to avoid any seeming inconsistency between the canons he adds that the women called deaconess were blessed so that they could perform some function which was not open to other layfolk. What this function might be was not very clear. His gloss on *Sacratas* suggests that it was the power to read the Gospels or homilies at a Matins service.[44]

John Teutonicus' interpretation of *Diaconissam* will become standard for later canonists and theologians, but it did not in fact originate with him. His gloss has an earlier history. John's text appears in a slightly more detailed form in the commentary of Huguccio.[45] In his commentary on Gratian, Huguccio also puts forward the authority of "Ambrose" which denied any ordained status for deaconesses, and notes his view that it was the Cataphrygians who had adapted Paul's words in order to argue that women too ought to be ordained as deaconesses in the church. Huguccio then goes on to say that this is impeded by the constitution of the church and by reason of sex, and adds the significant phrase, "that is, a constitution of the church made because of sex."[46] If a woman should *de facto* be ordained (undergo an ordination ceremony is presumably what is meant), she does not acquire the order and is prohibited from exercising its functions. Lest there be any mistake about the physical origin of the ecclesiastical prohibition of orders, Huguccio takes up the somewhat obscure point of the ordination of an hermaphrodite to emphasize that only someone obviously male is capable of receiving orders.[47] But what are we to make of the clear statement about deaconesses found in the canons of the Council of Chalcedon? Huguccio gives two answers, one flowing from the principles which he obviously holds, and a second which is the opinion of some "others." In the light of his views Huguccio is forced to conclude that the deaconesses mentioned in *Diaconissam* are not ordained individuals, but must be women chosen and instituted with a certain amount of solemn ceremony so that they can perform some functions normally reserved to deacons. This might possibly include singing or saying the Gospels at a Matins service, or reciting prayers, or exercising the sort of leadership which would fall to a deacon.[48] He then goes on to give a second opinion, added almost as an afterthought. There are "others," he says, who think that there were women who were ordained up to the diaconate in former times. This practice was prohibited by Ambrose, was reintroduced at the time of Chalcedon, and is now again abandoned. For Huguccio, it is this last view which now prevails throughout the church.[49]

The gloss of John Teutonicus, written almost a generation later, still echoes Huguccio's earlier text. In fact it is easier to grasp John's comments on *Diaconissam* after reading Huguccio's more expanded gloss. It is of great interest, moreover, to note what has been dropped. John does not mention that the constitution of the church which is a bar to a woman being ordained was a constitution made with the question of sex in mind, although it could be argued that John's readers would not have to be told this since it was presumed.[50] In John we find nothing about the problem of the hermaphrodite. By saying nothing he again need not bring up the question of sex. Finally, when John quotes the opinion of the "others" who think that women might be ordained up to the level of the diaconate, he does not give the same reason as Huguccio. As we have seen Huguccio gave a history of deaconesses being ordained until the time of Ambrose, then prohibited, reinstated again, and finally suppressed. John says nothing of all of this. What John omits leaves us with the impression that he is more interested in the current legal status of the question rather than in presenting any explanations.

While the canons *Presbiter* and *Diaconissam* (to which we might add *Si quis rapuerit*) suggest some sort of clerical status for women in the early church, they called forth a commentary which was more negative than positive in their regard. In examining the legislation of the *Decretum* in the light of what the *Glossa Ordinaria* had to say, theologians who drew on that material in the following century were at pains to show that these canons were not to be thought of as loopholes or exceptions to the general rule laid down in *Sacratas*.

We can conclude this section by looking at the passage in the *Decretum* where Gratian allows himself to make a direct statement of his own about the ordination of women. In the prologue to question 3, *causa* 15, he writes a brief preface to canons which have to do with the trial of criminous clerks. One of the legal preliminaries which had to be cleared up in the prologue was who had a right to testify against a cleric, and, to be precise, could a woman testify as a witness in a trial against a cleric? Gratian notes that according to Pope Fabian priests could be accused and testimony could be taken against them in a court only by someone "of their own order." The point that Fabian makes is the general one that anyone who is ordained has a status in society which puts them in a privileged legal position. With this privilege in mind Gratian then draws the conclusion and states that women cannot testify against priests, since "a woman cannot be promoted to the priesthood or even to the diaconate."[51] Our interest here is not in the justice of the legal procedure which would not commend itself to a modern court, but to the reasons behind Gratian's remark. His statement is clear enough—women cannot be ordained to the higher orders. While the phrase in the prologue is Gratian's *own* comment, not a part of any canon, it still would appear to represent something more than his simple personal viewpoint, still less an innovation of his own. Gratian was, after all, functioning as a lawyer when he drew up his collection of laws. It is not at all unreasonable to assume that his intention here is first of all to report the legal views common in his own time, rather than promote a purely personal opinion of his own.

Gratian is sometimes taxed with having injected his personal views about women into the laws of the medieval church, and thus is seen as a prime mover for the growth and development of an attitude which was hostile to a woman's role in the church. This is not an easy matter to assess. It may be useful to point out in this connection, however, that there were collections of canons circulating in Gratian's day, collections which were known to him, which were even more negative toward a clerical status for women than his own. In the *Hispano Collectio* for example, there are canons which say that "women should not minister at the altar," "they should not do anything which men are assigned to do," "they should not approach the altar or enter the sanctuary," "they should not preach," and "they should not presume to baptize."[52] The *Decretum* of Burchard, in addition to mentioning *Sacratas,* has canons which say that "only holy men may touch the sacred vessels," and that ". . . no woman should presume to come to the altar, or to administer with the priest, or to stand or sit in the chancel."[53] These decrees are also to be found in the *Decretum* of Ivo, Gratian's near contemporary.[54] While Gratian made extensive use of Ivo, he did not incorporate into his own *Decretum* a number of these restrictive decrees, many of them less muted and more directly against the role of women than those found in Gratian. From indications such as these, it seems too much to say that the initiative of Gratian was responsible for intensifying a negative attitude toward the status of women. It would perhaps be more accurate to say that his *Decretum* reflected an existing mentality among canonists, an attitude which Gratian simply mirrors.

Even a brief treatment of canon law at the time of the *Decretum* would be incomplete if some mention were not made of an ecclesiastical institution where women undoubtedly did exercise authority, and authority over men. This is the phenomena of the "double monastery" a prominent feature of the Celtic church, but also present on the Continent as well. In Saxon England a number of abbesses were firmly in charge of monasteries which included men and clerics in their numbers. The Abbess Hild (or Hilda) was the most famous among them.[55] In Ireland there was the celebrated monastery of St. Brigid of Kildare.[56] These monasteries were religious communities where monks and nuns, often with lay retainers, lived side by side. While the arrangement was unusual by later medieval standards, it was an established feature of early medieval life. In these communities leadership, and this included both spiritual and temporal administrative leadership, was frequently in the hands of an abbess who became the mother of her subjects, rather than in those of a masculine abbot. The explanation offered by later theologians who looked back at this custom was a curious one. By their standards the situation was peculiar so a rationalization had to be given to justify it. It was argued that a woman leader was needed in cases where men and women lived closely together so that the purity of the monks and woman religious might be preserved unimpaired.[57] The assumption which seems to have undergirded this line of reasoning was that women, being weaker by nature and unstable in mind and in affections, would be in no position to resist improper advances in the enclosed situation of a double monastery if they were put forward by men who held authority over them. Men, on the other hand, so the reasoning went, by nature had greater inner resources of spirit and more strength of character, and so would be able to resist advances made by women, even women in authority. While an explanation of this sort would be congenial to later authors who felt that they were explaining an awkward and unnatural style of religious life, there is no reason to suppose that contemporaries who lived in double monasteries actually saw the situation in this way.

We cannot know how the inmates of the monasteries of Ireland and Britain felt about the matter. In any event by the ninth-century they had died out along with much else in that indigenous church at the edges of Western Europe.[58] Their failure was largely the result of the continuous Viking raids of the ninth-century which impoverished the countryside and disrupted all cultural activities. Monasteries were particularly hard hit since they were storehouses of food and of communal wealth. While the double monastery did not make a comeback when peace was restored again in the tenth-century, the memory of them did not quite die out. In addition there were a few continental examples which also continued in existence. Faced with these examples canonists and theologians were forced to take account of the situation where women exercised a religious authority over men. It was agreed that abbesses could at times possess a legitimate authority over a community which contained both men as well as women. In addition to examples from a distant past, canonists were faced with a revival (or perhaps "establishment" would be closer to the truth) of a mixed style of community life in the twelfth-century. In 1119, the reforming Abbot Robert of Arbrissell, founded the Order of Fonterault with men and women members under the direction of a leader who would always be a woman. Papal approval was soon to follow.[59] In the same century the Camaldolese and the Gilbertines organized joint monasteries with some feminine leadership although, it is true, the chief ruler was always to be an abbot.[60] Isolated examples of women abbesses in Italy and Spain who exercised what amounted to episcopal authority provided still other instances of what must have been to later authors an anomalous situation.[61]

Canonists and theologians had to offer some theoretical explanation for a custom which undercut the general belief that the successors of Adam were designed to exercise leadership, and the followers of Eve were to remain submissive. It became necessary to examine the ultimate sources for the religious authority of a woman who ruled in a religious community, whether in a double monastery or in a community composed simply of women. Was a woman's authority parallel to the authority of a male ecclesiastic?[62] In the case of male clerics the basis for their authority was well established. A bishop or an abbot, even the priest-pastor of a parish, governed his community because he was ordained, or at least was *about to be* ordained. He was ordained with a title to preside over his community which was subject to him. As an ordained individual he was described as a member of the priestly or episcopal order. In later usage he was simply described as "having orders." Flowing from his orders came certain sacramental powers, such as authority to forgive sin in the Lord's name, or to preside over the Eucharistic meal, but in addition to his sacramental powers he also acquired a share in the power of *jurisdiction*.[63] That is to say he obtained the right to guide and govern the flock formally entrusted to his care. The power of jurisdiction was seen as something which flowed from Holy Orders, from that special grade of eminence in the church which Holy Orders signified. A double monastery presented a special problem. In a double monastery its woman superior *did indeed* possess authority to guide and govern her people, of that there was no doubt, but did she possess that authority in precisely the same way as her male counterpart? That is to say, did she really possess jurisdiction? To suggest that a woman could possess jurisdiction seemed to say that she was in a certain sense ordained, or at the very least it seemed to imply that she, *too,* had that special grade of eminence which Holy Orders was said to bestow. While a case for this might possibly be made, the canonists of the twelfth-century, and their successors, did not think in these terms.

They preferred to ground the basis for the authority which a woman religious superior possessed in other ways. The formula they used was carefully phrased so that it did *not* imply that women possessed true jurisdiction. If a woman superior seemed to excommunicate or to suspend clerics under her care, or to appoint pastors in churches in her charge, all acts implying possession of jurisdiction, she was not in fact really exercising jurisdiction. This was because she was not doing these things in her *own* name. Despite appearances, she only functioned as a delegate of someone else who did possess jurisdiction. This was either a nearby bishop or the Holy See if her community was exempt from episcopal control. When a woman seemed to appoint clerics in her community to give sermons or to hear confessions, she was not exercising jurisdiction herself, so the argument ran, but was simply designating particular clerics who would then automatically receive the jurisdiction needed to do these things from some higher church authority who ultimately possessed the jurisdiction. The authority which an abbess or other woman religious superior possessed in a solemn and permanent manner did indeed bind her subjects to obey, but it was not, properly speaking, a jurisdiction. In the literature of canonists and theologians it became known as "dominative power." the private, domestic authority necessary to run the affairs of her community.[64]

The distinction between jurisdiction and dominative power was a useful one for theologians struggling with the clerical role of women in the church. Jurisdiction, and that grade of eminence in the church which it implied, could be reserved for those who were ordained (or who were about to be ordained), while the domestic authority needed by a women in charge of a religious community could be institutionalized and regulated under the title of dominative power. Under such an arrangement a woman could, and sometimes did, exercise a great deal of very real power, and could become an influential, even an eminent figure in her neighborhood, and at the same time not possess the *symbolic* eminence which was associated with the "jurisdiction" that came with Holy Orders. The same distinction was also pressed into service to explain the anomalies to the general practice of the church which were sometimes found in particular legal privileges and in local customs where women seemed to be entitled to exercise the kind of authority normally reserved to clerics. By the twelfth-century the distinction between dominative power and jurisdiction was well established, as was the more general distinction between the "power of orders," (i.e., the right to celebrate the sacraments) and the "power of jurisdiction" (the right to guide and govern).

Influence of the Canonists on the Theologians

Toward the middle of the thirteenth-century the attitudes of the canonists as expressed in the *Glossa Ordinaria* on the *Decretum* of Gratian began to make their way into *Sentence* commentaries written by theologians. One of the earliest discussions that I have been able to find which takes up the ordination of women comes from the English theologian Richard Fishacre, who incepted at Oxford under his friend Robert Bacon.[65] Fishacre's commentary on the *Sentences,* which is a full-length commentary, has long been recognized as an innovative and pioneering work. He completed his lectures on the *Sentences* in 1240 and is credited with being the first Dominican at Oxford to do so. In his *Sentences* he concentrated on dogmatic aspects of theology, preferring to leave the *moralitia,* the moralizing aspects of theology, to commentaries on the Scriptures. This action was regarded as novel enough in his own day to gain a reprimand from Grosseteste, the bishop of Lincoln, and only the intervention of Innocent IV enabled him to continue lecturing *ordinarie* on the *Sentences.*

Where Peter Lombard had only given age requirements when discussing qualifications for ordination in the *Sentences,* Fishacre presents an expanded list. "Many things are required for this sacrament," he tells us, "first of all is the masculine sex; and it follows from this that a woman is incapable of receiving orders." In a following paragraph he expands on his statement. "Let it be noted," he says, "that if she should be ordained" (presumably if a woman were to go through an ordination ceremony is what is meant), "she would not receive the character [of Order], nor would she be ordained." Fishacre, in line with Huguccio, says that these conclusions flow from "the impediment of her sex and from the constitution of the church." Lest anyone be still in doubt about a woman's status, he adds, "abbesses are not able to preach, or to bless, or to excommunicate or to absolve, or to give penances, or to judge, or to exercise the office of any order."

Fishacre's statement is crisp, blunt, and leaves no room for any uncertainty about his opinion. Since we have seen nothing like this before in a *Sentence* commentary, only in texts of canon law, it is a surprisingly specific statement. One has the impression that it might be the result of some actual case, or concrete agitation on the matter.[66] The arguments he uses are still heavily dependent upon canon law, however. He begins by citing *Sacratas* which says that women may not touch the sacred vessels or linens. He "knows" that the canon was by Pope Soter to the bishops of

Italy, something which he would have read, of course, in the title to the canon in contemporary editions of the *Decretum*. He adds two other canons from the *Decretum*, *Mutier quamvis* (D. 23, c. 29), and *Mulier debet* (C. 33, q. 5, c. 19), but without quoting their contents. They state that a woman, however learned, cannot teach in a male assembly, and that a woman should keep her head veiled in the church because of reverence for the bishop; nor does she have the right to speak since it is the bishop who takes the place of Christ there.[67] He also adds a third canon, *De monialibus*, one which will become a part of the *Decretales* of Gregory IX, but which in his day was still listed as among the *Extravagantes*. This decree states that nuns who have fallen into excommunication should be absolved by the authority of the *bishop* of the diocese in which their monastery resides. The canon is concerned, of course, simply with establishing what authority has the power to absolve, but it is for him a convenient witness to the fact that a woman superior of a community of nuns cannot absolve, the nearby bishop must.[68]

In his reply Fishacre also cites the canons *Diaconissam* and *Presbiter,* the canons which seem to suggest that there once were deaconesses and women priests in the early church. Following John Teutonicus he reports that deaconesses were simply women who were allowed to read out a homily at a Matins service or to perform some other function which other nuns were not allowed to do. The feminine title, *presbytera*, refers to the wives of priests, or to widows who were given care of things about a church somewhat like the mother of a household might be. He also mentions a decree coming from the *Novella* of the Emperor Justinian, but this too is something found in the *Decretum*. Like *Diaconissam* it speaks in passing of deaconesses, but, for Fishacre, it, too, really refers only to unordained women who have been given some special function around a church.[69] Fishacre's canon law comes, quite obviously, from the *Decretum*, and the *Decretum* seen through the *Glossa Ordinaria* of John Teutonicus. As we have already mentioned, the *Gloss* appeared in 1216 or 1217. In the 1240's it would represent the conventional canonical wisdom of Fishacre's days as a student. He also knows of the canon *De monialibus* which would appear in the *Decretales,* and perhaps knew of the work itself published in 1234. That canonical collection, however, must have been something which was still quite new when he wrote his *Sentence* commentary in as much as he cites the decree appearing in it as still among the *Extravagantes*, i.e., the uncodified laws. Fishacre's debt to the *Glossa Ordinaria* is in fact even deeper than might at first appear. The phrase which he uses in his commentary to prove that women cannot be ordained—"it is because of the impediment of sex and by reason of the constitution of the church," is itself a quotation from the *Glossa Ordinaria* on *Dianconissam.*[70]

In all probability it was also from the John's Gloss on *Diaconissam* that Fishacre learned about the Cataphrygians. It was only this group, he reports, who claimed that women could by rights be ordained and receive a priestly and diaconal character. Although the Cataphrygians will be mentioned from time to time in *Sentence* commentaries their views need not detain us. Their tenets were not very well known by the theologians, and what was known was that they were an heretical sect in the early church. The fact that this third-century off-shoot of Montanism, as we now recognize them, happened to ordain women would not be any kind of witness to the acceptability of the practice in the church as far as medieval theologians were concerned. In succeeding centuries when this practice of the Cataphrygians is brought up it will always be as an example of something false and tainted with heresy.[71]

After listing the canons which prove to him that women cannot be ordained, Fishacre goes on to say that "Christ did not even give the keys to the blessed Mary but to Peter, although she was more excellent than the apostles."[72] The force of this argument is to separate personal worthiness and ability to minister in the church from the right to receive orders. The theme of the excellence of the Virgin and her unordained status will be taken up frequently in later authors. Fishacre may have read of this opinion in the letter of Innocent III, issued in Dec. 1210, to the Bishop of Burgos and Abbot of Morimundo, where the Pope complains about the women in that Spanish diocese who appear to have usurped clerical functions. A portion of Innocent's letter made its way into the *Decretales* where Fishacre may well have seen it. If so, it is curious that he did not cite the Pope's authority, which would have strengthened his conclusion. The phraseology of Innocent, or a close approximation, will appear in a number of commentaries on the *Sentences*, but as far as I have been able to find he is never cited as an authority in this connection, nor is reference ever made to the fact that the text appears in the *Decretales.*

After Fishacre, discussion of the ordination of women becomes more common, and the reasons given against it become more elaborate. Simon of Hinton, Fishacre's probable successor at Oxford, mentions it in his commentary. Simon's work is not a full-blown commentary, rather a practically minded synopsis of current church teaching written for students, who were not overly curious, but simply wanted a short manual that contained everything essential which a cleric ought to know. Hinton lectured at Oxford from 1248 (the year he became a Master of Theology) until 1250, or possibly 1254.[73] If his commentary was not actually composed at the time, it was certainly finished shortly after. He employs virtually the same phrases as Fishacre to record his opposition to the ordination of women. The text is of no great intrinsic interest, but is significant because of its popularity. A large number of manuscripts are known to have survived, both on the Continent and in England, four of which are to be found in Oxford alone. For a time Simon's work was attributed to John Gerson, the famous Chancellor of the University of Paris, and it appears in editions of Gerson's work giving it a latter day popularity.

One Oxford manuscript of Simon's manual also happens to contain a similar sort of manual on the sacraments by an anonymous Franciscan lector at Oxford, explicitly dated 1261. This Franciscan author says, quite as a matter of routine, that, "masculine sex is required for ordination, or else the order is not received."[74] No further explanation is given, but this is hardly unusual in a manual of this type which is designed to summarize doctrine, not to defend it. The English Dominican lector, William of Rothwell, who composed a summary-commentary on the *Sentences* around 1255, handles the matter in much the same way. He says simply that the female sex impedes ordination, because a woman cannot teach nor should they be put in charge of men.[75] His *Super Sententias,* like Hinton's, was quite popular as a manual and survives in twelve manuscripts scattered through England and down the Rhine Valley in Germany. Texts such as the ones cited above are useful as witnesses to the common opinion held by theologians at the time.

In the light of the evidence examined so far we can say that before 1240 no theological text (at least none that I have come upon) touched on the ordination of women although the canonists had addressed the issue. After the 1250's, on the other hand, almost all theologians if they spoke extensively about orders at all had at least something to say on the matter. By the middle of the thirteenth-century, then, it was customary to teach that the masculine sex was one of the requirements for orders, and that women were to be excluded entirely from them. If a reason was assigned, it was said that this was from "the constitution of the church," and various decrees from canon law were put forward to bolster that view. The great *Sentence* commentators adopted that conclusion as their own, but they also began now to put forward theological arguments by way of explanation.

Articulation of a Theological Position: Sacramental Symbolism and the Non-Ordination of Women

One of the great commentators on the *Sentences* in the middle ages was the Franciscan Master, John Fidanza, better known as Bonaventure.[76] He was already a Master of Arts in 1234 at Paris, and spent the next twenty years of his life going through that long course of study which led to the degree of Master of Sacred Theology. He completed the degree at Paris in 1253. His lectures on the *Sentences* were given between 1250 and 1252, and form the basis for the published version of his ample and popular commentary. By 1250, the *quaestio* format used in the *Sentence* commentaries had become standardized. His commentary, like those of his contemporaries and later colleagues at the universities, is a series of these formal *quaestiones* or articles. The format is well-known. Each *quaestio* opened with a statement of a thesis, usually beginning with the word *an* or *utrum*, i.e., "whether" something or other was true or right. The author then assembled a number of objections against his thesis and set them down at the beginning of the discussion. The objections would normally be followed by a series of statements by authorities which supported the author's own opinion. After these preliminaries, which were designed to focus the issues at stake in the article, the author would put forward his own views and give his explanation for them. This explanation formed the "body" or *corpus* of the *quaestio*, and it was its most important part. At the end of the *quaestio*, the author would refute or "solve" all the objections which had been raised in the first place. While an author took responsibility for everything said, it is worthwhile to keep in mind that the core of his teaching would be found in the body of the article. It was here that the author presented his public, magisterial opinion. Thoughts which were less well digested, tangential ideas, or peripheral matters were usually put forward in replies to the objections, or occasionally through the mouths of the authorities that he presented in support of his opinion. The material found in replies to objections and in the authorities an author chooses to quote, are invaluable, of course, in revealing his overall point of view and in filling out the skeleton of an argument, but normally the author's own best judgment, where we find him most precise, is in the body of his article, i.e., the *corpus* of the question.

In his *Sentences* Bonaventure explicitly asks "whether the masculine sex is required for receiving orders." In the article he begins by gathering together the prevailing canonical arguments. Following common opinion, he notes that a woman cannot be admitted to sacred orders because this is expressly ruled out by the canon *Sacratas*. *Sacratas* states that women cannot touch the sacred vessels and linens or perform functions at the altar, and therefore everyone agrees that women ought not to be promoted to orders.[77] But a doubt seems to remain in Bonaventure's mind. While they may not be ordained now, in the present discipline of the church, is it theoretically possible for them to be ordained? As we might put it, is *Sacratas* merely an expression of ecclesiastical legislation which might be changed, or does the prohibition expressed there rest on something deeper? For Bonaventure the doubt is a legitimate one. It is this doubt which he examines in the body of the article.

Continuing with the canonical part of the discussion, Bonaventure says that some have held that women could be ordained. Those who have held this view supported their contention by bringing forward a number of canons, such as *Diaconissam*, *Si quis rapuerit*, and *Presbiter*, which seem to suggest that there were ordained women in the ancient church. Without dismissing the doubt itself, Bonaventure dismisses these canons as offering valid proofs that women were ordained at one time. A close examination of them, particularly of the canon *Presbiter* and what follows, shows that words like *presbytera* (which we might translate as "priestess") that appear in some of the canons are really nothing more than references to widows, senior women, or elderly ladies of a church. The expression "deaconesses" likewise refers only to women who have been blessed and who share with deacons the right to read out a (prepared) homily. We can never suppose that there ever were women promoted to Holy Orders, at least, Bonaventure cautiously concludes, going by what *these* canons have to say. The state of the canonical argument leads Bonaventure to add that the better opinion, the one more in line with the thinking of the more prudent doctors is that women are incapable of receiving orders both by reason of church law and in actual fact.[78]

It is the state of the canonical argument which moves Bonaventure to the opinion that only men can be ordained. The canons which he cites, *Sacratas*, *Si quis rapuerit*, *Diaconissam*, and *Presbiter*, all are to be found in Gratian and will be continuously referred to by theologians throughout the rest of the medieval period. We have already seen what Fishacre had to say about them. Not only do references to these canons become commonplace, but they are given a standard interpretation by theologians.

Bonaventure, like Fishacre, follows the path of the popular *Glossa Ordinaria* of John Teutonicus. In interpreting *Diaconissam,* for example, he says that while the canon states that, "no one is to be ordained as a deaconess until they are forty years of age, and once ordained they lose their right to marry," this does not mean that deaconesses were *really* ordained. Deaconesses do not receive a sacramental character, he insists, because of the impediment of sex and the constitution of the church, nor are they able to exercise an order. The canon means only that such women are blessed so that they can then perform a special service such as, perhaps, reading out homilies or the Gospels at morning prayer, which other people would not be permitted to do. Comparison of Bonaventure's interpretation of *Diaconissam* with the *Glossa Ordinaria* shows it is simply a shortened form of the *Gloss* of John Teutonicus.[79] In Bonaventure, our friends the Cataphrygians again appear, but he agrees with the *Glossa* that their peculiar views run counter to the authority of Gratian, and are to be rejected.[80] Theologians writing after Bonaventure will routinely take their interpretation of church law from Gratian, and the Gratian as expounded in the early thirteenth-century in the *Glossa Ordinaria.*

Bonaventure is a theologian, however, and not a canonist. After reporting the canonical arguments he goes on in the article to sketch out some theological justification for the church's law and practice. In this endeavor he is much less indebted to canon law than was Fishacre. Bonaventure turns to sacramental symbolism and develops an argument which ultimately flows from a Christian understanding of the relations between God and the human race, and between man and woman. In the sacrament of Orders, he begins, the person who is ordained must symbolically represent Christ, the mediator. Now the mediator appears in masculine form and only in that form. In consequence, Christ as the mediator can be represented only by a man. It is for this reason that the possibility of receiving orders is restricted to men.[81] In a tense and very compact passage he points out that there is a double reason for such symbolic values. Only men are *naturally* able to represent the mediator and, in accordance with the character they receive, be a sign of this in actual fact. Bonaventure then concludes the body of the article somewhat cautiously, announcing that this is the more probable opinion, and the one which can be proved by numerous authorities from among the saints.[82]

At the end of the article Bonaventure leaves his readers with two crucial questions which do not find any immediate answers in the article itself. First, just what is the ability to "naturally represent" what is received in orders? Second, what is the precise quality of that sign which is conferred through the character of orders which restricts it to men? Bonaventure obviously connects orders with the activity of Christ as a *masculine* mediator. But why does he do so? A deeper understanding of his attitude can be found in two key *questiones* of his *Sentence* commentary. The first, found in the second book, deals with the right relation that should be found between man and woman. The other passage occurs in the third book, where he speaks about the masculine role of the incarnate redeemer.[83] The creation story of Genesis provides Bonaventure with the series of images that he uses in connection with both *quaestiones*. Looking to the second chapter of Genesis, Bonaventure finds that God, after He had created Adam as the unique, primordial human individual, caused him to fall into a deep sleep, and then create Eve, the woman, out of his rib. In common with other medieval theologians, Bonaventure sees this story as a paradigm which enables him to untangle the relations which should exist between man and woman, while at the same time allows him to talk about the symbolic values which are projected by each sex in other realms of existence.

Why was Eve produced from Adam's side? What value did that express? Bonaventure replies that this was entirely appropriate, as are all of God's works, especially the forming of rational creatures, for the wisdom of God was so wonderfully displayed in this event. This is particularly apparent when we consider the harmonious order which was preserved in producing woman from the side of man. Such harmony can be found *both* in the relations between man and woman in the human species, and also in other areas where man and woman can serve as appropriate symbols.[84]

Bonaventure agrees that a symbolic order is not identical with the physical order of things, but much symbolism is squarely based upon it, so it is appropriate to begin by looking at the order which appears in physical nature. He finds that in nature (the order *secundum rem*) men and women were created as beings which were mutually interdependent. The masculine and feminine expressions of human life each complete the other. To be more precise, Bonaventure says that it is the purpose of woman to give rest and fulfillment to man, while the masculine function is to nourish and sustain the woman. Man and woman are thus mutually joined by an intensive bond so that a woman is related to a man, and a man to a woman, with the result that each sex is life-giving to the other. The woman is to give tranquillity and a sense of worth to man, the man to be a support and a provider for a woman.[85] From his description of relationship it is obvious that Bonaventure does not have in mind a society of individuals each independent and equal. That would be far from his vision of a living society which is rather a set of interlocking and self-giving relationships. He looks rather to a kind of equality characterized by mutuality. Each sexual expression is necessary for the well-being of the other, even for the very existence of the other.[86] Self-giving will be equal in the relationship, but it will not be a giving of the same things. For Bonaventure mutuality is found in the real world, in the real diversity present in man and woman. It is on this foundation that we can discern what maleness and the feminine truly signify; beginning from that foundation we can apply that significance to other aspects of human life. It will be from an analysis of what fulfillment and rest (the feminine role) mean, and from analyzing nurture and support (the masculine role) that we will discover the full range of symbolism which sexuality projects in consciousness. Mutual dependency, which is so well expressed by the unity, the cooperation of man and woman, finds important applications in other aspects of Christian experience. Bonaventure points to three such areas: the relation between God and the individual soul; the relation between Christ and his church; and finally between inferior and superior reason (today we would probably prefer to say higher and lower consciousness).[87] In drawing out the symbolism of the mutuality found in the relationship between God and the individual soul Bonaventure draws an extended simile. He presents God as a masculine figure, the one furnishing all spiritual nourishment and support to the human soul which in its turn always remains feminine to God. The soul, following out his imagery, also has its role to play, for God is said to rest and to take delight in the human soul. As the author of Proverbs has said, "when his delights are to be with the sons of man."[88] The symbolism of mutuality can also be extended to describe the relationship which exists between Christ and the church. Just as Eve was formed by God from the rib of Adam, so the church was born from the body of Christ when blood and water flowed from His side (lanced by the soldier's spear) while He lay sleeping on the Cross. Moreover, Bonaventure adds in an aside, it was from Christ's creative action on the Cross that the sacraments of the new-born church gained their efficacy, i.e., the sacraments on which the church is founded. In this symbolism Christ's activity is masculine.[89] Bonaventure extends the imagery of mutuality to illustrate the states of consciousness which are found in every human psyche and which medieval authors, following Augustine, were accustomed to call "higher and lower reason." The phraseology takes us back to an interpretation of the temptation and the fall of Adam and Eve which is given by Augustine in his *De Trinitate*, an interpretation which medieval theologians were fond of using.[90] Augustine speaks of a marriage in the human psyche between an Adam and an Eve, that is to say between a kind of higher and a lower reason. Lower reason judges according to appearances, i.e., according to the conditions and the needs of mundane earthly existence, while higher reason judges human experience according to true or Divine standards. Now the sin committed in the Garden by the first parents of the human race was a primal sin. We find, in consequence, in every sin a repetition of the pattern whereby an Eve (our "lower" pragmatic and worldly reasoning) allows herself to become tempted with the result that she withdraws the "Adam" in us (our "higher" contemplative and God-directed reasoning power) from reflecting upon its true, heavenly goals and pulls it down toward the object of temptation. The result is that the pattern set up in the Garden where Eve tempted Adam is now repeated. In this imagery Adam (that higher reason which is found in *every* human being whether male or female!) is drawn away from due subordination to God and shifts its choice toward transitory and earthly goods to such an extent that they become temptations that totally absorb him. In the imagery of the Genesis story Adam goes along with the concerns of Eve so as not to disappoint her, while Eve is said to be seduced by the wiles of the devil, i.e., the transitory, even fleshly, concerns of life.

While Adam and Eve are both present in every human soul according to the terms of this imagery, and while each is an indispensable help to the other, Bonaventure introduces into his work a certain amount of that pejorative characterization of women which was a part of so much theological literature since at least the time of Augustine. In this imagery Eve inevitably appears as that part of the soul which is inferior, weak, unstable and incapable of any direct approach to heavenly wisdom unless aided by the mediation of that higher and better part of the soul which is Adam. The danger here, of course, is to pass from the symbol to begin to think of women themselves as inherently weak, unstable, less wise as human individuals. This is not to say that medieval theologians did not ever fall into this trap—indeed they often did—but it is important to remember that when they refer back to the Genesis story they are talking about symbols and their significance in tracing God's plan for salvation, they are not talking directly about men or women. As a consequence medieval authors are fond of using expressions like the presidential status of men, or the subject status of women. These phrases are not necessarily to be taken as a description of the skills or abilities of any given man or woman. Bonaventure's language should be read in that spirit.

When Bonaventure turns his attention to Christ as the mediator, the author of human salvation, he continues to employ symbolic language. In the third book of the *Sentences* he asks whether it would have been appropriate for Christ to have assumed flesh in female form. He replies that it would not have been appropriate for Christ because the masculine sex is of a greater dignity, and, therefore, the sex more suitable for the mission of the mediator.[91] This dignity can be shown in three ways. Our first consideration is the origin of the human race. Adam was, of course, the first human being created and is, in consequence, the unique and the supreme source for the entire race. Inasmuch as all later generations flow from him, in a peculiar sense he resembles God the creator. Just as all creatures flow from the one God who is the principle of all, so Adam in a sense represents God as the font and source of all humankind, both men and women. For Bonaventure this argument implies that the dignity of Adam is greater, and the sex which he represents is also of a greater dignity. A second consideration is the differing roles of man and woman. The role of a man is to be active and of a woman to be passive. This is evident, he says, because a man is more robust than woman both in name and in fact. Finally, the greater dignity of the masculine sex rests on its authority to preside. If a correct order is to be maintained, it is appropriate that a man oversee a woman "as the head oversees the body."[92] We recognize a common theme of medieval literature, but it is worth noting that in the heart of his article Bonaventure does not resort to biological or philosophical arguments, or even to bits of his own experience to prove his point. He simply relies on the "words of the Apostle."[93]

From the preceding passages it is quite obvious that Bonaventure envisages the Incarnate Christ as a masculine figure, not as feminine, and certainly not as impersonal. The sex out of which the Christ will play his role as mediator will be masculine. From the terms of his remarks it is an active, a directive, and a presidential one.[94] Following this line of reasoning it goes without saying that anyone who is to act in the church *in persona Christi* must also fulfill a masculine role. This is precisely what Bonaventure says, as we have seen, when he comes to discuss candidates for orders in the fourth book of his *Sentences*. Only a man can naturally represent Christ, and only a man can be a sign of the order he has received.[95] On the natural level, the masculine role is to nourish and support while the role of the woman is to provide rest and a sense of fulfillment. The woman's role is to be receptive, and so she becomes the obvious symbol of the soul before God, and of the church before Christ. The imagery given in orders is very different and not feminine. Order is concerned with spiritual power, that is, with direction, supervision, and with continuing the mediation of Christ. This is a necessity, Bonaventure points out, because the church contains a multitude of people. It would fall into confusion unless directed, and lapse into error without leaders. Divine wisdom has provided the church with a well structured constitution and with good leadership (otherwise, being the kind of institution it is, it might fall into error and lack leadership). As a consequence, it is quite appropriate that there be a sacrament where power is conferred so that ministers of God may provide the sacraments and maintain proper order.[96] From what Bonaventure has already said it is obvious that, for him, this role is more suitable to men than to women.

The sacrament of Order has several levels (grades) each conferring a particular power to exercise leadership in the church. While these powers may differ, some degree of configuration with Christ is conferred with each of the grades of order. Hence anyone who is ordained at all is a sign of Christ, and represents Christ before the church to some degree. In Bonaventure's eyes these powers can be exercised, these roles fulfilled, only by a man. While masculinity is required for all grades of Order, it is especially so for the higher or the sacred orders, and most especially so for the priesthood where the minister not only handles sacred things, but actually confects what is sacred, i.e., consecrates the Eucharist.[97]

When speaking about sacred orders Bonaventure is, of course, continuing to employ symbolic language. The innate ability or the acquired skills enabling someone to lead or to direct others is beside the point. No one can receive orders unless they bear within them the image of God. The masculine sex is, for him, more suited to receive orders because it reflects that special imaging of God in the more appropriate way. In a somewhat flamboyant passage he says that in the sacrament of Orders the ordained individual is to a certain extent "made God," being a participant in God's power. Such a status quite obviously does not depend upon anyone's skill or ability, but must be based upon symbolic factors. Referring to a text common among medieval authors, Bonaventure says that it is the man by reason of his sex who is made in the image of God. As a consequence of this a woman cannot be ordained.[98]

Bonaventure is aware that a number of objections can be raised to the logic of his position. What shall we make of the fact, he has an objector ask, that the character given in orders is a spiritual reality, and that spiritual realities are received in the soul, not in the body? There is no distinction of sex in the soul, sex is purely a bodily matter. If orders are received in the soul, why shouldn't a woman be just as capable as a man of receiving them? Bonaventure handles this objection (which was raised quite commonly in *Sentence* commentaries), by pointing out that orders is not a matter of the soul alone, but of the "soul as it is conjoined to the flesh."[99] This remark reflects, of course, the general medieval viewpoint that sacramental life of the church was not simply a cerebral affair, a matter of words and ideas, but rather an activity which involved the whole human personality and had to include physical body and the life of the senses. Sacramental practice inevitably involved washings, meals, anointings, and the like. Activities such as these could never be carried out by a soul at an impersonal or disembodied level. Holy orders, like all the other sacraments, required some visible sign which involved the body. Not the soul, but the body, which must be either masculine or feminine, had to be our point of reference for these signs. For this reason the sacramental character and the activity flowing from it could not escape bodily identification, and with that identification the patterns of feminine and masculine symbolism.

Because Holy orders was so closely identified with notions of representation, rather than with ability to perform ministerial functions, Bonaventure felt called upon to conclude that the masculine sex was an essential requirement not only for receiving the higher orders, such as priest or bishops, but for all orders. For him there was a certain symbolic unity among all levels of Order, high or low. While a bishop alone should be called the spouse of the church, since he alone represents Christ to the church in a complete and perfect way, nevertheless, he goes on, all the grades of order are a preparation for the episcopacy. It follows from this, if anyone considers the question carefully, that those who receive any order at all should be capable of becoming a bishop. Since a woman cannot be called the husband of the church, i.e., cannot be a bishop, it follows logically that it is not appropriate for her to receive any of the other orders either.[100] At both the natural and the sacramental level imagery and symbolism combine in Bonaventure's theology to favor the ordination of men. It is only in this way that a right symbolic order will be maintained in the church. Hence he concludes his article by saying "this position is the more probable and the one which can be proved by many authorities among the saints." It is obviously the opinion which he has made his own.[101]

Bonaventure's younger contemporary and colleague at the University of Paris, Thomas Aquinas, also saw the question of ordination as a problem rooted in religious symbolism, but he did not develop that symbolism in quite the same way. Thomas taught at Paris from 1255 to 1260 in the

Dominican chair reserved for strangers, that is for non-French members of the Order.[102] He takes up the question in his commentary on the *Sentences* in the usual place. Close readers of Thomas usually expect to find at least two separate treatments of major theological issues in his writings, an early discussion in his *Sentence* commentary, and a later, occasionally contrasting one, in his *Summa Theologica*. Regrettably the *Sentence* commentary treatment is Thomas's only statement on this important question, if we except a brief mention in his *Summa Contra Gentiles,* a treatise not directed to Christian theologians.[103] The discussion in the *Summa* has always been regarded as his definitive and more considered view of a question. In the *Summa* Thomas approached issues as part of his overall vision of theology without being restricted by an order of questions and methodological considerations dictated by someone else's arrangement of questions. The *Summa* was not a commentary with all the restrictions that that form of writing implies, but a presentation of his own. While there is a unity in Thomas's thought which is evident enough from the beginning of his career, especially his philosophic outlook, he did change his mind, sometimes significantly, from the *Sentence* commentary to the *Summa*. Unfortunately we do not have a second statement of his views about ordination questions, since Aquinas did not finish his treatment of the seven sacraments in his *Summa.* This is indeed unfortunate. Thomas's theology of the sacraments in the *Summa* turns upon the power of symbolism where he is concerned with the power of symbols and how they affect the human psyche in order to mediate God's presence to the individual and to society. In the last part of the *Summa* Thomas began to apply his ideas about symbolism, both natural and Divinely appointed symbolism, to the seven ceremonial rites of the church which are called the sacraments. His analysis breaks off, however, in the discussion of the sacrament of penance. This is at the very point where a discussion of holy orders would normally begin.[104] A certain incompleteness is in fact already evident in his discussion of the sacrament of the Eucharist. Thomas explains the problem of the real presence of Christ in the bread and wine of the Eucharist in great detail, and the Communion service is also covered, but discussion of the Mass as a sacrifice appears overly brief and curiously truncated. It is precisely at this point that we would expect notions about priestly offering and ministry to be taken up.[105] In order to give some answers to the questions which Thomas did not cover, later medieval and modern editions of his *Summa Theologica* regularly add a section to the original text known as the *Supplement*. This *Supplement* was constructed by a fifteenth-century editor, Henry of Gorkum, who rearranged material taken from Thomas's earlier *Sentence* commentary to fill out the original plan of the *Summa*.[106] Thomas' entire treatment of the sacrament of Orders, found in contemporary editions of the *Summa Theologica,* is from the *Supplement*, and is simply a reprinting of the ideas which Thomas had at the beginning of his theological career when he was writing his commentary on the *Sentences*.

Thomas takes up the ordination of women under the general heading of "deficiencies of nature in those proposed for ordination."[107] (This was the customary way of posing the question when Thomas was working up his commentary on the *Sentences* in the 1250's. He then asks, "Does feminine sex interfere with the reception of orders?" When Bonaventure raised the question he was concerned, as we have seen, not only with whether a woman *should* be ordained, but whether she *could* be ordained. Thomas taught at Paris shortly after Bonaventure, and begins his reply by clarifying his own position on this point. Some qualities, he says, are so essential in the recipient of a sacrament that neither the grace (*res*) of the sacrament, nor the sacrament (*sacramentum*), is received without them. There are other qualities, however, which should be in a recipient of a sacrament, but which are less essential. In these latter cases the sacrament can be received, although not the grace (*res*) which is promised in the sacraments.[108] For Thomas, the masculine sex is one of those requirements which is necessary not only for receiving the grace promised in the sacrament of Orders, but for receiving the sacrament itself. To avoid any ambiguity he adds that even if a woman went through the formality of an ordination service she would not receive any order.[109] The reason which Thomas gives for this is that a sacrament is a *sign*, and, more precisely, a sign of what is symbolized in the sacrament itself. The recipient must be able to be seen as a living sign, a living symbol of what the sacrament claims to be offering. To use an example which Thomas himself offers, in the sacrament of the anointing of the sick (extreme unction) what is offered to a recipient is the grace of healing from illness. But to be healed a person must first be sick in some way. A healthy person, however well intentioned, cannot receive the sacrament of the anointing of the sick because there is no way in which he can signify being in need of a cure.[110] This is precisely the situation of a woman seeking orders. In Thomas' opinion, she is incapable of symbolizing what is signified in orders.

What precisely is the quality of the feminine sex which renders a woman incapable of orders? In his reply Thomas lists only one such quality, and it illumines for us his entire understanding of the nature of orders. He says that a woman cannot receive orders because she cannot effectively symbolize any degree of eminence inasmuch as her status is one of subjection.[111]

In his article in the *Sentences* Thomas does not discuss the symbolic value of eminence any further beyond a brief quote from 1 Timothy 2:12, "I do not allow women to teach (*docere*) in church, or to be given authority over a man;" and reference to the eleventh chapter of 1 Corinthians. In default of any further treatment of the ordination of women in the *Summa,* it might seem that Thomas's commentaries on the Epistles of St. Paul would be the next best place to look for an account of his views of the symbolism of ordination, especially since he refers us to Paul himself. Thomas is known to have commented on the Epistles of St. Paul more than once, and to have had a greater respect for them than for any other writings, except for the Gospels. A promising place to look, but not without difficulties. Thomas's major commentary on the Epistles of Paul is his *Expositio*, which is a work either dictated by him or corrected by him. Curiously enough, the *Expositio* of Paul also breaks off. Moreover, it does so precisely at the point where we would be most interested, at 1 Corinthians, Chapter 10. This is the famous passage where Paul commands women to pray with veiled heads because women are subject to men. To fill out the commentary by Thomas on the remainder of Paul's Epistles (i.e., after 1 Corinthians 11 through Hebrews) we must rely again on one of his youthful works. This is the *Reportatio* made by Reginald of Piperno of an earlier commentary on Paul by Thomas. According to Weisheipl, the *Reportatio* is the report of an early *lectura* given when Thomas was in Italy, sometime between 1259 and 1265. It is possibly part of another complete commentary on all the Epistles of Paul.[112] A *Reportatio* by Reginald would, of course, communicate Thomas's essential ideas, but it would present them in an uncorrected and undigested form. Such a transmission of Thomas's remarks might very well emphasize, by word or phrase, thoughts which appealed to the reporter, perhaps more than they did to the original master himself. By a curious coincidence, we once again have no mature statement of Thomas on the matter.

In Reginald's *Reportatio* over the key passage from 1 Timothy, "I do not allow women to teach in the church or to be given authority over men" (and this is Reginald's report of Thomas's ideas), we find a distinction between what Paul thinks is appropriate behavior for women, and what they should not be doing. Women *should* be silent (tight-lipped might be a better translation), eager to receive instruction, and submissive. Why are these particular qualities appropriate for women? They are fitting for those who are "deficient of reason." The *Reportatio* goes on to say that the words of women are inflammatory, and those who don't have native acumen should be eager to receive instruction. As Aristotle says, whenever two realities are mutually related, as for example, body and soul, or sense and intellectual knowledge, the partner more endowed with reason should take the lead, while the other member of the pair should be submissive.[113]

The *Reportatio* of 1 Corinthians, ch. 11 (Thomas's second reference in the *Sentences*), pursues these themes. Over the statements of Paul that women should veil their heads when praying in church as a sign of their subjection to men, the *Reportatio* agrees that this is surely the case. Nature itself conspires to reveal this to us, since it is in accord with nature for a woman to cultivate long hair as a kind of natural veiling.[114] In ch. 14 (verses 33-36) of the same Epistle, where Paul gives his celebrated admonition that women should be silent in church, the *Reportatio* gives as the reason that teaching involves presidency over the public assembly. Prelacy, presidency, is inappropriate for women in view of their subject status. This status is a fitting one because women are deficient in reason as (the *Reportatio* notes) "Aristotle has said in his *Politics*."[115]

The *Reportatio* of Thomas's commentary on 1 Corinthians and 1 Timothy clearly adopts the theory that women are subject to men and inferior to men. In a medieval biblical commentary this is not especially surprising, but linking the subject status of women with the general Aristotelian theory of the mental and physical weakness of women was something new. Aristotle held the view that in the process of generation nature always intended to produce the best. In human generation nature's intention was to produce a man (who was the best), and if a women happened to be born that was a kind of oversight of nature. This gave rise to the well-known phrase that a woman was a *vir occasionatus,* i.e., an accident and hence slightly deficient.[116] The ease with which this idea was introduced into the commentaries on Paul tends to obscure the radically new basis which is given to the role of male and female in traditional symbolism. In earlier patristic works, even in the *Glossa Ordinaria* or in the commentaries on the *Sentences*, the symbolic relationship between man and woman was denied from biblical imagery, for the most part from the imagery of Genesis. Adam was presented there as the human being created first by God's free choice, and Eve as a second creation, designed to be Adam's helpmate. Although Eve was created by God's choice just as Adam was, man was given a natural primacy by God over woman from the beginning. Later when Eve was seduced into sin (hoodwinked, so to speak) by the Tempter this relation was confirmed. Adam followed Eve into sin, not so much seduced by her as misled by slightly higher motives[117] and by God's further determination Eve was placed in a subject status. Without setting this biblical imagery aside, the *Reportatio* now sets about giving an explanation which has a more biological foundation. The *Reportatio*'s repeated emphasis on the intellectual inferiority of women (the phrase is repeated several times) is now based on the Aristotelian analysis and less on biblical symbolism. This line of reasoning becomes a new factor in justifying a woman's subject status and her natural inferiority. Because of the novelty of the argument placed in the traditional symbolic context, and because it appears in an uncorrected *Reportatio,* it will be useful to examine how Thomas evaluated the new argument in different questions of his *Summa* and in other key passages from 1 Timothy and 1 Corinthians where the status of women come up.

In the *First Part* of his *Summa,* when Thomas discusses the appropriateness of God creating woman in the beginning before the Fall, he argues that Eve was created as a helpmate for Adam since, as Genesis says, it was not good for the man to be alone. She was to be a companion not in every area of life, but primarily in bringing forth offspring.[118] In answer to an objection which suggested that God should not have created Eve before the Fall because God created nothing superfluous or imperfect then, and a woman is imperfect, Thomas replies with an assist from Aristotle. Since nature always attempts to produce a perfect copy of itself, the birth of a woman must be an accidental event, a particular event which is less than perfect action. On the other hand, looked at from the view of human life as a whole, femininity is by no means accidental or imperfect, but part of the Divine order of things.[119] While Thomas does indeed admit that women are subordinate to men, man is not to use woman for his own personal advantage, but rather for her own best advantage. The masculine sex is better at deciding what is best, and therefore should preside.[120] But rather than stressing the weakness inherent in a woman's nature, Thomas prefers to talk about the need for subordination and for order if two individuals are to work together in harmony as a community. For him, the image of God is to be found in both women and men, since they both equally possess an intellectual nature. Intelligence is, to his view, the principal reason why we say that human beings have been made in the image of God. In Scripture it is sometimes said that the image of God is found in man and not in woman. Paul, for example, says that a man is the image and glory of God, and that woman is the glory of man. But this is to be understood in a very specialized sense, not that a woman is not made in God's image. What Paul means is that, just as God is said to be the source and the goal of all creation, so a man, in an analogous sense, can be said to be the beginning (he was created first) and the goal of woman (she relates to God through him).[121]

Later, in the *Second Part of the Second Part* of the Summa, Thomas takes up the sensitive question of whether a woman can preach in public in the church or not. Before answering that question directly he is careful to distinguish what is meant by "preaching." "Preaching" can be done privately before a small group of people in familiar conversation, or it can be carried on in public before the church at large.[122] When Paul says in 1 Timothy and 1 Corinthians that women are to keep silence in the churches and are not permitted to speak, it is this latter kind of preaching which he has in mind. There are three reasons, Thomas believes, why Paul has spoken as he has. The first reason, and it is the principal one, flows from the status of the feminine sex.

As Genesis teaches, a woman ought to be subject to man.[123] Other considerations are added, but they are secondary. A woman's speech sometimes arouses desire, as Ecclesiastes reminds us, and common experience suggests that women are not as perfect in wisdom as men, so the burden of public preaching cannot be conveniently entrusted to them.[124] While ability is certainly a factor in Thomas's argument as to why women should not be preaching, the symbolic status of women as proposed in the Genesis passage is the more important factor. Those who are charged with teaching and persuading in a public forum ought to be *prelates* (i.e., those naturally in charge) and not persons of subject status.[125] Later in the same article, through the mouth of an objector, Thomas takes note of the obvious fact that women have gifts of wisdom and of knowledge which should be shared, and that this can really only be done through preaching. Thomas replies that women so endowed should certainly do this, but in a private capacity and not in public. Divine gifts are given in different measure, but they ought to be shared in accordance with the condition of those who have received them.[126] For Thomas, even a supernatural charism does not escape his passion for order.

Thomas is quite prepared to recognize that some women have superior talents which make them capable of teaching and preaching. As a medieval theologian he could hardly overlook the exceptional grace given to a woman. One woman, the Virgin Mary, was endowed with wisdom as well as the gifts of knowledge and prophecy beyond what was given to anyone else. When he speaks of Mary in the *Third Part* of the *Summa* he acknowledges her unique gifts, but the mere possession of gifts does not confer on anyone the right to make indiscriminate use of them. Even

Divine graces must be used, Thomas argues, in accord with one's condition. The Virgin Mary, he notes, was not given the mission of preaching and evangelizing despite her undoubted insight and wisdom, inasmuch as that activity is never appropriate for the feminine sex, as witnessed by Paul's remarks to Timothy.[127]

As we have seen, Thomas accepts the notion that man has been put in charge of woman by God, and this belief certainly colors his stance toward a question like the ordination of women. His attitude about women appears to be based on his interpretation of biblical imagery, reinforced, no doubt, by his reading of the naturalistic arguments which he had found in Aristotle. Biblical imagery seems to predominate in his description of the status of women both in the *Summa* and in relevant passages in the *Sentence* commentary, while it is in Reginald's *Reportatio* of his *Commentary on Paul* where arguments based on the skills and innate abilities (or lack of them) are most sharply in evidence. In the questions of the *Sentence* commentary dealing with ordination, sparing use is made of the notion that women are somehow deficient in mental abilities, and when Thomas comes to conclude he simply makes reference to the well-known passages of Paul to 1 Corinthians and 1 Timothy and makes no mention of Aristotle at all.

Both Thomas and Bonaventure fell under the influence of the biblical creation stories and the interpretations of them put forward in the standard biblical apparatus in use in their day, but they handle the imagery in somewhat different ways. Both agree, of course, that Adam was created first by God's set purpose, and that Eve was created afterward (taken from Adam's side) because God had freely chosen to proceed in this way. For them, the story thus teaches the primacy of men over women. They also both share the view, repeated in the *Glossa Ordinaria*, that it was Eve who was seduced by the Tempter, not Adam, and that that event was a contributing factor in placing Eve in a subordinate position. While they agreed in broad outline, Bonaventure chose to stress the complementary nature of the roles assigned by God to men and women even after their Fall. As we have seen, the man was to nourish and support, the woman to receive the love offered by her husband and to provide a place of rest for him. Christ, then, in his role as the new Adam, quite obviously comes to nourish and support the church—which flows from his side on the Cross, much as Eve emerged from Adam—while the church, like a spouse, is to receive and be an object of Christ's love. Anyone acting in the place of Christ (*in persona Christi*), in Bonaventure's eyes, must also pursue that sort of role, the masculine role of nurturing and supporting. Thomas, for his part, looks upon the role of Adam in a slightly different sense. He emphasizes the role of Adam as the leader, the organizer and director of the human race. Adam's role is that of the fountainhead the first ruler of the race. Eve's role, in contrast, becomes one of obedience and submissiveness. When Thomas comes to describe the role of Christ, as we might expect, he speaks of Christ as directing, teaching and even battling for his bride, the church. Thomas's answer to the hypothetical question would it have been possible for Christ to enter into history as feminine, is illuminating. He replies that it was perfectly possible for God to assume any bodily form he wished to, but it would have been inappropriate for him to assume the form of a woman. Why would this be so? It would be unfitting because Christ's role is to be teacher, a champion (*propugnator*), someone who came to fight a battle for the human race.[128] For Thomas, this is the masculine role *par excellence.* Such a role demands leadership and presidency—these are images which Thomas is fond of bringing forward whenever he talks about the symbolism of the sacrament of Orders.

The theology of Thomas and Bonaventure makes it clear that both would have been uncomfortable with a feminine priesthood. Holy Orders was one of the seven sacraments and in their understanding of sacraments considerations of symbolism predominate. Although they nuanced their arguments somewhat differently, as we have seen, they both struggled with the natural and historic symbolism of the priesthood and the feminine and found them incompatible. It was in this light that they evaluated the witness of the constant practice of the church which had never accepted the ordination of women, at least as far as they could see. While both theologians agreed on the ultimate conclusion—that women could not be ordained—they did not offer the same symbolic arguments. (Bonaventure talked of mutuality while Thomas spoke of leadership and eminence.) Their differences here reveal that in this area the church's tradition appeared to be much less fixed. In the next generation when theologians lost interest in the natural symbolism of the different sacraments and began to regard them as examples of God's gracious, even his arbitrary, favor toward his people, the *practice* of the church would be looked upon as decisive. In the following century, as we shall see, the ordination of women was again examined from a legal, i.e., a canonical, point of view. When Bonaventure and Thomas retired from their chairs of theology in 1274 they left behind them in their great commentaries on the *Sentences* theological constructs which would dominate discussion in the schools on all major points of faith until the end of the century.

Thomas Aquinas died on his way to the Council of Lyons while Bonaventure arrived there to become a Cardinal of the Roman Church and the Minister General of his Order. In different ways they were both removed from the academic scene. While Bonaventure did write occasionally on particular issues after becoming General, his theological initiative in the schools was ended due to the press of administrative duties. Their immediate followers were content to summarize their teachings, and here, as on other issues, their commentaries were regarded as a systematic statement of the commonly held belief of Christians.

In the years immediately after their *Sentences* were published the state of the question concerning the ordination of women did not change in any obvious way. Very brief summary-commentaries on the *Sentences* sometimes passed over the question altogether. An example of such a summary-commentary from this period is from the pen of Cardinal Hanibaldus de Hanibaldis, a student of Thomas. It is of incidental interest today because it was once believed to have been an *abrege* of Thomas's *Sentence* commentary made by Thomas himself.[129] More typical is the commentary of Peter of Tarentaise, the future Innocent V, written between 1259-64.[130] Peter's method was to follow Thomas's and Bonaventure's arguments very closely, siding sometimes with one author, sometimes with the other. As a result, his commentary is virtually a montage of quotations from the two great mendicant masters. It is especially valuable as a witness to the theological attitudes commonly accepted by members of the two orders. In dealing with the sacrament of Orders Peter repeats the distinction, widely held, that some things are so necessary for receiving a sacrament that it cannot be conferred at all if they are not present, while other things are needed only in the sense that the sacrament could not be conferred in a suitable way without them. The masculine sex happens to be one of those things which is necessary on both counts, so it is clearly required. The reason for this is that the duty of preaching is attached to orders, and this is something which a woman is not allowed to undertake. Peter adds a second reason—that it is unfitting for a woman to be preferred to a man in ministering before God since, as he puts it, a man is closer to God than a woman is. Women should be led to God by men, not the other way around. By way of support for this Peter refers to 1 Corinthians, ch. 11, "Man is made in the image and is the glory of God, a woman, however, is of man." To this he adds his own gloss, saying that women should be led to God by men, not the other way around.[131] Peter uses the same biblical symbolism as his sources, the symbolism which depicts women as closely related, but subordinate, to men.

From his sources, and no doubt from his general education as well, Peter has heard of the texts which suggest that women may have been ordained in the church once upon a time. It is true, he agrees, that there may once have been women prophetesses in the church and that this implies leadership, but it really proves nothing here. The gift of prophecy does not confer power such as the sacrament of Orders does, so the example does not apply. To the well-known cannons in the *Decretales* that talk of deaconesses, and even "*presbyterae*" in the church, he replies that these words should not be taken literally. They were only titles given to some women who had acquired permission to read in church, such as deacons do, or to the wives of married priests.[132] Peter also takes up the conventional objection suggested in Galatians. In the eyes of Christ, Paul says, there is no distinction made between "slave and free, man and woman." If this is so, why should there be any distinction made in conferring the sacraments? Peter replies that this passage simply refers to "gaining merit and not about holding office." A good woman may surpass a man in merit, but that does not mean that she outranks him in nature or in office. Another objection argues that, inasmuch as order is rooted in the soul (where presumably men and women do not differ) while sexuality is a bodily matter, sex should present no obstacle to receiving orders. Peter admits all this, but argues that, even though orders is a spiritual gift, it is one which has to be exercised through means of the body. We are left to conclude that sexual differences do have a place here, and, as a consequence, the sacrament of Orders is not an impersonal power. Finally, if someone should argue that women are sometimes made prelates, and that prelacy carries with it more authority than the authority which would be given in orders, Peter answers that we are only talking here about power given to some women over other women. It is given to them (and here we are perhaps listening to an echo of the situation thrown up by the institution of the double monastery) because it would be dangerous for women to live in the same community which was governed by men.[133]

The brief, but very popular, summary commentary of Ulrich of Strasbourg, the *Summa Theologiae Veritatis*, is another example of the genre which is of particular interest because it has been attributed at one time or other to Thomas Aquinas, Bonaventure, and Albert the Great.[134] Composed about 1278, it obviously had something to offer to all shades of theological opinion. It is a valuable witness to the standard teaching of mid-century theologians. In his *Summa* Ulrich notes that there are five sacraments given for personal sanctification and two for the church at large. Of the latter two, marriage and orders, matrimony is for the carnal generation of new members of the church while orders is for its spiritual propagation. There are six requirements for receiving orders which are substantial. The first is the need for a bishop; next, the proper matter; then, the appropriate form of words; the candidate must be male; have the correct intention; and be baptized. In elaborating on the need to be male Ulrich simply says that one must be male, "because a woman does not receive the character of order." From the context it seems clear that by order, not simply the priesthood, but all levels of orders is meant.[135]

Commentaries like these, brief as they are, show that what was articulated by canonists in the twelfth-century had become the conclusion taught by theologians in the thirteenth, and then after. The reasoning which the theologians employed did not remain static, however, and the change in argumentation provides us with an insight into their changing image of woman.

Psychological and Physiological Factors and the Non-Ordination of Women

For an appreciation of the newer spirit regarding women it will be useful to examine the writings of the secular Master, Henry of Ghent.[136] As a Master of Theology we can assume that he wrote a commentary on the *Sentences* while lecturing at Paris. Unfortunately it has not been identified. Perhaps he never re-ordered for publication. He is remembered instead for his *Summa Theologica,* an important work known and used by Duns Scotus and William of Ockham. Like the work of Thomas Aquinas, the *Summa* of Henry of Ghent remained unfinished. In the part which remains Henry dealt in great detail with philosophic themes, particularly with the nature of God, and with the way in which the human mind might have an appreciation of the Divine nature, and how it could speak with certitude about the created world. Speculation on these problems seems to have absorbed most of Henry's energy and attention, leaving him no time to present a balanced view of the totality of Christian theology. This would have included, of course, a treatise on the work of Christ, the redemption, and the entire sacramental system. These topics were promised by Henry in a overview, but in fact were never written. In the first part of his *Summa* where he discusses who has the right to teach doctrine in the church we can gain a picture of what he would have said about the ordination of women. Henry followed the Divine illumination theory popular among thirteenth-century Augustinians, so we know that the teaching of doctrine held an important place in his system. Preaching, as distinct from a simple reporting of the contents of the Gospel, was an activity restricted to those who possessed orders and who proceeded under the direction of their local bishop. The Gospel was one of the principal ways in which God has chosen to illuminate the minds of the faithful and it was critically important that its teaching be in the hands of suitable preachers. In order to preach doctrine effectively, four things were required in the preacher: *constancy*, so that there be no deviation from the truth in what is preached; *effectiveness*, so that the personal weakness and lassitude of the preacher may not interfere with the work of preaching; *authority*, so that the faithful may have reason to believe what they are being told; and finally, *a vivacity of mind*, so that people will turn away from sin and adopt virtue. In Henry's eyes, women fail to some extent in all of these areas. The "weaker sex," as he phrases it, is inconstant, so the task of preaching has been given to men; women are fragile and so are ineffective in conducting discussions or when appearing in public; they do not have authority, since they have no liberty of action being placed under the command of men; and they do not have the needed vivacity of mind which draws people from sin toward virtue, but rather something of the reverse seems true of them.[137] Henry agrees that a women may possess sound doctrine and the fervor of charity may prompt her to speak out. All this is praiseworthy enough, but it can be done privately, and need not be in public in a church assembly.[138] What is appropriate for a woman is to teach other women and children, not men. When we read the words of Solomon that "he had been taught wisdom by my mother from my youth," this is the sense in which we should understand them. This is also how we should evaluate the work of the prophetesses who are mentioned at times in Scripture. Besides, the letter of Paul to Timothy which says that women should not preach in the church is decisive.[139] Henry is forced to admit that there do seem to have been prophetesses raised up in the Old Testament, but their task was to embarrass warrior men who proved too faint-hearted. In the New Testament, we find figures like Mary and Martha, and the daughters of Philip who were sent to preach, but this was when the "harvest was plentiful and the laborers few."[140] These examples are exceptions and are not to be construed as precedents. Since it is the duty of a priest to preach by reason of the order he has received, and since a woman could preach only as the result of an extraordinary grace bestowed by God in special cases, in Henry's mind priestly ordination was obviously not for them. In presenting his conclusion we find that Henry relies less on the symbolic status of women and bases his opinion on their supposed intellectual and emotional deficiencies. For Henry, it is men who are innately more able, more stable, so much so that the task of public preaching logically should be given to them. Henry's work will be influential. His turns of phrase as well as his general attitude will reappear in numerous *Sentence* commentaries of the century.

A junior contemporary of Henry of Ghent is the influential Franciscan theologian, Richard of Middleton (*Mediavilla*). His *Sentence* commentary has been dated at 1283, and is the result of his lectures at Paris which fall sometime between 1280 and the outside date of 1284.[141] His theological viewpoint perhaps can be best described as transitional. He maintains the basic insights of Bonaventure toward Augustine and Aristotle, yet in his works many can see interpretations of Aristotle which will be brought to flower in the thought of Duns Scotus, who wrote in the succeeding generation. When dealing with the ordination of women, Richard preserves the distinction used by Bonaventure, that by church law (i.e., *de iure*) women *should* not be ordained, and from the law of nature (i.e., *de facto*) *they* cannot be ordained. To make the point clear, he adds, as others before him, that if a woman went through the entire ordination ceremony it would have no effect. Richard offers only one essential reason for his conclusion. Sacraments are effective, they gain validity, from their institution by Christ. In instituting this sacrament, Christ ordained only men, not women. The arrangements in force in the church are the responsibility of Christ, and rest there. Richard admits that the question of who is to be ordained, and who is not, is a legal matter, but the answer acquires its force not from church law, but from Divine law. The theologian can do no better than offer some congruous reasons why these arrangements are appropriate. The arguments which are offered by a theologian prove nothing in an apodictic way, they can only be persuasive.[142]

The line of reasoning which Richard offers to shore up the Divine law, or perhaps it would be better to say to give some explanation of it, is familiar enough to us by now. All orders, he tells us, in some way or other involve doctrinal preaching. But women should not preach publicly on account of the weakness of their intellects and fickleness of their emotions, something which we observe more commonly in women than in men. Moreover, teachers must exhibit a certain vivacity of mind (a phrase which we have seen in Henry of Ghent) and an emotional stability to enable them to persevere in confessing the faith.[143] As a second consideration, Richard adds that a person who is in orders is placed in a position of eminence over others. Now eminence should flow from the natural leadership qualities found in the ordained. But women are subject to men in the natural order of things since, as Richard blandly puts it, "the feminine sex is naturally imperfect in relation to the male." He concludes his remarks in his *Sentences* by noting that these two considerations can be drawn from the first letter of Paul to Timothy where Paul says that women should learn by silence and in submissiveness, and that he does not permit them to preach or to exercise authority over men.[144] In Richard's hands the argument against the ordination of women assumes a far more naturalistic and much less symbolic form than we have seen heretofore. The motive for the prohibition is still a regulation given in Scripture (the prohibition against preaching and being in charge over men), but Scripture presenting essentially what is an induction of the Divine will. The symbolic character appropriate for an ordained person as an Adam figure (the primal imaging of God), or even as a representative of Christ, is not dwelt on at all. Instead simple folk wisdom about the supposed superiority of men over women, observation of women's abilities in leadership roles, are put forward to account for the Divine legislation and to provide an apologetic for it.

The central point which Richard of Middleton had concentrated on, that reception of ordination depended upon arrangements instituted by Christ, was taken up at the turn of the century by his fellow Franciscan, John Duns Scotus. During the course of his commentary Duns Scotus developed the point with greater precision. It may also have inspired him to inquire about the value of orders not only for the holiness of the church, but for the personal salvation of those who received them. His formulation was to have a lasting effect in the schools. Duns Scotus commented on the *Sentences* both at Paris and at Oxford. His first lectures at Oxford, given sometime between 1297 and 1302, covered only the first three books of the *Sentences,* and so are not of immediate interest to us. In Paris, between 1302 and 1303, he lectured on books one and four, book four presumably, although not necessarily, being covered in 1303. At the end of June of that year he was expelled from France for refusing to sign an appeal to a General Council demanded by Philip the Fair in his quarrel with Boniface VIII. It is believed that Duns Scotus then withdrew to Oxford and in the following year (1304) lectured there on book four of the *Sentences,* thus completing his *Opus Oxoniense.*[145]

The fourth book Duns Scotus's *Commentary,* given verbally twice, has come down to us in three written forms. Two versions of the published *Ordinatio* represent the Oxford lectures, the *Opus Oxoniense,* one version represents Paris lectures, or the *Reportata Parisiensia*. These do not represent substantially different lectures, but are basically the same set given at Oxford and at Paris. The seventeenth-century editor Luke Wadding, following the opinion of his earlier colleague Ferkic, held that Duns Scotus produced only one *reportatio* (as he put it) found in two slightly different forms. In 1639 he published an edition of Scotus's work which was a blending of these two versions. This was reprinted by Ludwig Vivès in Paris in1893-94, and is the edition now most commonly in use except for the completed volumes of the masterful critical edition now being published under the editorship of Carolo Balic. While the Vivès edition of the *Sentences* which we must use is not critical, it is all authentically Scotus and sufficiently accurate for our purposes.[146]

Duns Scotus begins his comments in a somewhat old fashioned way by turning to the place in the *Sentences* where Peter Lombard asks if children or infants can ever be ordained. This enables Scotus to raise the larger question of what impedes reception of orders, and how absolute can impediments be. He replies, that someone can be prevented from being ordained if it was unfitting to confer orders upon them for some reason. They can also be prevented from receiving them if it is against a precept of some sort, and they can also be incapable *de facto*. (As he would put it, someone may be prevented by "necessity of law, or by necessity of fact.") Extreme youth prevents someone from receiving orders fittingly, i.e., worthily, because children cannot receive them with appropriate reverence. Children are prevented from receiving them by the laws of the church as well. On the other hand, extreme youth does not prevent reception of orders *de facto*. If a boy should be ordained (however wrong that procedure might be), he is ordained and would never be reordained at any later time.[147]

The situation is not parallel, however, in the case of women. It is not appropriate to ordain them (although at this point Scotus does not go into any particular reasons why) and it is, moreover, against ecclesiastical law to ordain them, and in addition they are *de facto* incapable of receiving any. Unlike children, women are impeded from receiving orders *absolutely,* or as Scotus will say, they are prevented *simpliciter*. But what is the basis for this strict prohibition? Scotus agrees with Richard of Middleton that this rule must ultimately rest upon a disposition made by Christ who instituted the sacraments in the first place. He cannot believe, Scotus insists, that the structures against ordaining women rest solely on a church law, or even on a precept handed down from the Apostles. It is at this point that Scotus's argument takes a surprising turn. I cannot believe, he says, that the church or the Apostles could deprive even one single person, let alone an entire sex, of a status [his word is *gradus*] that would be beneficial to someone's personal salvation! Neither the Church nor the Apostles could in justice, he reasons, deny to anyone something which was of use for their salvation, unless the church and Apostles were acting under the direction of Christ himself. He, who is Lord of all, is the only authority capable of issuing such a prohibition.[148] In a more sophisticated manner, but not unlike Richard of Middleton, Scotus places the question of the ordination of women beyond the limits of the church's jurisdiction. With this argument two important themes enter into the discussion. First, Holy Orders are now viewed in terms of a grace which is useful for one's salvation. They can be seen as a personal possession, something of value to be striven for even independently of the strict needs of the church community. The importance of orders as something given to individuals who will be of service to the church is not denied, of course, but that ecclesial purpose can easily become overshadowed by the thought of orders as a personal grace, a grace that might justly be sought, even deserved, by all. Secondly, with Scotus the institution of the sacrament is seen more sharply as an action here as arbitrary; nonetheless, Christ's actions do not require the same amount of explanation or justification as we would require of the church or any created human agency. The value of symbolic arguments is now obviously less important for the theologian and it continues to fall away.

Scotus is a theologian, however, and we would not expect him to abandon all explanation for the prohibition against the ordination of women. Like Richard of Middleton he resorts to congruous arguments. These arguments do not try to show why Christ had to act as he did—that would be to attempt to examine the absolute power of God which is beyond human analysis; they simply suggest why the Divine choice was not inappropriate. Following the arrangement which we have already seen in Richard of Middleton, Scouts says that all the grades of order are related to the priesthood and to doctrine. But as Paul has said to Timothy, ". . . I do not permit women to teach," which is a command that excludes women from preaching sermons that teach a doctrine. In line with his general theme, Scotus notes that the *Glossa* on Timothy adds, "Not only I, but the Lord does not permit this."[149] This prohibition flows from a woman's weakness of intellect and the fickleness of her affections, and from the fact that a teacher should have a certain vivacity of mind and stability of emotion. (This phraseology, which we have already seen, was by now becoming standard in the schools and will be repeated later as a matter of course.) To underline his basic point Scotus observes that any further restrictions on ordination which may be found in the *Decretum,* or things added to the precepts of Paul, are to be regarded as extensions of a primitive law which Christ had initially laid down.[150]

In order to gain a deeper insight into Christ's own mind in this matter Scotus examines the figure of the Blessed Virgin. He applies an argument which is in the same form as the one used by him to defend the Immaculate Conception of Mary. The Mother of Christ was most holy and most worthy of all grace. No one could be equal to her in sanctity or honor, yet the power of orders was not conferred upon her. Scotus leaves us to draw the obvious conclusion that the grace of order was not appropriate for her for some reason. If this be true for Mary, then, it would be all the more true for women less holy and so less worthy than she. In raising the question of the Virgin, Scotus must also deal with the legend of Mary Magdalene. There was a tradition which held that she was a preacher in the early church and was called an *Apostola,* in addition to being counted as the protectoress of all sinful women. Scotus makes reference to this story in the Paris version (and only in the Paris version) of his *Sentences.* He handles the tale somewhat abruptly. The Magdalene was, he tells us, a single, individual woman who happened to enjoy a personal privilege given to her by Christ. Personal privileges, as canon law teaches, die with the person possessing them, and cannot be taken as precedents for a contrary practice.[151] Whatever the truth of the legend of the Magdalene might be, it has no general application. The remarks which Scotus makes about the position of Christ's mother are somewhat tentative and brief. They will be extended, and occasionally the Mary Magdalene story as well will be developed by *Sentence* commentators of the Scottist school throughout the rest of the fourteenth-century as confirming evidence that Christ did not wish women to be ordained.

A second line of reasoning which Scotus uses to explain why Christ did not choose to ordain women is the familiar one that women must not be put in charge of men. By nature, his argument runs, the status of women is to be subject, and never to be in a position of eminence. This becomes even more appropriate after the Fall, for as a result of the Fall in Eden Genesis teaches that women were placed under the special power of men. If a woman were to be ordained, she would of necessity have to preside and to dominate which is a quality foreign to her present condition.[152] Since these teachings are present in Genesis, Scotus seems to suggest, it would be incongruous for Christ to change the Divinely instituted arrangements.

Toward the end of his discussion Scotus turns to a philosophic argument taken from the *Metaphysics* of Aristotle.[153] The argument will appear regularly in later commentaries. Here we find an objector using a text from Aristotle to favor the ordination of women. The objector's argument runs (or can be paraphrased) as follows: When cause and effect are of the same species, the cause should be able to produce its effect in *every member* of the same species. (For example, a human being always generates another human being, not something other.) When a bishop ordains, therefore, the effect—the character—should be transmitted to women as well as to men inasmuch as sexual differences do not render a man and woman different species. (As we would say today, both men and women are equally human beings.) Scotus replies that this line of reasoning is perfectly correct when we talk about causes in the natural world. Natural agents do have the power to produce effects, and so they do. But this is hardly the case where we talk about an agent who is acting out of free choice, and who also employs a *secondary* cause as instrument to boot. The relation of a bishop before God at the moment of ordination is precisely an example of causality of this latter type. When conferring orders a bishop is not a *primary* cause imprinting a character on the soul, a bishop is only a *secondary* cause, an *instrumental* cause of that effect. For that reason a bishop can only imprint the character which is given at ordination on someone who is properly disposed to receive it, i.e., disposed in a way determined by God who is, after all, the *primary* cause that imprints the sacramental character. God for his own reasons has determined that one of the necessary dispositions for receiving orders is to have masculine sex. In the Oxford version Scotus's text goes on to say that the argument presented by the minister of sacrament does not mechanically (*ex necessitate*) produce the effects called for in the sacrament. What the minister does is contingent, that is to say, he only "causes" something to happen in a "majority of cases" (*in pluribus*) following the Divine good pleasure, or as Scotus himself phrases it, "in accord with the *pactum Divinum*."[154]

Scotus's careful answer to the objection which he poses is no doubt placed here by him in order to reinforce his view that the will of God is what is truly operative in the sacramental system. Considerations such as the subject status of women, their supposed weakness of intellect and their emotional instability, favorite themes of medieval theological and secular literature, can be taken over as supporting arguments to help make the rule of the Divine will more plausible. These arguments are not, however, the basis for the structuring of the sacrament of Orders, nor are they the real reason why women cannot be ordained. As a result of this emphasis, the symbolic character of sacraments assumes considerably less importance. The notion that this world is somehow the image of the Divine, that the Divine is reflected through the sacramental symbols, both major themes in the theology of Bonaventure and Thomas Aquinas, recedes from view. Quite logically, little effort will be made to try to construct arguments based on the symbolism involved in the sacrament of Orders. The way in which the minister of orders does or does not represent Christ in his sacramental actions will be of less interest. Instead justification for a masculine priesthood will be placed on authority, power and the ability to function effectively.

The influence of the arguments of Duns Scotus can be traced in his own generation, as we might expect, in *Sentence* commentaries written by fellow Franciscans, but they also appear sometimes in those of Dominicans as well. Four commentaries which have been edited will be considered: Antonio Andreas writing at Lerida about 1315 and John of Bassolis at Rheims in 1313, both Franciscans, and the Dominicans, Durrandus of Saint-Pourrain, Master at Paris in 1310, and Peter de la Palude, who succeeded Durandus. Their works show that arguments of the type Scotus offered were well-diffused in the first quarter of the fourteenth-century.

Antonio Andreas may never have been a Master, but the number of manuscripts of his *Commentary* show that he was an influential author nonetheless.[155] He argues that a woman is incapable of receiving orders both by reason of appropriateness and *de facto*. One should not believe that this stricture is merely an ecclesiastical norm he argues, for the church on its own authority could not exclude the whole of the feminine sex from such a dignity without falling into sin itself. This is especially the case when we reflect that such a status (*gradus*) is given not only for the sake of others, but is a perfection of the soul of the person who possesses it. For this reason, he concludes, the rule must have been introduced by Christ. Evidence for this can be found in Paul's letter to Timothy where he states, or rather where Christ states, that women may not preach. Antonio then points out that a sign of this is that Christ did not bestow any grade of order upon his own mother who exceeded every creature in sanctity. The reason for his choice is suggested by the Apostle in 1 Corinthians. After the Fall, God did not want any woman to assume a status of this sort since they had been placed under the authority of men as a penalty, according to the teaching of Genesis.[156]

In his brief *Sentence* Commentary, John of Bassolis draws the same conclusion.[157] Women are excluded by law, simply and absolutely, from receiving orders of any sort. We must not, however, presume that the church would deprive all women of such a dignity unless Christ had instituted the sacrament in this way. A sign of this is that Christ did not wish his mother to be ordained even though she was the most worthy woman. In this particular *Sentence* commentary Paul is now described as the promulgator of a statute in his letter to Timothy where he says that women are not to teach. Bassolis adds the phrase, not teach "doctrine in public." He ends by offering the conventional reason that after the Fall, according to Genesis, women were placed under the power of men in accord with the sentence called down upon them by God.[158]

Writing in the same years the Dominican, Durandus, offers the same type of argument. Durandus lectured on the *Sentences* at Paris in 1307 to 1308, but revised his commentary twice at the instigation of the members of his Order, once to accommodate their criticisms, and a second time to partially reinstate his original views. We are using the third edition of his *Sentences,* written between 1317 and 1327.[159] Orders can be impeded, he says, either by the necessity of the conditions of the sacrament (*de necessitate sacramenti*) or on account of the fittingness or propriety needed to receive them. The feminine sex fits into the first category of impediments. The principle reason for this is the way in which Christ instituted them. Christ ordained only men at the Last Supper when he gave the power to consecrate the Eucharist, and again after his Resurrection when he imparted the Spirit giving the power to forgive sin. Moreover, he did not ordain his mother to any grade of order even though she was the most holy of women. In this matter the Apostles have simply handed down to us what they received from the Lord. We find this in 1 Corinthians 11, where it is indicated that women should not be ordained, or placed in a position in the Church involving *doctrinal* authority. But this is precisely the charge given to all who are being ordained.[160] Durandus goes on to argue that it would be wrong to hold that this is only a regulation given out by the Apostles. They could not withhold a dignity useful for our salvation and granted by Christ without being guilty of prejudice. Durandus thinks that this prejudice would be all the more reprehensible because the dignity of Orders is not some secular matter, but rather is something valuable for promoting one's salvation if used rightly. If Christ had wanted women to be ordained, such an honor could not be withheld from them without prejudice. As a consequence, we must hold, Durandus insists, that the inability of women to gain Orders comes from Christ himself.[161] Only one reason is cited for this in the text, and again it is a congruous reason. Anyone who is ordained is by that very fact put in a position of excellence (we might say of leadership) over the non-ordained. Such an arrangement is inappropriate for women, however, because their status is one of subjection. As Durandus puts it in his text, "this is because of the weakness of their body, imperfections of mind, etc." The tenor of this remark, the offhand way in which it is presented, may perhaps suggest that Durandus had less confidence in the ability of women than some other authors we have been considering, but it is significant to observe that when he draws his final conclusion he does not rely on those supposed inabilities, but returns to the more basic argument that a woman cannot be ordained because of the requirements of the sacrament (i.e., *de necessitate sacramenti*).[162]

Durandus's Dominican successor at Paris, Peter de la Palude, lectured on the *Sentences* from 1309 to 1310, although the definitive version of his work did not appear until a little later, 1318-19.[163] Peter closely follows the line of Durandus, but makes the added point that inasmuch as women are excluded from orders in a *de facto* manner not even the Pope can dispense from this restriction because he is never entitled to change the "matter of a sacrament."[164] He then goes on to make the point that in his opinion every order is a sacrament, and not simply a kind of sacramental. It had been commonly agreed among medieval theologians that, in addition to the sacraments which had been instituted by Christ, the church had introduced into worship services numerous ceremonies, blessings and consecrations which were placed under the general title of sacramentals. Unlike the sacraments, sacramentals were subject to change and modification under ecclesiastical supervision. Certainly the priesthood was one of the sacraments in the strict sense, but what about the other orders, the lesser orders? If you happen to think, Peter readily agrees, that all the orders except for the priesthood are only sacramentals and do not pertain essentially to the sacrament itself, then it is perfectly true that the Pope could change their "matter," their "form," and those who would be eligible to receive them.[165] However that may be, Peter goes on, the male sex is a necessary requirement whenever we speak of the sacrament of Orders properly so-called. The male sex is, for him, something *de necessitate sacramenti*. In explaining why this is so, Peter argues, as had Durandus, that this depends upon the institution by Christ, as we can see from the fact that Christ ordained men and not women, and from the Epistle of Paul. This portion of Peter's article is in fact textually identical with that of Durandus. The only difference, and it is a minor one, is an added clause making explicit mention of Genesis as the Scriptural warrant for saying that women were placed "in a status of subjection after the Fall."[166]

Peter's general line of argument is unremarkable in a *Sentence* commentary written about this time, but it is of some interest because of its implicit suggestion that women might possibly be ordained to minor orders, perhaps even to the diaconate. While Peter does not advance that view himself, he recognizes that it is inevitable if the view that all orders before the priesthood are simply regarded as sacramentals. Peter was quite aware, of course, that this was the opinion held by a respectable number of theologians in his own day.[167] While foreseeing such a possibility, Peter does not pursue it himself. In answering the conventional objection that deaconesses must have existed in the church at one time since the canons, *Deaconissa* and *Presbiter* speak of them, Peter gives as reply (also conventional in this literature) that such "deaconesses" were not really ordained (as deacons would be), but were women allowed to give a blessing and to read out homilies at a Matins service.[168]

While dealing with issues of canon law Peter also brings up the case of the hermaphrodite, i.e., the person who has physical characteristics which are both male and female. In practice this is not in fact a serious problem to solve since such a person would be regarded as deformed, and so be ineligible for receiving any orders by that reason alone. In theory, however, it was of interest to Peter since it allowed him to state that the basis for determining sexuality was physical. If a candidate had sexual characteristics that were predominantly masculine, then the individual was regarded as being capable of receiving orders; if, on the other hand, feminine sexual characteristics prevailed, the individual was regarded as a woman, and in consequence could not be ordained.[169]

The State of the Controversy in the Fourteenth-Century: Repetition of an Established Theme

By the first quarter of the fourteenth-century interest in the problem of the ordination of women seems to have begun to wane, at least among theologians who wrote commentaries on the *Sentences*. This lack of interest paralleled a lack of interest in sacramental theology as a whole. During the century commentaries on the fourth book of the *Sentences* became progressively shorter while introductions and commentaries on the first book grew longer and more elaborate. Discussion of the sacraments, the major interest of the fourth book, was now squeezed into fewer and fewer folios with the result that many traditional *quaestiones,* and at times whole *distinctiones,* were omitted. Some commentators did not even get around to treating all of the seven sacraments. In these circumstances it becomes increasingly difficult to find a balanced treatment of the sacramental system. The theology of Baptism and the Eucharist predominated while orders received only passing attention, if any attention at all.

The *Commentary* of William of Rubio, who was writing at Paris about 1325, is of interest to us then for he still does say something about ordination, and the ordination of women.[170] Rubio was a Franciscan and a committed disciple of Duns Scotus; but only some of Scotus's discussion on the ordination question is brought forward here, because Rubio's main attention is focused on the relation between Divine and ecclesiastical law. Unlike the previous commentaries we have examined, Rubio organizes his remarks around the concept of legitimacy, possibly because it permits him to handle a number of small problems under one convenient heading. In a more roundabout way he reaches the traditional conclusions, however. Some individuals, he says, are illegitimate respecting orders simply and absolutely, while others are said to be illegitimate only in the sense that they cannot receive them fittingly or worthily. Those in the latter category, if ordained, do receive the order although they commit a sin in doing so; those in the first category do not receive orders at all.[171] Now the first form of illegitimacy is something permanent and irrevocable. Rubio makes the point that the church on its own authority simply does not have the power to render anyone illegitimate in a permanent way, i.e., simply and absolutely. This is true not only for the sacrament of Orders, but for any of the sacraments. The reason for this is that the sacraments are conferred by God; all that the church contributes is her ministerial activity. If any individual, or any group of individuals, is said to be simply and absolutely incapable of receiving something, that peculiar kind of illegitimacy comes from God; it cannot originate with the church.[172] Having established this point, Rubio then goes on to say that the feminine sex does impede the reception of orders simply and absolutely. Since this is the case, the impediment is obviously of Divine, not ecclesiastical origin.[173] Picking up the threads of the argument from justice which he finds in Scotus, Rubio says that it seems implausible that the church would deprive a whole sex of the ability to receive orders—something both valuable to them and an aid to their salvation—if women were in fact capable of being ordained. It is quite certain, he adds, that orders would be useful and helpful for salvation to women just as they are to men, if women were in fact able to receive them. The church would not be without sin if she unilaterally deprived a whole sex of open access to orders.

In fact no statute resting simply on the authority of the church could bar a women from actually receiving an order if she were truly capable of receiving them. But we happen to know that this presupposition is false, because a statute of the church does stand in the way. We are left to conclude that the church's prohibition, which certainly does exist, is not simply something which can be reduced to mere ecclesiastical law.[174]

The commentary of Francis of Meyronnes, composed about 1320 to 1323, is even more compact and schematic than his predecessor, Rubio.[175] Although brief, it does manage to cover all the *distinctiones* given in Peter Lombard, and it does have something to say about all the main problems of sacramental theology. In the traditional place in the *Sentences* for raising questions about who can be ordained Meyronnes asks, Can the sacrament of Orders be conferred upon any Christian? A preliminary consideration would seem to suggest that women can be ordained since the faithful are the appropriate matter for the sacrament. He immediately parries this thrust, however, by saying that there are many among the faithful on whom this sacrament should not be conferred. This question is introduced here, he goes on to say, to resolve six *dubia*. The *dubia* turn out to be quite familiar, the six classical impediments to receiving orders. They are defect of age (ie., youth), defect of sex, bigamy (i.e., more than one marriage), physical mutilation, being perpetrator of a homicide, and irregularity (i.e., exclusion from the sacrament as a penalty for violating a positive law of the church). In discussing these points Meyronnes compresses his text so much that it is at times difficult to grasp the full context surrounding his clipped remarks, but his general meaning is clear enough. The feminine sex is clearly an impediment to orders. This conclusion follows from the teaching of the Apostle who did not permit women to preach in the church.[176] To the conventional objection that the *Decretum* mentions deaconnesses and *presbyterae,* Meyronnes gives the conventional answers, which he has found as he tells us in the fourth book of Scotus's commentary on the *Sentences.* The burden of the argument is that such titles do not imply actual ordination, but are merely honorifics given to women in various ministerial situations.[177]

As we have indicated a change in the format of *Sentence* commentaries was noticeable from the early part of the fourteenth-century. This tendency was continued and perhaps accelerated with the advent of the theological movement known as "Nominalism," or "terminism" as it was sometimes referred to by contemporaries. The movement, philosophical in origin, soon began to influence theologians as they applied its new conceptions to doctrine and to biblical interpretation. The force and rapidity of the growth of Nominalist ideas so impressed thinkers of the time that they began to speak of it as a *new way,* the *via moderna.* Nominalist theology was then contrasted with the *older ways* of thinking, the *viae antiquae* associated with the philosophical approaches of Thomas Aquinas and Duns Scotus. The basic philosophical insights at the heart of the *via moderna* are credited to the English Franciscan, William of Ockham.[178] Under his influence theologians in the schools rethought what could be said about the nature of God, or rather how the human mind was capable of knowing God and of understanding his creative activity. In the hands of those who followed the *via moderna* the distinction between God's absolute power (*potentia dei absoluta*) and his ordered power (*potentia dei ordinate*), already in use since the mid-thirteenth-century, was expanded and applied much more generously. Theologians agreed that Christians through Scripture and through the teachings of the church knew a great deal about God's actual workings in the universe. Because God had revealed himself to Christians, they could know his ordered or ordinary ways, the *potentia dei ordinata.* They were privileged to know what God had done and what he would, no doubt, continue to do. But this knowledge did not give Christians a complete insight into the limits of God's power over creation. Much less was known about the absolute power of God, i.e., the *potentia dei absoluta,* since God could in theory do anything at all which did not imply a flat contradiction. For Ockham and for those who followed him, the human mind was ill-equipped to penetrate beyond what could be know through God's ordered power, for God's absolute power was a mysterious realm without created precedents. Arguments based on human experience, or from philosophic ways of examining the created universe, were, for the men of the *via moderna,* uncertain guides for talking about the nature of God, or about his ways in dealing with humanity. The congruous arguments, dear to older theologians, lost their persuasive force and approached the category of metaphor.

Sacramental theology, which had often based itself on symbolism garnered from the imagery found in created things, found it hard to flourish in the new mental climate. The congruous arguments of the sacramental theologian could hardly offer any valid insights into the absolute power of God which was, by definition, beyond such limited vision. They could at best offer a kind of confirmation of what pertained to the ordinary power of God, something which was already known anyway, and known to us more clearly and exactly through revelation and the church's legislation. It is not surprising that we find much less interest in sacramental theology, in the use of sacramental symbolism in Ockham and his followers. The *Sentence* commentaries on the fourth book continue to be very brief, with the discussion of the sacraments incomplete and undeveloped.

The *Commentary on the Sentences* of William of Ockham himself certainly fits into the pattern. Its fourth book is by far the weakest. This book is the result of lectures given, most likely, in 1319 just before Ockham was called to Avignon to answer charges about h doctrine.[179] It is in the form of a *Reportatio*, and so is not the final, polished version. Only the sacraments of Baptism and the Eucharist are covered in any detail.[180] Nothing at all is said about the sacrament of Orders, and so, as a consequence, the question of the ordination of women never comes up for discussion. Ockham's *Sentence* commentary will set a precedent for the commentaries which come from other theologians who are identified as belonging to the Nominalist school. Among Nominalist authors whose works are characterized by brief surveys of selected sacraments, and who never around to discussing orders or the ordination of women, we can cite the English Franciscan, Adam Wodeham, who lectured at Oxford (1317-19) and possibly at London (1328-30); the English Dominican, Robert Holcot (1332-36); Henry Totting of Orta, at Erfurt (I 1363), and at Paris (1378-81); Cardinal Peter d'Ailly, who lectured at Paris about 1375; the Greek-born Franciscan, Peter of Candia, a Master of Theology at Paris in 1381; Marsilius of Inghen, Master of Theology at Paris in 1382 and later at Heidelberg; and Gabriel Biel, one of the Brethren of the Common Life, who completed his final version of his commentary at Tubingen in 1495.[181]

The silence of the Ockhamist commentators prevented them, of course, from making any positive contributions to the discussion such as the Scottists had done when they raised the question of injustice connection with withholding orders from women. The total effect of their silence went further than that, moreover. If we accept the common view of historians that Nominalist thought represented the cutting edge of philosophical and theological development in the latter fifteenth-century, and that it dominated the intellectual enthusiasm of Masters in many of the newly founded universities as well as Paris, then it seems quite clear that a large percentage of the students at those schools would have heard little about the possible ordination of women, or indeed would have had introduction to orders at all. They would inevitably have been left with the impression that the current arrangements of the church were mandates imposed by an infinite God about which little needed to be said, or even could be said.

The silence was not total, however. Theologians who followed one of the older ways of thinking sometimes brought the question forward. The Augustinian Friar and Thomist, Thomas of Strasbourg, writing toward 1337, for example, taught that the church's prohibition of ordination of women was not simply the result of ecclesiastical regulations, but followed from the nature of the sacrament itself, i.e., it was *de necessitate sacramenti*.[182] This was true because ordination involved an obligation to preach. This obligation obviously fell on priests, but it also bound deacons and those in lesser orders. Since deacons "proclaim the Gospel and those in lessor orders assist them," all were potentially preachers. Yet Paul in his letter to Timothy laid down that women should not teach in a church. On this ground, Thomas concludes that women cannot be ordained, an argument with which we are familiar.[183] Thomas also recalled that no one should be ordained who must pray with head veiled. This, too, was something which Paul had insisted upon for women. This added reason, although phrased in a curious and by now old-fashioned way, seems to be nothing more than a restatement of the notion that women should not be placed in a position of excellence over others in the church.[184] When Thomas comes to speak of Mary, he makes the point, even more strongly than Scotus, that, if Mary was not ordained by Christ, then all women must be ineligible. He remarks that Christ "as a good son honored his Mother before every other creature," and would never had withheld this honor from her if in the Divine plan she were capable of receiving this sacrament.[185] Turning to the conventional objections that deaconesses and *presbytera* were mentioned in the ancient laws of the church, he gives the conventional answer that these were merely honorific titles. To another conventional objection that orders should be open to all, men and women, because orders is a spiritual reality of the soul, and the souls of men and women do not differ, he again answers in the conventional way—orders is a spiritual reality, but one which is related to a body.

Thomas emphasizes only one point regarding the status of women, but it is one of some significance. To the suggestion that women must be able to render judgments because Debora ruled Israel as a judge for many years (with the implication that such a judgeship put her in a position of excellence, and hence in a position to be ordained), he replies that we can speak of the power of giving judgment on two different levels. We must keep in mind that there is a spiritual realm and a temporal realm. Nothing prevents a woman from exercising temporal power, he agrees, and indeed many women have, and in some parts of the world still do have, great temporal power. This is the type of power which Debora had when she "judged" Israel. Authority to hand down judgments in spiritual affairs, however, is quite another matter. In this realm, the power to give judgments does not pertain to women, hence neither does ordination. This is clear to him since in his eyes the power of orders is strictly spiritual.[186] In Thomas of Strasbourg we clearly find an openness toward women holding positions of authority and being placed in a position of "excellence" over men in the civil sphere. It would be interesting to discover if he had any contemporary women rulers in mind when he came to write his article. In order to defend the traditional view against ordination of women, a view which he does not relax, he is obliged to separate the temporal and sacramental spheres. Women may have political skills and ability, but that is not for him what is required for exercising orders. In his hands orders are detached from that kind of competence, since, as he tells us, they are strictly spiritual. The competence required for orders is, presumably, of an otherworldly sort.

In the latter half of the fourteenth-century a few discussions of the question can be found. Three treatises from the period which I have examined make a brief reference. The Thomist, Denis the Cistercian, who was author of a *Summary-Commentary* dated about 1375, says simply that a woman cannot be ordained either *de iure* or *de facto* to any of the seven grades of order. The reason for this is that Christ instituted this sacrament for men and not for women. How do we know this? We know this because we never read of a case (in Scripture) where Christ ever ordained a women, however holy, not even his own mother.[187] Another *Summary-Commentary*, a compilation of texts reflecting the lectures of Henry of Gorchum (who was at Paris from about 1395 to 1419, and later at Cologne), Giles of Rome and a certain Henry of Wurimaria, contains only a single line which says, "Six things are substantive with regard to orders, and the first of them is male sex in the ordained since a woman does not receive the character [of Orders]."[188] In still another set of *quaestiones* (this time following the plan of the *Summa* of Thomas Aquinas rather than the *Sentences* of Peter Lombard), Henry of Gorchum once again reports the prohibition against the ordination of women, but he expands on his reasons slightly, referring us to the importance of sacramental symbolism. The sacrament is not only an event (a *res*), it is a sign of what is involved in the event. Since a woman cannot occupy a position of eminence because her status is one of subjection, she cannot be a sign of leadership, and so the sacramental symbolism cannot be fulfilled. This is also the reason, he continues, why abbesses are not truly prelates as other ordinaries are. Instead, their authority is given to them by special commissions.[189]

These late-fourteenth-century treatises do not make stimulating reading, at least with regard to our question. They are content with describing the situation then in force, one which had been in force as far as they were concerned from time immemorial. They offer no new reasons nor make any attempt to give a fresh explanation for the old reasons. In short, they show uniformly little interest in the issue.

When these treatises were being written, the church was absorbed with another theological issue of pressing urgency, and one which had prior claim on the creative thinking of theologians and canonists. In 1378, a double papal election produced a schism in the Western Church which was to last for forty years. A divided church with a double hierarchy led by one pope resident in Rome and another claimant living in Avignon might suggest that a through going discussion of authority, ministry, and orders was called for, but this was not to be the case. The questions raised were the grand ones of the role and powers of the pope, the cardinals, and the bishops both as they were scattered throughout the earth and when they were gathered together in general council. At the universities, interest fell on the then immediately practical questions of how a council might be summoned in such an extremity, who its members ought to be, and what were its powers vis-à-vis a pope, or even before two or three of them. During these years, questions about the strictly sacramental aspects of orders were hardly touched upon in the schools beyond report of traditional teaching. The surviving works of leading theologians of the day, like Peter d'Ailly or Jean Gerson, who dealt so extensively with ecclesiastical policy and administrative reforms, did not go into matters concerning the fine points of ordination at all.[190]

Traces of a different set of attitudes can be felt, however, in the writings of authors who were out of the mainstream of the theological establishment. At Oxford, Wyclif held anticlerical opinions which recast traditional sacramental and institutional notions of the priesthood.[191] In consequence, his ideas encouraged more religious initiative by the non-ordained. Some elements of his teaching, therefore, did seem to encourage, if not the ordination of women, at least increased ministerial activity on their part. His attitudes were picked up later in Lollard circles which looked back to him for theological, if not for personal, leadership. Wyclif advanced two general arguments which could be interpreted as advocating a new view of priesthood. First, he spoke of the absolute power which God always held over the administration of the sacrament, and, second, he brought into new prominence the notion of the common priesthood of all baptized. In the hands of his "followers," this teaching began to take on a new thrust. If we take into consideration the absolute power of God (the power which the Almighty has to do anything which does not involve a contradiction), then, the argument ran, nothing prevents a woman from being ordained. Absolutely speaking, God could communicate the power of administering all the sacraments to a layman, to a woman or even to an irrational animal, just as he has now chosen to restrict this power to men, but, over and above considerations of God's absolute power, we also have the authority of the Apostle Peter (and of Chrysostom, too), who speaks of the baptized Christians as the "Holy people, the royal priesthood." This group includes both men and women. Augustine, too, speaks to the same effect where he says that "the priests of God and of Christ will reign for one thousand years." Augustine does not simply mean priests and bishops who are sacerdotal priests in the church, but he means all Christians. They will reign because of their mystic chrismation. Under this supposition, a woman as well as a man could be referred to as a priest. At least this is the way the arguments of Wyclifites sounded in the ear of Thomas Netter of Walden when he wrote his *Doctrinale Antiquitatus Fidei Catholicae* against them in the 1420's.[192] Netter was indignant at the whole thrust of Wyclif's theology in this and on many other questions, and he was aware of the influence which Wyclif's views were having.[193] The *Doctrinale* is an elaborate effort to blunt the power of that influence at a time when the Lollards were still a major cause of concern. Netter warns that on many occasions Wyclif did not blush from doing battle in favor of women as suitable candidates for priestly, episcopal or even papal office. He thinks that this is shameful, a source of derision among the Jews, and a scandal to the Saracens, but nonetheless Wyclif's Lollard followers take this as a warrant for ordaining women who will celebrate Masses and other sacraments, and preach and read the Scriptures in their gatherings.[194] What Wyclif has done is to spin a subtle web using the concept of God's absolute powers to suggest that God could confer power on a woman, or even on an animal. To defend the Catholic opinion, Netter brings forward in polemical fashion a series of arguments, many of which we have seen before. In the first place, Netter argues it is highly significant that Christ did not ordain his mother to the priesthood. She is one of the predestined and also a virgin. He chose Judas instead, a man linked with so monstrous a sin and one which was foreknown. It is also significant for Netter that in their first plenary synod the Apostles did not choose any women when they selected the seven deacons. Further, Paul in his letter to Titus says that priests should be chosen from men of one wife, but he never speaks of the reverse case of choosing a wife of one man. Following the exegesis of Ambrose over Romans 16:13, Netter goes on to make the somewhat obscure point that Paul was forced to address the mother of Rufus as his mother too, since she deserved respect as a holy woman, but could not be called a priest since a woman had no place in priestly administration.[195] In this list of arguments, as we might expect, Netter also brings up the injunction of Paul to Timothy that women should not preach. He knows of the Cataphrygians and their vain presumption in defending the ordination of women to the diaconate. Finally, he makes the point that from the beginning we never find women priests among the holy people, neither from Moses to Christ, or from Christ and his Apostles, nor in the time of primitive church through the Fathers up to our own day.[196]

After presenting these arguments, Netter turns to Wyclif's other main line of reasoning that women are priests just as much as men since they, too, are part of the holy people which is a kingdom of priests. For Netter, Wyclif's suggestion is clearly ambiguous and deceptive and is not faithful to Augustine. It is perfectly true that women are priests as members of the church, but this does not mean that they are priests in the sense that they offer holy gifts as virtue of their public office in the church. This is the type of activity that properly describes the priesthood.[197] Those who are uncomfortable with a special ministerial priesthood and say that all the people are equally holy and equally priestly run the risk of going the way of Dathan and Core, who rose up in this way against Moses. They were punished for their presumption. In this latter sense, the priesthood is no longer open to women. This is the result of the temptation and the Fall in the Garden. Netter argues that both Adam and Eve sinned in their encounter with Satan, but that they sinned differently. This difference is the root of the present difference in the role of men and women in the plan of salvation. Eve not only fell, but she was deceived by the devil in her fall. Through Adam's sin, our whole human nature has become infected, but the penalty meted out by God to the woman affected her sexual role, her femininity. In the current plan of salvation, a woman's role is to give physical birth to children and to secure the education of them; a man's role is to bring forth children in the spiritual sense by means of the gift of the priesthood.[198]

The *Doctrinale* of Thomas Netter is interesting not only because of the space which he allots to the question of ordinations, and the number of arguments which he piles up concerning the ordination of women, but because of the obvious intensity of his feeling. Netter obviously sees Wyclif as a dangerous innovator who must not only be refuted before academics, but must be convincingly defeated in the eyes of the ordinary educated reader. Netter's arguments are not particularly new, nor far-reaching if we accept the comparison which he draws between the different salvific roles assigned to men and women. His discussion strongly suggests, however, that in England at this time the question of the ordination of women was a real and a lively one.

The influence of the ideas of Wyclif in theology and in political theory made their way into Bohemia in the later fourteenth-century to be picked up by the Czech leader, John Hus.[199] On the question of ordination, as in much else, Hus was something of an independent thinker. In his *Sentence* commentary, written about 1404, he too draws the traditional conclusion that women should not be ordained. He agrees that the masculine sex is required, not simply because of a prescription of law, but as a necessary part of the conditions surrounding the sacrament (*de necessitate sacramenti*). A woman is, therefore, someone incapable of receiving orders.[200] On the other hand, he finds that the reasoning customarily offered by theologians is inadequate. The statements found in Paul's letters to the Corinthians, that women must pray with their heads veiled, and the injunction to Timothy, that a woman may not preach, do not seem to be sufficient reasons. Hus points out that before the prohibitions were issued by Paul they would not have sufficed. The question which should be asked is why can't a woman pray with her head unveiled, why can't she preach? The only answer to this must be to return to the primary cause for these rules. It is the Lord who has issued them in the first place. In both the Old and New Law, the Lord has never indicated that that sex (i.e., women) should receive orders. Scripture is clear enough, but as to why this should be so, Hus exclaims simply, "God knows!"[201] Later in a phrase reminiscent of Wyclif, he suggests that ordination is not, after all, the touchstone of everything. The Lord, he notes, did not confer orders on the most holy Virgin although he did upon Judas Iscariot who he damned.[202]

A discussion of the ordination of women lingered on in the latter part of the fifteenth-century, but without notable innovation or development. The question is taken up only by a few authors, and they for the most part handle it briefly. Paradoxically, where we do find discussion it can be explained as a result of that general revival and renewal of the past which characterized a great deal of the intellectual life of the latter fifteenth-century. The healing of the Great Schism in 1415 secured by the election of Pope Martin V, who was recognized as Pope throughout Europe, brought with it the end of the emergency situation which had hung over the life of the church for a full generation. With a return to normalcy at the highest levels of government, the church looked forward with hope to a time of renewal. With the advantage of hindsight, we are painfully aware that those expectations of reform were not to materialize. Historians can now easily trace how disappointed expectations gradually built up a reservoir of mistrust and bitterness as the century progressed. Many became convinced that the structures of the church and of civil society too had become unworkable and were in need of a thorough going reorganization. The religious Reformation of the sixteenth-century, in large measure a reaction to the failure of reform in the late fifteenth, produced substantive changes in religious belief and practice for Reformers as well as those who remained loyal to the Roman Church. Both sides often looked to the late fifteenth-century as a time of corruption and decadence. Their negative attitudes should not blind us to the fact that many of those living in the fifteenth-century viewed their own times quite differently. To many, the age appeared to be one where reform and renewal were at hand, or just around the corner. The same kind of enthusiasm which embraced humanism and the artistic revival of the Renaissance, and which found an outlet in the study of the ancient scriptural languages and the writings of the Fathers, also inspired numerous theologians to review and restudy the writings of the great masters of theology of the thirteenth-century. It was the same spirit which motivated new editions of the writings of Bonaventure, Thomas Aquinas, Duns Scotus and William of Ockham and commentaries on them. As a consequence, ideas of the thirteenth and fourteenth-centuries were re-examined and provided the basis for a lively, if secondary, theological discussion. A theologian writing in this spirt is Denis the Carthusian.[203] Denis began his studies with the Brethren of the Common Life, a group noted for its innovation and lay spirit. In 1421, shortly before he was 20, he applied to enter the Carthusian Order, an enclosed Order devoted to contemplation and study, but on account of his age was sent to the University of Cologne to do his theological studies. At Cologne, he enrolled in the *via Sancti Thomae* which flourished there, and remained faithful to that philosophical and theological orientation all his life. He was allowed to enter the Carthusians in 1524 or 1525, probably before he completed his theological studies. This enables us to date his commentary on the *Sentences* sometime after 1525, and his voluminous commentaries on Scripture sometime later than that.[204]

In asking whether the feminine sex is an impediment to orders, Denis begins with a series of statements which are quite different in tone and spirit than what we have been reading and reflect a more positive image of women. He says flatly that some women, both by their natural qualities and by God's grace, are a lot more worthy and suitable for ordination than many men. Many women are wiser and more virtuous and have a greater devotion to openness toward God. Sex, it would seem, should not be an impediment to orders. Moreover, if anyone should argue that women belong to a sex that should be subject, it should be kept in mind that many women are leaders (*praesidentes*), and one of them was made queen and ruling-lady (*domina*) over the whole world. She was, of course, the Virgin Mary, the most holy and the most transcendent (*supermundissimi*) mother of the Incarnate God.[205]

After these positive statements, Denis turns to the writings of Thomas Aquinas to resolve the question. Some things are necessary for a sacrament because they flow from the nature of the sacrament itself (they are *de necessitate sacramenti*), while some things are necessary because they have been commanded (they are *de necessitate precepti*). If what is lacking is required only by law, then a person might indeed receive the sacrament although they would not receive Divine grace associated with the sacrament. On the other hand, if something which flows from the nature of the sacrament is missing, then the person involved receives neither the grace given in the sacrament nor its sacramental character. For Denis, the masculine sex is one of those requirements demanded by the nature of the sacrament itself. In consequence, someone who is not male simply cannot receive the sacrament of Orders, whatever ceremonies might be performed. By way of analogy, Denis argues that just as a person who is not truly sick cannot receive the sacrament of Extreme Unction (the sacrament of the sick), so a woman cannot receive orders. The reason for this is that a sacrament is a sign of what is referred to in the sacrament. Grace (i.e., the *res*) is not the only thing required here, but what the grace implies (*significatio rei*) must be present as well.[206] For Denis, a woman cannot really make present, i.e., she cannot truly signify what the sacrament of Orders symbolizes. When drawing this conclusion, it is interesting to note that Denis consciously returns to the theology of the earlier schoolmen. With regard to the sacraments, the fundamental point to be considered is the significance, the sign value, of the sacrament, not simply the fact that is has been instituted by Christ. Denis certainly believed that the sacraments had been instituted by Christ, but not in an arbitrary fashion. A sacrament must always be a symbolic gesture, an instrumentality. When instituting them, even God must respect the natural world so that what is chosen to be used by Him as instrument may truly be a sign of what is intended. In returning to this point of view, Denis was being faithful to the schoolmen of the mid-thirteenth-century, such as Thomas

Aquinas and Bonaventure, both of whom speak continually of the sign values inherent in the rites of the sacramental system.

With these premises in mind, Denis can complete his argument, of course, only if he find some inherent difference between man and woman which will show that one sex is an appropriate sign, a suitable instrumentality for orders, and the other sex clearly is not. Arguing as so many medieval theologians before him, Denis finds that the difference between man and woman which is critical here is their status. A great deal of the symbolism present in the sacrament of orders would be exemplified, of course, by both men and women, but the question of status is the area where this is not the case. The sacrament of Orders confers upon its recipients the status of eminence, it endows them with leadership in the Christian community. But leadership is something which is unsuitable for women. Why is this so? Denis replies that the natural status of woman is to be subject. A woman cannot be ordained, we are left to conclude, because femininity of itself does not proclaim leadership, an essential ingredient in the symbolism of orders.[207]

In putting leadership (status) at the center of his argument against the ordination of women, Denis was guided, doubtless, by the long *Sentence* commentary tradition and by the standardized glosses on Paul which constantly return to the notion that women have a subject status. Despite this long tradition, the choice of leadership as a central symbol is not all that obvious. Other symbols were also deeply imbedded in the understanding of orders, and Denis was well aware of their existence. We come upon some of them when Denis discusses orders from other vantage points. His remarks about the canonical impediment known as bigamy enable him to relate the sacrament of Orders to the symbolism of matrimony. (For purposes of ecclesiastical law, a bigamist is said to be anyone who has married more than once, whatever the reason, as, for example, a remarried widow or widower.) According to Paul, in 1 Timothy and in Titus, bigamists were not to be admitted to orders, but he gives no clear reasons himself for the prohibition.[208] In defending this rule, Denis builds an argument which is based on matrimonial symbolism. He is not the first to do so, for as he himself says he has found the argument in Bonaventure. Both the sacrament of Orders and the sacrament of matrimony, he notes, are exceptionally rich in symbolism. Not only are the ritual ceremonies symbolic, but the persons who enter into these sacraments must be symbolic figures as well. The one ordained, whether to the grade of bishop or priest, must be able to signify Christ. Now Christ took as his bride the church. The primary signification of the sacrament of Orders is that the person in orders signify Christ, and signify Christ precisely in the sense in which Christ is the bridegroom of the church, which is his bride. Since Christ espoused himself only to the one church (he takes no other bride), it would be inappropriate for a person twice married to present themselves for ordination. Hence, we have Paul's prohibition in 1 Timothy and in Titus.[209] We are not interested here in the cogency of these arguments, or even the consistency of the imagery, as providing reason for not ordaining individuals who are many times married. What is of significance here is Denis's statement that the primary signification of orders is that the ordained person symbolizes Christ, and Christ as he is the bridegroom of the church. If this symbolism is adopted, and if it is regarded as in some way primary, it is a small step to say that only someone of the masculine sex could carry through this sacramental symbolism. Only a man could be the bridegroom in the church. When talking about the ordination of women, however, Denis makes no move to introduce what seems to be an obvious argument. In all probability, he was guided here by the long commentary tradition which did not make any such connection. It is curious that he did not do so, nevertheless, especially in view of his emphasis on the sign value of the sacrament of Orders.

How does Denis integrate the statements made at the outset of his article that some women are wiser and more virtuous than many men and that they are sometimes found in positions of leadership? Admissions such as these would seem to undermine his assertion that women by nature have a subject status. Denis apparently finds no difficulty since he never challenges his initial statements later. Not for him are remarks about the weakness of a woman's intellect and the fickleness of her emotions. For him, the point at issue is the symbolic status of women, not concrete abilities. In the terrestrial world, women, like Debora, can be called to govern.[210] Women can be wise and virtuous. The sacraments, however, are not concerned so much with worldly rule or abilities, but are essentially signs of a spiritual reality. Emphasis is placed on this level. Where the sacraments are concerned, matters like eminence and subject status involve a symbolic relationship, the right ordering that leads human beings back to God and to salvation.

The Decline of Interest During the Fifteenth-Century

Later in the fifteenth-century, there was a decided falling off of interest in the question, not only among Nominalist theologians who had rarely raised the issue, but with theologians from all of the schools. At mid-century, William of Vorrillon, a Franciscan and a close follower of Scotus, simply says in his major *Commentary on the Sentences* that women cannot be ordained either canonically or in actual fact.[211] This can be proved, he says, "by a number of laws, etc." Moreover, Christ did not ordain his own mother to any order. He then takes note of the conventional answer (this time quoted from the Subtle Doctor) that these "presbiterae" refer either to the wives of priests as occurs in Greece, or among the Latins to a pious elderly widow in charge of other women, or to an abbess in charge of some nuns.[212] In his shorter *Compendium on the Sentences,* William makes no mention of the issue at all!

Two other Franciscan authors, Gui Brianson, who was at Paris in 1450, and the Observant, Nicolas Orbellis, at Angers in the second half of the century, both usually described as representatives of the Scottist school, restate the arguments of the thirteenth-century Master, Richard of Mediavilla.[213] Women may not be ordained in law or in fact inasmuch as Christ instituted this sacrament to be conferred on men. Two reasons can be assigned for this: first, it is not appropriate for women to preach in public due to the weakness of their understanding and fickleness of emotions; second, women have a subject status in relation to men, as we find in the dictum of Paul, "I do not permit a woman to teach, or to be in charge of men."[214] The only significant addition to Mediavilla's argument is the Scotus touch that Christ did not ordain his mother, a person unequalled and unsurpassable in holiness.[215] In all of these authors, the discussion is quite perfunctory and shows no spark of originality, or even of particular interest. A portion of their texts is closely copied from the much earlier *Commentary*. One is left with the impression that, since these questions were customarily asked in the schools, one had to say at least something about them, if only for the sake of appearances.

Authors from other theological schools also seem to be uninterested. In the important *Summa Theologia Moralis* of Antoninus of Florence, one of the most influential authors of the latter fifteenth-century, I have been able to find only one brief, almost accidental, reference to the question. Antoninus, always a careful writer, wrote extensively on the sacraments and upon orders.[216] In speaking of those who are going to be ordained, he talks about those who are unworthy of the sacrament, about the examinations to be made of the *ordinandi* and what to do about the failure to carry them out, about the age of ordination, about the place where they are to occur, and what to do when ordinations have been forced upon someone. He later speaks of impediments to orders and discusses the state of those who have committed murder, are mutilated, are illegitimate, bigamous, or of servile status, or have had reputations. In all of this lengthy discussion, mention of women is made only once, and that in the very special and quite rare case of a person who is physically an hermaphrodite. He solves that question, too, in the customary manner. No hermaphrodite should be ordained (they are imperfect individuals), but, if they happen to be ordained, those who are predominantly masculine will receive orders; but, where feminine characteristics prevail, no ordination occurs. If this is true, then, all the more so in the case of a woman. An indication that this aside is actually Antoninus's main discussion of the issue is the fact that he cites the familiar canons *Presbytera* and *Diaconissa* here, and gives the conventional answers.[217] It is obvious that for Antoninus the tradition is well known, clearly uncontroversial, and apparently in no need of any particular discussion. The Nominalist theologian Gabriel Biel writing toward the end of the century, as we have already noted, does not discuss the topic of orders. The humanist author Paul Cortensius also fails to consider the problem.

The last theologian we will consider in this long series of authors is the Scotsman John Major. Major was at Paris between 1503 and 1518 and was well known as a voluminous writer of the older style.[218] In his *Sentence* commentary, or rather commentaries, since he produced more than one, Major asks all the old questions, but his works do contain evidence of new currents of interest and new ways of thinking. We find his solid theological comments laced with chatty stories, references to classical authors, and at times, information about current happenings. In this he is more the Humanist than the Medieval. His article on the ordination of women expresses interest in the question, although no apparent deep concern. Who is able to be ordained, he asks in the 1509 version of his commentary? His answer is that women and the non-baptized are among those who cannot be. The answer is to be understood absolutely. If any bishop should attempt to ordain a woman, he would accomplish nothing. The cause for this is simply Divine institution, although, he adds quickly, this rule is quite in conformity with reason.[219] In the 1516 edition, he notes that there are many things which we hold on the authority of Divine law which are not expressly found in that law, nor can they be obviously deduced from it. By way of examples, he lists the belief that the Supreme Pontificate was given to the successors of Peter by Christ, the origin of the individual orders, and that women are not to be ordained.[220] The truth of these beliefs is demonstrated by means of some arguments showing their congruity. The argument which we can make for not ordaining women is the example of Mary. The virgin-bearer of Christ did not receive any order because this was unsuitable for the feminine sex. For this reason, too, the Apostle says rightly in his letter to Timothy, "I do not permit women to teach, nor to be in charge of men." This is the substance of the argument Major gives in his 1516 version of the *Sentences*.[221] In an earlier edition, written in 1509, he goes on to expatiate on the problems with women. They are an imprudent and garrulous lot, he thinks, and bearers of tales. He then quotes the story of some honest women who complained loudly that they were forbidden to hear confessions. They visited the Roman Pontiff, who gave them a pix to keep overnight in which he had hidden a bird. He then gave them strict instructions not to open it. As we customarily say of a woman, Major goes on, she is always quick to do the very thing which is prohibited. One of them opened the pix and the Pope's bird escaped. In the morning, when he asked whether they had opened the pix, and they denied they had, he concluded that they would not know how to keep secret sins detected in confession. It would be shameful for them to gad about the countryside and to spread gossip in town, but rather they ought to remain privately at home.[222] This story is doubtless not original with Major, but a bit of folk "wisdom" about women which circulated as an *exemplum*. It illuminates tellingly the underlying negative attitude toward women prevalent in some quarters. That it appears in Major's work and not in other commentaries I take as an example of Major's literary style rather than a shift in theological attitude. In both versions of his *Sentences* he tells us, somewhat irrelevantly, that in describing the customs of the Egyptians Herodotus records that they had no women priests for either their gods or goddesses. At the opening of the sixteenth-century, it was a time for making classical allusions, and so Major dutifully makes them. Stripped of the story and the classical reference, Major's discussion is in fact quite spare, repeating the same arguments which we have heard since the thirteenth-century. The ordination of anyone depends upon the institution of Christ, and he instituted the sacrament of Orders without reference to women. We know all this from the belief that his mother, the Virgin, was not ordained herself, and from the statements of Paul in Timothy and 1 Corinthians that women should not preach or be placed in authority over men, at least in spiritual matters.

Major's final version of the fourth book of the *Sentences* was written in 1516 when he was at Montaigue College, Paris, one year before new developments in theology inaugurated by Martin Luther. In Luther's theology, as we know, the whole question of ministry and orders would be reviewed again in a radical fashion. The notion that the Christian priesthood involved placing the ordained in any degree of eminence over fellow baptized Christians in spiritual affairs would be sharply attacked by him and by all the Reformers. Special powers to celebrate the Eucharist, to hear confessions and to preach the Gospel which did not stem from the priesthood of all believers conveyed in Baptism would now be denied. Individuals might well be appointed to perform certain specific functions to assist fellow believers, but that followed from the need for good and reasonable order in the community, not from a spiritual character conferred once and for all upon selected individuals. When Luther was asked if women could be ordained and could preach the Gospel he, quite naturally, answered yes.[223] But his answer was to a new and a different question.

Conclusion

In drawing conclusions from the present study it seems obvious that the treatment given to the question by theologians from the thirteenth to the sixteenth centuries was an exercise in restating arguments that would defend the already accepted conclusion that women could not participate in the sacrament of Orders. This conclusion, as we have seen, was clearly stated by canonists in the West in the previous two centuries. They in their turn had relied on earlier collections of canons and on selected statements of the Church Fathers who had regarded the practice of nonordination of something that had been settled time out of mind. Variant views or isolated examples of a different practice were dismissed as one of the more bizarre of the opinions held by heretics living at the fringe of the Christian community. Even the notion that women had at one time been deaconesses was hedged in with so many reservations that they could reasonably say that, whatever the office of deaconesses may have once involved, it did not involve participating in the sacrament of Orders. Inasmuch as the practice of the church was normative (for just as the church could never fail to teach the truth, so she could never be unjust in the practices which she enjoined as a matter of policy), a theological justification for the practice of nonordination was appropriate, but it was not particularly urgent. It would not become urgent unless the practice were to come under sustained attack. Whether the introduction of properly theological arguments into the *Sentence* commentaries at the beginning of the thirteenth-century represented a response to pressure for the ordination of women, or whether it was simply a desire to fill out a theological discussion of the sacrament of Orders, is a matter which is still unclear. Dissident groups, such as the Waldenses and the Cathars, did, it is true, make some allowance for women in their ministries, but then neither of them had a view of ministry which implied a priestly ordination in the first place. It is quite possible that the discussion of the ordination of women in the 1220's and 1230's in the *Sentence* books is simply a response of general theological interest of the sort which touched on all sorts of questions about that time.

Since the practice of the church was normative by itself, it was also unnecessary to develop theological arguments about nonordination of women that were apodictic, any more than it would be necessary to find apodictic arguments for the existence of the Trinity. All that the theologian would feel called upon to do would be to show that the current nonordination practice fit in with the statements of Holy Scripture and with other considerations of the church's tradition. It was precisely in this spirit that the theologians argued. A number of passages from Scripture which were traditionally associated with ordination, taken mostly from the canonists, were discussed and commented upon, but no general search through Scripture can be said to have been made. The relation of men toward women, both as this appeared in the state of nature before the Fall, and after the primordial sin in the Garden of Eden was also taken up, but more in an effort to show support for a practice already in force rather than to establish the practice itself. This attitude helps to explain the variation in argument which the theologians used as the centuries progressed without producing any corresponding changes toward the nonordination conclusion, a conclusion which remained quite constant.

The most prominent Scriptural passages which were used through the period were taken, as we have seen, from Paul, especially 1 Corinthians 14 and 34, and 1 Timothy 1 and 2, passages which incidentally represent the earliest and the latest strata of the Pauline material. The passages do not refer to the actual celebration of the Eucharistic meal, which had long been regarded as the central point of Christ's own ministry and of the sacrament of Orders. It is, of course, not surprising that no passages talk of the Eucharist inasmuch as the Scriptures themselves are silent about whether men or women presided at that community event. The passages of Paul which are cited refer instead to the authority to preach the Gospel, an activity attached to and restricted to those in orders, especially in higher orders. After citing these passages and others like them, theologians had to give reasons why women could not in fact preach in the churches. Why couldn't women preach? It was not entirely obvious even to theologians at the time why they should not since it was clear that some women could do so better than some men. Women could not preach, however well prepared they might be, so the argument ran, because this would imply the equality, even the superiority, of the woman preacher over the male members of her congregation. In the eyes of some theologians, the rejection of a woman preacher was justified by resorting to arguments taken largely, although not exclusively, from Aristotle. According to the philosopher, women were physically, emotionally, and mentally inferior as a class to men. Although this sort of argument appears frequently enough in medieval texts, especially after the middle of the thirteenth-century when Aristotle began to be admired, theologians were not entirely happy with it. There were too many examples of exceptional women in their own midst; there was the tradition that women could be, and in ancient times often had been, civil rulers. The argument was also vulnerable to the accusation that it was philosophy attempting to decide a theological question. A more telling argument, even for the more misogynistic theologians, was the notion derived ultimately from Genesis that woman had been made a helpmate for man. This original state was confirmed and to some extent intensified by Divine decree as a result of the Fall of Eve in the Garden of Eden. Medieval theologians ultimately rooted the church's practice of nonordination of women in the religious symbolism concerning women found in the Old and New Testaments.

In the hands of theologians, such as Bonaventure and Thomas Aquinas, who felt that the created world, however imperfectly, in some way nonetheless reflected Divine wisdom, natural symbolism could be presented to help clarify church practices. Women, for example, should not cut their hair, for it was a covering which naturally expresses their subject status. On the other hand, anyone who is to be ordained must trim their hair with the tonsure, which is an implicit denial of any subject status. Even nature itself hints at the relation which should prevail between men and women. The sign is dramatic perhaps, but as an argument for the nonordination of women it is in fact quite weak if we compare it with statements of the Divine disposition expressed in God's written Word and in the practice of the church. The subject status of women revealed in nature and in Scripture was significant, however, since it made clear that orders was a sacrament appropriate to those who occupied not a subject, but an elevated, state. Hence it was to be regarded as a sacrament which gave authority and superiority in spiritual matters to those who received it.

In the hands of theologians who felt that the physical world and human affairs generally were not avenues for comprehending the Divinity, such as Duns Scotus and the Nominalist thinkers following the leadership of William of Ockham, the significance of arguments from natural symbolism died away. For them, the question of whether women should be ordained or not was very much a question to be decided by the practice of the church. The answer might be supported to some degree by considerations of inferiority and superiority of men over women gleaned from stories related in the Scriptures. As a consequence, it was quite logical for such theologians to wonder if the legislation of the church was just or unjust. Since the sacraments were not so much symbols rooted in the physical reality of the world, as such they were expressions of the Divine will, the practice of the church could be justified only if it were clear that its custom was in fact an expression of the Divine will. Obviously, arguments could no longer be drawn from the realm of nature. Even human nature itself was inadequate for that purpose. Only concrete examples of Divine action toward individuals or groups of individuals would really do. For theologians of this persuasion, the fact that men only had been chosen to be ordained (i.e., had been chosen to be Apostles or Disciples), and the fact that the Blessed Virgin, the woman to whom all possible graces had been given, had not been so chosen, was a fact of great significance. The Marian argument against the ordination of women had been broached before their time (it appears as early as decretals of Pope Innocent III), but in the fourteenth-century it began to receive much more prominence, especially among the followers of Duns Scotus and William of Ockham.

While examining what theologians between the thirteenth and sixteenth-century positively had to say, it is also worthwhile to consider what they did not get around to saying in their commentaries. Medieval theologians were very much aware that human salvation came about through the humanity of Christ. United to the Person of the Word, Christ acted in each of the sacraments which he had established. It was quite common, therefore, for theologians to argue that in the sacrament of Orders the function of the ordained minister was to act in the person of

Christ. The expression was slightly stronger than the parallel English phrase, "to act in someone's name." To act in someone's name implies a legal right to do so, whereas to act in the person of another implies becoming a kind of substitute for the original individual. So, for example, when a celebrant of the Eucharist was said to act *in persona Christi*, it was implied that the individual was substituting, playing the role of Christ himself. It was a commonplace for authors of *Sentence* commentaries of the period to say that an ordained person when performing the sacraments acted *in persona Christi*. Under these considerations it would have been quite easy for theologians to develop the argument that only men could be ordained, and not women, since they alone were in a position to substitute for Christ, who was a male figure. As far as I have been able to discover, this argument was never made at the time. While all the major medieval theologians spoke of bishops and priests as acting in the person of Christ in other contexts, they never brought up the issue when talking about the ordination of women.

The theologians of the period also maintained silence in another important area. It was commonly agreed that Christ is the bridegroom of his people, the church, which is then described as his bride. The symbol is a powerful one, and was popular, because it dramatizes the intimacy of Christ, the Savior, with the community of the church. The symbol has good credentiality since it is found in Paul, especially in Ephesians 5:29-33. The imagery of Ephesians along with its insistence that the male assume a Christlike role in loving his wife, was, of course, well known at the time. On the whole, it was reserved for describing a bishop vis-à-vis his community rather than for a priest or other ordained minister. It would be an easy step to argue that a priest, or at least a bishop, must be male since only a male could logically be a bridegroom for the church, the bride. Although the imagery is known it is not brought forward as a proof to defend the practice of the nonordination of women during this period.

The last two considerations, that a priest acts precisely in the person of Christ, and that Christ and presumably his representative is the bridegroom of the Church, were certainly part of the medieval context which would have made it seem plausible and the just course to exclude feminine candidates from orders. The major consideration, the one which exercised the most powerful attraction over the minds of medieval theologians, seems to have been, however, elevation and subordination. Individual, personal abilities aside, a woman's place was to be a helpmate for man, not his leader. An inescapable goal of the sacrament of Orders was the formation of Christian community, an activity which required and implied a role of leadership. In this matter, questions of skills, ability, or equality were kept severely to the side. For them, the fundamental issue was one of hierarchy, of maintaining the right order in the church.

Notes

1. Tim. 2:12-13; I Cor. 11:5-10; 1 Cor. 14:33-36.

2. James A. Weisheipl, *Friar Thomas d'Aquino: His Life, Thought, and Work*, (Garden City, N.Y.: Doubleday, 1974) 67-68, for an overview of the function of the *Sentences*. Also Gordon Leff, *Paris and Oxford Universities in the Thirteenth and Fourteenth Centuries: An Institutional and Intellectual History*, (New York: Wiley, 1968) 160-67.

3. Weisheipl, *Friar Thomas*, 110.

4. For a brief discussion of some bachelors and their work as "cursors" on the Bible and the *Sentences*, see Weisheipl, *Friar Thomas*, 59-67

5. *Magistri Petri Lombardi Sententiae in IV Libris Distinctae*, 3rd ed. 2 v. in 3, Spicilegium Bonaventurianum; 4, 5 (Grottaferrata: Editiones Collegii S. Bonaventurae ad Claras Aquas, 1971-1981) 3:393-416.

6. Humbert of Silva Candida had raised the issue of the validity of simoniacal ordinations in his *Libri Adversus Simoniacos* in the midst of the investiture crisis, a novel theological view but a politically powerful one. See Gerd Tellenback, *Church State and Christian Society at the Time of the Investiture Contest*, trans. R. F. Bennett (Oxford: Basil Blackwell, 1966 [1959]) 109-12.

7. He gave 14 years as the minimum age for subdeacons, 25 for deacons, and 30 for priests, *Petri Lombardi Sententiae*, 3:415-16. He cites as his authority two decrees of Pope Nicolas and Pope Fabian. The citations cannot be found in their writings nor do they appear in the *Decretum* of Gratian (c. 1140), although they are mentioned in the *Panormia* of Ivo of Chartres (d. 1115) (Jacques Paul Migne, ed., 217 vols. and indexes, *Patrologiae cursus completus . . . Series latina* [Paris: Garnier Fratres and J.P. Migne, 1878-90] [hereinafter *PL*] 161:1135, 1136-7). Gratian gives a slightly different age for the subdiaconate (20), giving the same ages for deacon and priest as is given in Peter Lombard, but he cites different authorities (*Decretum*, dist. 77-8 [Emil Friedberg, ed., *Corpus Iuris Canonici*, (Graz: Akademische Druck- u. Verlagsanstalt, 1959) (hereafter Friedberg) vol. 1, col. 273-6]). The editors of the *Sentaentiae* suggest that the Lombard found the decrees listed in an unknown Paris collection. The ideas about age for ordination set out in the "decrees" Lombard quotes have a long history that predates the medieval period. Cf. *Petri Lombardi Sententiae* 3:415.

8. *PL* 176:431-4.

9. *PL* 210:303-430.

10. Alan reported that they allowed "mere women" to preach with them (bk. 2, ch. 1, *PL* 210:379). According to Alan, the Waldenses said that they could consecrate the Eucharist as well as a priest because, "priests bless not according to their own power, but because they put on the figure of Christ, and by means of Him who is in them, they bestow the fullness of blessing." Bk. 2, ch. 8 (*PL* 210:385). Shulamith Shahar points to the rights granted women in Waldensian communities and their activity, but notes that ordination of women as clerics was not a particular interest of the movement which did not try to evolve a new theology running counter to that of the Roman Church. *The Fourth Estate, A History of Women in the Middle Ages,* trans. Chaya Galai. (London: Methuen, 1983) 254-8.

11. Peter of Poitiers, *Sententiarum Libri Quinque,* bk. 5, ch. 14 (*PL* 211: 790-1280, esp. 1257 sqq).

12. William of Auxerre, *Summa Aurea in Quattuor Libros Sententiarum. . .* (Paris, 1500, rpt, Frankfurt/Main: Minerva, 1964). Cf. bk. 4, fol. 283r for a discussion of qualities required of those ordained.

13. Guidonis Orchellus *Tractatus de Sacramentis ex eius Summa de Sacramentis et Officiis Ecclesiae,* Damian and Odulph Van den Eynde, eds., (Franciscan Institute Publications, text series, 4) (St. Bonaventure, N.Y.: Franciscan Institute, 1953). Although this work has survived in only three manuscripts, it has influenced later writers of more importance, like Hugh de Saint-Cher and William of Auxerre. See K. F. Lynch, "Some 'Fontes' of Alexander of Hales," *Franciscan Studies* 13 (1953) 119-46.

14. *Magistri Alexandri de Hales Glossa in Quatuor Libros Sententiarum Petri Lombardi* (Florence: Collegium S. Bonaventurae, 1957).

15. *Alexandri de Hales Glossa,* 4:434.

16. For a discussion of the date of composition and the editorship of Alexander's *Summa,* see the Prolegomena by V. Doucet, in *Alexandri de Hales Summa Theologica* (Florence: Collegium S. Bonaventurae, 1948), 4.1, esp. lxxx, cccxxxiv, cccxxvix-ccclxi. For his views on part 4 of the *Summa,* p. lxxxb. Following a papal directive to the Franciscan Order, which Alexander had joined in 1236, William of Melitonia attempted to complete the *Summa* by piecing together bits of the *Glosses* and other writings of Alexander along with material taken from his Franciscan colleagues, such as Jean de la Rochelle and Odo Rigaud. The work would have provided a valuable witness, not only of Alexander's views but of several representatives of the early Franciscan school. Unfortunately, it was not brought to completion either. It is to be particularly regretted that William, the collector, failed to reach the section in the *Summa* devoted to orders before he stopped work on the project in 1260. We must rely, then, on glosses of 1230 to represent Alexander's thoughts.

17. Hugh de St. Cher (c. 1200-1263), the second Dominican Master of Sacred Theology, taught at Paris from 1230 until 1236. In this work he briefly discusses the seven grades of order, and questions whether or not heretics could

confer them, but he does not go beyond the questions raised by Peter Lombard. His great commentaries on Scripture were still before him. Cf. Van den Eynde, *Tractatus de Sacramentis,* [141] for the date of Hugh's work. I have consulted Bodley Ms. Can. Pat. Lat. 208, fol. 46v. For his life, see *New Catholic Encyclopedia,* 18 vols. (New York: McGraw-Hill, 1967-89) (hereafter *NCE*) 8:193A.

18. *Hugonis de Sancto Charo . . . in epistolas omnes D. Pauli . . .* (Lyon, 1669). Over 1 Cor. 9, he makes the point (already commonly accepted but reinforced by him as the common exegesis) that woman was created by God to be man's helpmate, and that man's glory was to command her well (fol. 102ra). Over 1 Cor. 14, he says that, "in the presence of men women should not teach or preach publicly, or expound the Sacred Scriptures, in the mode of doctrine or preaching," (fol. 114rb). If women sometimes seem to do so, such as Debora, the prophetess, that was the result of a privilege given to her, and such exceptions do not generate a rule; or else we can say that the prophesying was really singing or praising such as nuns do (fol. 114rb). Over 1 Tim.1, he repeats that women should not speak or dominate men, and for two reasons: First, it would be against the order of creation since man was created first; and second, because it was Eve (the woman) who was seduced into sin and from her fall, "the nature of all women was made in transgression through that." (fol. 211vb). Hugh's work helped fix these ideas as standard exegesis.

19. Beryl Smalley, *The Study of the Bible in the Middle Ages,* 3rd ed. (Oxford: Blackwell, 1983) 270-3.

20. *Sancti doctoris ecclesiae Alberti Magni Ordinis Fratrum Praedicatorum Opera Omnia,* Bernhard Geyer, ed. (Cologne: Ashendorff, 1951), *De Sacramentis,* Tract. 8, 26:135.

21. Peter of Poitiers, *Sententiarum Libri Quinque,* bk. 4, ch. 14, *PL* 211:1257b: " . . . concerning the laws, nothing is said here about those things the arguments about which are more of service to the decretists [the canonists who commented on the *Decretum* of Gratian] than to the theologians."

22. "Dionysiana," J. Rambaud-Buhot, *NCE* 6:876. This collection was to become the preferred collection of the Roman Church, forming the basis for the "*Hadriana Collectio*," *NCE* 6:887. A collection given to Charlemagne by Pope Adrian I in the ninth-century is the "*Hispana Collectio*," G. Martinez Diez, *NCE* 6:1. This collection appeared in Gaul in the eighth-century and helped to conceal the fraudulent character of the ninth-century Pseudo-Isidore. Cf. C. Duggan, "Decretals, Collection of," *NCE* 4:709-11; *Dictionnaire de Droit Canonique,* 7 vols., (Paris: Letouzey and Ané, 1935-65) (hereafter *DDC*) 8:409-18.

23. Burchard prepared his *Decretum in Twenty Books* between 1007 and 1015, published in *PL* 140; for Ivo's *Decretum,* see *PL* 161:59-1022. Another collection made under Ivo, an abridgment of the *Decretum* known as the *Panormia* and dated c. 1095 was his more popular work, *PL* 161:1045-1344.

24. For the formation and plan of the work, see *L'âge classique: 1140-1378: sources et théorie du droit,* Histoire du droit et des institutions de l'Église en

Occident, 7) G. Le Bras, Ch. Lefebvre, J. Rambaud, eds. (Paris: Sirey, 1965) 52 sqq.

25. A discussion of the clerical status of women in the first six centuries can be found in Roger Gryson, *The Ministry of Women in the Early Church*, trans. Jean Laporte and Mary Louise Hall (Collegeville, Minn.: Liturgical Press, 1976). A treatment of the historicity of much of the early legislation appears in Paul-Henri La Fontaine, "Le sex masculin, condition de l'accession aux ordres, aux IVe et Ve siecles," *Revue de l'universite d'Ottawa*, 31.1 (1961), 137*-82*, and Ida Raming, *Der Ausschluss der Frau vom priesterlichen Amt; gottgewollte Tradition oder Diskriminierung? Eine rechtshistorisch-dogmatische Untersuchung der Grundlagen von Kanon 968 1 des Codex Iuris Canonici* (Cologne: Böhlau, 1973). A second edition of this work has appeared under the title *Priesteramt der Frau — Geschenck Gottes für eine erneuerte Kirche* (Munster, Lit Verlag, 2001). This edition will appear in English as volume two in this series *A History of Women and Ordination* by Scarecrow Press.

26. L. E. Boyle, "Decretists," *NCE* 4:711-13, and, A. M. Stickler, "Joannes Teutonicus," *NCE* 8:998.

27. These can be found in Friedberg 1:86; 765; 86 and 1367; 1255; 1055 and 1057, respectively. Gratian's own words of comment appear in 1:750.

28. The decree, which is not from Soter, can be found in the *Decretales* of the Pseudo-Isidore, where it would have been regarded as genuine by contemporaries. Gratian would have read the text in Burchard and Ivo. The canons immediately preceding and following *Sacratas* in the *Decretum* of Gratian are the same in Ivo and Burchard's work. *Sacratas* appears in the notice of Boniface I, according to L. Duchesne, *Le Liber Pontificalis,* 2nd ed. (Paris: E. de Boccard, 1955-57) 135; 227-29. We are not particularly interested in its historicity, but in the fact that it was accepted by Gratian and his readers as an authentic canon of the Church.

29. Hence Thomas Aquinas was told, "in this same handing over of the chalice, under the prescribed form of the words, the sacerdotal character is imprinted." *Summa Theologiae*, Suppl., q. 37, a. 5. (Editor's note: the Supplement to the *Summa* was added to complete the Summa by his students, see p. 163 below).

30. *Adicimus* reads: "We add furthermore that because of the audacity of certain religious monks, you ordered in our place, transmitted by your word through our vicars, decreeing especially that no one dare to preach aside from the priest of the Lord, regardless of whether he might be monk or lay person who boasts of his reputation for whatever learning." *Decretum, Causa* 16, question 1, c. 19. For the full text of Pope Leo, cf. *Epistola* 120 (*PL* 54:1054). The letter is to Bishop Theodoret, who had opposed Dioscoras and championed Chaldedon. He was regarded as a pilar of orthodoxy by Leo. In the letter, the Pope encouraged him to be vigilant in pursuing the theological victory that had been won, and not to allow monks to preach. Monks, especially Egyptian monks, would have been regarded as likely sources of anti-Chalcedonian agitation at this time.

31. "A woman, however learned and holy, ought not to presume to teach men in an assembly. A lay person ought not dare to teach in the presence of clerics (except in petitioning)."—or as found in an alternate form—"A woman, however learned and holy, ought not to presume to baptize others or to teach men in an assembly." *Decretum*, dist. 23, c. 29, and *Decretum, de con.* dist. 4, c. 20. Charles Munier has shown that the canons are not from the fourth or fifth Council of Carthage, as their titles given in the *Decretum* would have it, but come from a document known as the *Statuta Ecclesiae Antiqua*, which is of Gallic provenance. In all probability, the *Statuta* were put together by Gennadius of Marseilles, a priest zealous for the prerogatives of his own priestly order, and somewhat "anti-deaconal" as a result. Munier finds that the program of reform put forward in the *Statuta* met a real need in Gaul, which was then facing the invasion of the Visigoths. He dates the text, which he finds very unoriginal in character, between 476 and 485, but incorporating earlier material. *Les Statuta Ecclesiae Antiqua, Edition etudes critiques* (Bibliotheque de l'institut de droit canonique de l'université de Strasbourg 5) (Paris: Presses universitaires de France, 1960) 209-12, 235-77, and 240-42. The canons falsely attributed to the Councils of Carthage appear in the *Decretales* of the Pseudo-Isidore, and were picked up by Burchard and Ivo. The latter is the probable source for Gratian. For the text as it appears in Pseudo-Isidore, see *Les Statuta Ecclesiae Antiqua* 306.

32. Gratian is quick to point out that this decree does not bind in an emergency when a woman can baptize. He adds, "except in an acknowledged necessity . . . ." *Decretum, de. cons.* dist. 4, c. 20. Hence Thomas Aquinas was told, "in this same handing over of the chalice, under the prescribed form of the words, the sacerdotal character is imprinted." *Summa Theologiae*, Suppl., q. 37, a. 5. (Editor's note: the Supplement to the Summa was added to complete the *Summa* by his students, see p. 163 below.)

33. Cf. *Glossa ordinaria*, causa 16, q. 1, c. 19 v. *Adicimus*. (Editor's note: The edition used for this translation of the *Glossa* is *Decretvm Gratiani emendatvm et notationibvs illvstratvm: vna cum glossa* . . . [Venice . Apud Magnam Societatem vna cum Georgio Ferrario & Hieronymo Franzino, 1584,] hereinafter Ferrario and Franzino.) In explaining the authority to preach which was traditionally attached to the deacon's office, John refers his readers to the canons, *Perlectis* (*Decretum*, dist. 25, c. 1; Friedberg, 1:89-90) and *In sancta* (*Decretum*, dist. 92, c. 2; Friedberg, 1:317). He adds, "or [a deacon] is placed here to preach by virtue of appointment. In a similar way, lay men or women preach by permission of a priest." In the same gloss, when speaking of subdeacons, he says, "They preach, therefore, by reason of preferment and not by reason of order because the place of priest persists as [it says in the canon] *Precipimus* (*Decretum*, dist. 93, c. 26; Friedberg, 1:330)." Ferrario and Franzino, 1:1461.

34. "A woman ought to cover her head because she is not an image of God. But as she is shown to be subservient and because the transgression began through her, she ought to have this sign in church out of reverence for the bishop; she should not have her head free, but covered by a veil; she does not have the power

of speaking because the bishop holds the person of Christ. Therefore, as though before Christ the judge, she is thus before the bishop because he is the vicar of the Lord; she ought to be seen to be subservient because of original sin." *Glossa* on *Decretum*, causa 33, q. 5, c. 19. The title of the canon refers us to Paul, 1 Cor. 14:1-10, although the passage in St. Paul does not read in quite this way.

35. *Glossa ordinaria* on *Decretum*, causa 33, q. 5, c. 19, *vv. propter reverentiam*, "That is out of reverence for the priest," Ferrario and Franzino, 1:2396. In *v. episcopum*, he refers to *Decretum, De Penitentia, dist.* 3, c. 35; (Friedberg, 1:1222-23) Ferrario and Franzino, ibid. This canon, *Inter hec hyrcum*, employs the image of the levites as the *vicars* of Christ, whilst Moses acts in the *person* of Christ. John's constant theme is that priests represent Christ.

36. "We decree that deaconesses ought not to be ordained before forty years of age, and this with diligent examination. If a deaconess truly had taken ordination and she had carried out this ministry for whatever length of time, and afterwards handed herself over to marriage, doing injury to the grace of God, she would be anathema along with him who joined her in this marriage." *Decretum, causa* 27, q. 1, c. 23.

37. "A certain prebyter was ruling the church entrusted to him with great reverence, who from the time of accepting this order, while loving her as a sister but fearing her as an enemy, did not permit himself to approach his female presbyter (*presbyteram*) and on no occasion permitted himself to coming near her. He cut himself off utterly from a communion of intimacy with her." *Decretum*, dist. 32, c. 18. *Diaconissam* appears as the fifteenth canon of the Council of Chalcedon, in John Dominic Mansi and others, eds., *Sacrorum conciliorum nova et amplissima collectio*, 54 v. in 57, (Paris: H. Welter, 1901-27) 7:363. But the form of the canon found in Gratian can be traced to the Pseudo-Isidore. For the forms of the canon, cf. Mansi 7:377, 388, 397.

38. *Si quis rapuerit* simply mentions deaconesses in passing and was rarely referred to in theological discussions later. See *Decretum*, causa 27, q. 1, c. 30.

39. "Women presbyters (*presbyteram*) whom truly we ought to accept, the Council of Laodicea saying, (c. 19), 'Women who among the Greeks are called "presbyterae", who among us, however, are called elder widows, once-married women and little mothers, ought not to be installed in a church as if they were appointed to it (*ordinatas*).'" *Decretum*, dist. 32, c.19.

40. The possible meanings of *diaconissae* in the early church have been canvassed by Paul Henri Labontaine, *Les conditions positives de l'accession aux ordres dans la première législation ecclésiastique (300-492)*, Ottawa, Éditions de l'Université d'Ottawa, 1963); by Gryson, *The Ministry Of Women*, and L. Rand, "Ordination of Women to the Diaconate," *Communio* 8 (1981) 370-83. Much of the material raised in these studies would, of course, have been unknown to Gratian and his Glossators.

41. *Glossa ordinaria* on *Decretum*, causa 27, q. 1, c. 23 *v. Ordinari* " . . . this is seen to be obviated by those [words] of Ambrose who preceded this council. He said in fact [commenting] on that place in the first letter of the Apostle to

Timothy, 'Women likewise should be respectable'. The Cataphrygians said that deaconesses ought to be ordained which is against authority, thus occasioning these words." Ferrario and Franzino, 1:1973.

42. This anonymous commentary, once attributed to Ambrose, is the oldest known commentary in Latin on the Epistles of Paul. It was written in the last quarter of the fourth-century, during the reign of Pope Damasus. The author writes, " . . . You shall be holy, because I also am holy, and he therefore wishes women, who are seen to be inferior, likewise to be without fault in order that the church of God might be clean. But the Cataphrygians, seeking a pretext for their errors, maintain by groundless presumption that these same deaconesses ought to be ordained because women are addressed after the deacons, even though they know the apostles to have chosen seven deacons. Were there then no suitable woman to be found even though we read that there were holy women among the eleven apostles?" *Ambrosiastri qui dicitur Commentarius in Epistulas Paulinas,* Henry Joseph Vogels, ed., (Vienna: Hoelder-Pichler: 1966-69). 3 vols. (Corpus scriptorum ecclesiasticorum Latinorum 81, pt. 1-3) 3:268. The Cataphrygians were seen as a sect within the Montanist movement centered in or about the village of Pepusa, hence the later name "pepusianists." They are mentioned by Epiphanius, Augustine, John Damescene, and Ambrosiaster among the Fathers.

According to Epiphanius they admitted women bishops and women priests, while Ambrosiaster spoke of women deacons but not of women in higher orders. All of these Fathers regarded the movement as an aberration and not as a precedent to follow. A brief discussion with a good bibliography can be found in Labontaine, *Les conditions,* 15-22.

43. *Glossa ordinaria* on *Decretum,* causa 27, q. 1, c. 23 *v. Ordinari* (Ferrario and Franzino, 1:1973).

44. " . . . but a certain blessing, for instance, is bestowed upon a woman from which a certain special office follows which is not allowed to others, for instance reading a homily or the gospel at matins." Ibid.

45. Huguccio (Hugh of Pisa), a Bolognese canonist of the twelfth-century, produced an elaborate and detailed commentary on the *Decretum,* and has been called the greatest of all the Decretists. "Huguccio (Hugh of Pisa)," A. M. Stickler, *NCE* 7:200-1. The major portion of his commentary appeared between 1188 and 1190. Internal evidence seems to confirm that his gloss on *Diaconissam* was produced at the time, or at least sometime before John Teutonicus' Gloss, which echoes its language.

46. " . . . the Cataphrygians say that deaconesses ought to be ordained, which is contrary to authority. But I say that a woman is not able to accept an order. What prohibits this? The constitution of the church and sex, that is, the constitution made because of sex." Admont Ms 7, fol. 337 rb-va. Reference made here to the Hill Monastic Manuscript Library, St. John's Abbey and University, Collegeville, Minnesota. I would like to thank the Hill Monastic library for making this text available.

47. "What if the person is an hermaphrodite? A distinction should be made according to the state of the recipient like it is according to the testimony given in a will [*Decretum*, causa 4, q. 3, cap. 3, par. 22 (Friedberg, 1:540)] . . . § *Item hermafroditus*. If therefore the person is drawn to the feminine more than the male, the person does not receive the order. If the reverse, the person is able to receive, but ought not to be ordained on account of deformity and monstrosity. *Decretum*, distinction 36, cap. 11 (*Illiteratos*) defends this . . . . If a person is equally drawn to both, the person does not receive the order." Admont Ms 7, fol. 337 va.

48. "I say that a woman was never ordained, that is, I say that at no time did any woman ever have the order of the diaconate. But they were ordained as deaconesses, that is, they were chosen and instituted with a certain amount of solemnity to some office that is appropriate to a deacon, for instance, they sing or say the gospel at matins and say prayer, and such office and such preference are said to be of the diaconate." Ibid.

49. As for the opinion of the others, Huguccio says, "Others say that women were at one time ordained to the diaconate, later during the time of Ambrose, they were prohibited, later again at the time of Chalcedon they were ordained; now they are not ordained." Ibid.

50. Where Huguccio has, "The constitution of the church and sex, that is, the constitution made because of sex," John has simply "by reason of the impediment of sex and the constitution of the church."

51. The pertinent phrase is "those who are not of their own order nor are able to be [of their own or] cannot accuse priests of the Lord, nor may they testify against them, nor are they able to do so. Women however are unable to advance not only to the priesthood but even to the diaconate, therefore they are intrinsically able neither to accuse priests nor to testify against them .. . ." *Decretum*, causa 15, 3. Prol. (Friedberg, 1:750)

52. Bk. 2. c. 9; bk. 7, c. 45; bk. 15, cc. 100-01; bk. 64, c. 142; bk. 82, c. 28. (*PL* 84:49; 133; 207; 581; and 805, respectively)

53. *PL* 140:808.

54. *PL* 161:259; 567; 1292.

55. According to Stenton, no woman in the middle ages held a position comparable in influence with Abbess Hild. She was a woman of the highest rank, the daughter of King Oswiu of Northumbria. She founded a monastery at Hartlepool and shortly after one at Whitby (657). It is sometimes said that she presided over the important Synod of Whitby (664), which was held in her monastery. The Synod had been called to adjust differences between churches following Celtic customs and those following Roman usage, notably about the date of celebrating Easter. In an informal setting of this sort (there was no prelate with the authority to preside), Hild as hostess of the place may well have occupied the presidential chair, although I have not been able to find this clearly stated. Hild's chief biographer is Bede. See *The Dictionary of National Biography*, Leslie Stephen and Sidney Lee, eds., 22 vols., (London: Oxford University Press, 1921-

22) 9:832-33, and E. M. Stenton, *Anglo-Saxon England*, 3rd ed. (Oxford: Clarendon Press, 1971) 162-63.

56. Brigid must be neither underestimated nor overestimated. To dismiss her as a mythological figure from the Celtic past who could not be representative of the Irish church in historic times is to underestimate her significance as a Christian personality. Cogitosus' *Life of Brigid* (*PL* 72:775-90), which is admittedly a hagiographical statement of her activity, is nonetheless a good description of the church in seventh-century Ireland. The church was a church where jurisdiction (i.e., government) was largely in the hands of abbots, with bishops exercising only sacramental functions. It is true that an abbot might sometimes also be the bishop, but he was usually not. This seventh-century situation was in fact a shift from an earlier time, for in the fifth-century the church in Ireland was divided into dioceses with well defined boundaries under the jurisdiction of a bishop, just like the church on the Continent. The *paruchia* of the seventh-century was not a territorial unit, but rather a group of houses recognizing one head, an abbot—or, at times, an abbess. Brigid was such an abbess. Moreover, she was an abesse "whom all the abbesses of Ireland venerate, and whose *paruchia* extends all over Ireland from sea to sea." (*PL* 72:777-78). In Cogitosus' *Life*, Brigid is an over-abbess and in charge of a tripart church structure. She is in charge, first, of the bishop and his clerics; next, of the abbess and her virgins and widows; and, finally, of the church laity and non-monastic clerics. To assume that this tripart model of church government was commonly in the hands of women in the seventh or any century is to go beyond our evidence. To assume Brigid is an archetypal model for Irish religious life is to overestimate her importance. The typical *paruchia* was likely to be in the hands of an abbot. The number of arch-abbesses like Brigid is historically few; she was perhaps unique. It is worth remembering that Irish secular society had concentrated authority in the male line, at least with respect to the transfer of property. Moreover, in ancient Ireland, as on the Continent, women were under legal disabilities; for example, their testimony as eye witnesses was not accepted in court. See Kathleen Hughes, *Early Christian Ireland: Introduction to the Sources* (London: Hodder and Stoughton, 1972), esp. 220-32.

57. This was the answer which Bonaventure was to give as an accepted commonplace in the thirteenth-century. ". . . Concerning abbesses, it is said that they do not have the place of customary preference, but they have been put somewhat in the place of an abbot because of the danger of [women] living together with men. . . ." He goes on to say, "'Office' . . . to which customary power is attached . . . , has the significance that it is not suitable to women, however much 'governance' may suitable to the feminine." *Commentaria in quatuor libros sententiarum*, bk. 4, dist. 25, a. 2, q. I ad 2, in *Doctoris seraphici S. Bonaventurae . . .Opera omnia* (Quaracchi: Collegium S. Bonaventurae, 1882-1902) 11 vols., 4:650b.

58. As Stenton notes, most of the evidence we have which proves the association of men with women in a double monastery comes to us accidentally

from narratives written for other purposes. *Anglo-Saxon England,* 161. Hughes argues convincingly that the Viking raids in Ireland (and presumably in northern Britain, too) had a major sociological impact on the whole structure of Celtic society in the ninth-century. *Early Christian Ireland* 148-59.

59. Robert of Arbrissel (1055-1117) founded a double monastery at Fontevrault about 1100, and gave *Constitutions* to it in 1116. He chose Petronilla to be its Abbess, who was accepted by a vote of the community, and thus came to be in charge of men and women. *NCE* 12:528. The Rule attributed to Robert and printed in fragments in Migne is a good witness to the rigorous separation between the sexes which was put into practice in a double monastery. Men were not to enter the women's quarters, nor vice versa. Even in church, the choirs were kept separate (*PL* 162:1083-4).

60. Gilbert of Sempringham began his Order with seven women in 1131, papal approval followed in 1148 under Eugenius III. Although Gilbert's Order included men and women, and women exercised important leadership roles (there were prioresses and scrutatoresses among the major officials) and held equal place at legislative chapters of the Order, it is clear that the principal authority was always to be a male leader. *NCE* 6:481; see also Rose Graham, *S. Gilbert of Sempringham and the Gilbertines; a History of the Only English Monastic Order*, (London: Elliot Stock, 1903), esp. 49-54.

61. Joan Morris has gathered together numerous examples of women religious who exercised broad religious authority in Europe in the Middle Ages. She points to monasteries and houses of canonesses which were exempt from local episcopal control, and hence dependent directly on the Holy See. In such houses (and this would be equally true of both male and female foundations) and in the territories dependent upon them the authority of the local superior would be all-embracing. *The Lady Was a Bishop: The Hidden History of Women with Clerical Ordination and the Jurisdiction of Bishops* (Cambridge: Cambridge University Press, 1978). In at least two cases, such arrangements lasted until modern times. The power of the Abbess of Las Huelgas de Burgos was not suppressed until *Quae diversa* of Pius IX in 1874 (Morris, 85-6), and the Abbess of Conversano's authority lapsed only in 1809. Haye Van der Meer, *Women Priests in the Catholic Church? A Theological-Historical Investigation*, trans. Arlene and Leonard Swidler (Philadelphia: Temple University Press, 1973) 115-201.

62. It is the contention of both Morris and of Van der Meer that a woman's religious authority (jurisdiction) was no different from a man's. Meer argues specifically that it shouldn't be described in restrictive terms, such as "quasi-jurisdiction" or "dominative power," or the like (*Women Priests*, 106-20). He seems to overlook the fact that this is the way medieval theologians themselves described the situation, at least by the thirteenth-century, see Bonaventure, n. 57. Morris admits that women with full jurisdiction, nonetheless, had to call upon male clerics for sacramental functions, among them saying Mass, hearing confessions, and issuing judicial censures in their names. But is quite true that

spiritual direction in such jurisdictions was *de facto* in the hands of women who governed the men, even the clerics in their charge. They were hardly "silent in their churches," even if they did not preach in public. See Morris, esp. 17, 20, and 86.

63. A good description of the present understanding of "jurisdiction" is J. R. Banks, "Jurisdiction (Canon Law)," *NCE* 8:61-62, and E. Schillebeeckx, *Ministry, Leadership in the Community of Jesus Christ,* trans. John Bowden (New York: Crossroad, 1981) 55-56. He suggests that the distinction between *potestas ordinis* and *potestas jurisdictionis* is a result of the rethinking of the notion of ministry in the twelfth-century, and that it cannot be found in the sense currently given much before the end of the eleventh-century.

64. In modern legal parlance, such authority is now called "dominative power," see *NCE* 4:963-64. It is the power given to the leader of an "imperfect community," i.e., to a community which cannot exist in its own right, but depends upon a larger unit. The idea also carries the connotation that such authority is *private* and not *public* since it affects only a portion of the society concerned.

65. For the life of Richard Fishacre (?1248), see *NCE* 12:479. I have collated two manuscripts of his *Sentences,* preserved at Oxford (Balliol Ms. 57, col. 302 ra, and Oriel Ms 43, col. 430 rb) in preparing citations from his work. Since it has not been edited, I quote the passage, *IV Sent.,* dist. 24, which deals with the ordination question in full. ". . . here and in the following are all the things necessary for this sacrament, which are many. First of all is the masculine sex; and it follows from this that a woman is incapable of receiving orders. If it is asked about those religious women who are called deaconesses, I answer that they are not so called because they share orders with a deacon, but only in so far as they share in some of his offices, *viz.,* because they are allowed to read the Gospel and other readings. Since it is not allowed to them to touch the sacred vessels as a deacon. Thus distinction 23 [*Decretum,* dist. 23, c. 25] Pope Soter to the bishops of Italy, 'It has been brought to the attention of the apostolic see that women consecrated to God, or nuns, touch the sacred vessels or blessed palls, that is in the presence of your company, and carry incense around the altar. That all this is blameworthy conduct to be fully censured can be rightly doubted by no wise person. Because of this, by the authority of this Holy See, lest this disease spread more widely, we order all provinces to most swiftly drive it out.'

Let it be noted that a woman, if she should be ordained, would not receive the character [of orders], nor would she be ordained, and this because of the impediment of sex and the constitution of the church. Therefore abbesses are not able to preach or to bless, or to excommunicate, or to absolve, or to give penances, or to judge, or to exercise the office of any order. See *Mulier sacratas* [*Decretum,* dist. 23, c. 29], *Mulier* [*Decretum, Causa* 33, q. 5, c. 19], *Extra., De Sen[tentia] Ex[communicationis],* De monialibus (*Decretales,* b. 5, tit. 39, c. 34 [Friedberg, 2:903])

Christ did not even give the keys to the blessed Mary but to Peter, although she was more excellent than the apostles. The Cataphrygians disagreed; favoring which certain laws which seem to say that a women is able to receive the presbyteral or diaconal character.

'We decree that deaconesses ought not be ordained before forty years of age, and this after diligent examination.' [*Decretum, causa* 27, q. 1, c. 23] This is from the Council of Chalcedon. Again the *Novellis* of the Emperor Justinian, 'If anyone raped or seduced or corrupted a female attendant, that is, a female recluse [monastriam] or deaconess or nun [monacham], the goods of that person and of anything else contaminated by this vicious joining with these women are to be sold in that religious place where the said woman had lived by the religious bishop, and the treasurer and the provincial ruler and the officials of the province. They, however, are to be handed over to the penalty and danger of capital punishment.' [Decretum, causa 27, q. 1, c. 30] On a woman priest (*presbytera*) 'A certain prebyter was ruling the church entrusted to him with great reverence, who from the time of accepting this order, while loving her as a sister but fearing her as an enemy, did not permit himself to approach his female presbyter [presbyteram].' [*Decretum*, dist. 32, c. 18]

The solution: A deaconess as described above is one who is fortified by a special blessing by reason of which the office of reading the homely in matins or some other thing which is not allowed to other nuns follows. Finally the presbytera was so called because she was the wife of a priest or even a widow 'matricuria,' that is having care of the goods of the church almost like the mother of a household. See the last chapter [*Decretum*, dist. 32, c.19] 'We decree that women who among the Greeks are called "presbyterae," who among us, however, are called elder widows, once-married women and little mothers, ought not to be installed in a church as if they were appointed to it (*ordinatas*).'" (Editor's note: Richard Fishacre quotes none of the above canons precisely or completely, although the meaning is retained.)

66. Cf. Balliol Ms. 57, col. 302 ra, lines 1-3; and Oriel Ms 43, col. 430 rb, lines 13-16.

67. For the text of the canon *Mulier Quamvis,* see n. 31 above; for the text of the canon *Mulier debet,* see n. 34 above.

68. "Your brotherhood had asked us concerning nuns . . . about this consultation of yours therefore we respond thus that they are to be absolved by our authority through the bishop in whose diocese their convent exists." *Decretales,* b. 5, tit. 39, c. 34 (Friedberg, 2:903). The decree is from Innocent III, given March 1, 1202.

69. Cf. Balliol Ms. 57, col. 302 ra, lines 22-4; and Oriel Ms 43, col. 430 rb; 32-4.

70. See ns. 43 and 50.

71. See n. 42.

72. Cf. Balliol Ms. 57, col. 302 ra, lines 19-20. Innocent's text reads, "Granted that the most blessed virgin Mary was more worthy and more excellent than all of the apostles, the Lord entrusted the keys of the kingdom of heaven not to her, but to them." *Decretales* lib. 5, tit. 38 c. 10 (Friedberg, 2:886-7). This

notion will be expanded, especially by Franciscan theologians following Duns Scotus.

73. The birth and death dates of Simon of Hinton are unknown, but he was a Bachelor at Oxford by 1239. From 1254 to 1261, he was the Dominican Provincial of England, but was absolved from that office by the General Chapter, apparently for refusing to admit foreign Dominican students to the studium at Oxford. The Chapter sent him to Cologne, but he was back in England within the year. *NCE* 13:221-2. His *Summa* has been studied by P. A. Walz, "The *Exceptiones* from the Summa of Simon of Hinton," *Angelicum* 13 (1936) 282-368; and A. Dondaine, "La Somme de 'Simon de Hinton," *Recherches de théologie ancienne et médiévale*, (henceforth *RTAM*) 9 (1937) 5-22; 205-18.

74. "Thus ends the summa which the brother reader of the Friars Minor composed at Oxford in the year of Our Lord, 1261." Oxford University, Bodley Ms. Laud 2, fol. 167 v.

75. The dates of William of Rothwell are uncertain. A Dominican lector, he wrote probably at Oxford sometime in the late 1250s. He composed a study on the principles of nature, which I have edited, as well as a *Super Sententias* or summary-commentary on the *Sentences* which is heavily dependent on the *Commentary* of Peter of Tarentaise. See A.B. Emden, *A Biographical Register of the University of Oxford to A.D. 1500* (Oxford, New York: Clarendon Press, 1957), 3 vols., 3:1596. "Whether the female sex prevents the reception of order. I respond yes because sex is numbered among the essentials of orders. Indeed, it is not suitable for women to teach nor ought they to be preferred to men in the Lord's ordinances." British National Library, Harley Ms. 3211, fol. 28 ra.

76. For a study of his life and work see Jacques Guy Bougerol, *Introduction a l'étude de Saint Bonaventure*, Bibliothèque de théologie, série 1, Théologie dogmatique, vol 2., (Tournai : Desclée, 1961); *Bibliographia Bonaventuriana (c. 1850-1973)*, J. G. Bougerol, ed., (Grottaferrata: Collegium S. Bonaventura). His *Sentences* have been edited, *Doctoris Seraphici S. Bonaventure . . . Opera omnia* (Quaracchi: Collegium S. Bonaventurae, 1882-1902) 10 vols., vols 1-4.

77. "Whether the male sex is required for reception of orders . . . I respond: . . . the common opinion holds that women ought not to be admitted to sacred orders. For it is said expressly by distinction twenty-three (canon 23): 'It has been brought to the attention of the apostolic see that women consecrated to God, or nuns, touch the sacred vessels or blessed palls, that in the presence of your company, and carry incense around the altar. That all this is blameworthy conduct to be fully censured can be rightly doubted by no wise person. Because of this, by the authority of this Holy See, lest this disease spread more widely, we order all provinces to most swiftly drive it out.' And thus all agree they ought not be promoted, but whether they are able to do so is doubtful." *Commentary on the Fourth Book of Sentences.*, dist. 25, a. 2, q. 1 (*S. Bonaventure . . . Opera omnia* 4:649b-650a).

78. ". . . mention is of '*presbytera* (women priests)' —but clearly, if one attends to what is said in the thirty second distinction [canon 19, *Mulieres*],

'Presyteram,' etc., it *is* held here that widows and senior women and ladies are called 'presbyerae' and from this, we can gather that those who were called deaconesses by some blessing share with deacons in reading the homily. Therefore according to the canons in no way was it believed that women were ever promoted to sacred orders. And according to the wiser opinion, and of the more prudent doctors, not only ought they not and can they not be [so promoted] by law (*de jure*), truly they cannot do so in fact (*de facto*)." Ibid.

79. Cf. notes 43 and 44.

80. "Certainly the opinion of those who are called Cataphrygians was that they [women] were able [to be ordained], indeed not only did they find support in the aforementioned authorities, but they clung to the canons as authorities and brought them forward in their behalf so that by this it appeared that women did take orders in antiquity. As was said in the first question of *causa* twenty seven, 'We decree that deaconesses ought not be ordained before forty years of age.'" *Commentary on the Fourth Book of Sentences*, dist. 25, a. 2, q. 1 (*S. Bonaventure . . . Opera omnia*, 4: 650a).

81. "Indeed in this ritual (*sacramentum*) the person who is ordained signifies the mediator Christ. Since the mediator was only in the male sex and through the male sex is able to be signified, therefore the possibility of receiving orders is appropriate only to males who alone are able to represent by nature, and, according to the reception of the character, actually to receive the sign of him." Ibid. A point made by J. Rezette, "Miscellanea," *Antonianum* 51 (1976): 522.

82. ". . . this position is more probable and is able to be proved from many authorities among the saints." *Commentary on the Fourth Book of Sentences*, dist. 25, a. 2, q. 1 (*S. Bonaventure . . . Opera omnia*, 4:650b).

83. *Commentary on the Second Book of Sentences*, dist. 18, a. 1, q. 1, (*S. Bonaventure . . . Opera omnia*, 2:434), and *Commentary on the Third Book of Sentences*, dist. 12, a. 3,q. 1 (*S. Bonaventure . . . Opera omnia*, 3:270a).

84. "I answer that it should be noted for the understanding of the above that the wisdom of God is shown to be admirable and worthy of praise in all of His works, most powerfully, moreover, it is manifest in the formation of rational creatures. This indeed is apparent most clearly when one considers the harmony of order that divine wisdom preserved when it produced woman from the side of man. It was fitting, therefore that women be produced from the side of man not only according the accustomed order that is perceived between men and women in the human species, but also according to the order and custom perceived among those things *signified* by men and women." *Commentary on the Second Book of Sentences*, dist. 18, a. 1, q. 1, (*S. Bonaventure . . . Opera omnia*, 2: 432b).

85. "A man and a woman were made according to the particular quality and nature of their sex in order that they might be joined together and from this [union], one might be calmed by the other and one might be supported by the other, for then a woman is joined to man by a strong bond and vice versa. Therefore, one sex was produced from the other. Because this union clearly gives man rest, it was accomplished, therefore from a man when asleep. On the other

hand, because a man give a women strength and sustenance, a women is said to be have been made from his bone." Ibid.

86. For treatment of the interdependence theme in Bonaventure, see Joan M. Ferrante, *Woman as Image in Medieval Literature from the Twelfth Century to Dante* (New York: Columbia University Press, 1975), esp. 105-07; Emma T. Healy, *Woman According to Saint Bonaventure* (Erie, PA: Villa Maria College, 1956) 3-8; 13-15. She presents the texts where Bonaventure argues that man and woman both enjoy direct creation by God and that woman was not created as the result of original sin as some Fathers seem to suggest, and that woman was to be a companion to man.

87. "Nevertheless it likewise agrees with those things that are *signified* through women and man. For truly by man and woman, God and the soul, Christ and the church, the superior part of reason and the inferior are signified." *Commentary on the Second Book of Sentences*, dist. 18, a. 1, q. 1, (*S. Bonaventure . . . Opera omnia*, 2:432b).

88. " . . . all rational spirits were produced immediately by God, as it were, from a first and immediate principle; and God rested in this and in some sense slept [Prov 8:31] 'when his delights are to be with the sons of men' and the rational spirit is comforted and strengthened by the divine indwelling of the spirit; the greatest harmony is fashioned, sign to that signified, according to which God and the soul are signified through man and woman . . . " Ibid.

89. "It is likewise fitting that Christ and the church are signified by man and woman. The Church certainly was formed from Christ when blood and water flowed from the side of the Christ sleeping on the cross, out of which efficacy overflowed into the sacraments (*sacramenta*) of the church, through which sacraments (*sacramenta*) the church is founded; and thus maleness accords with Christ . . . " Ibid.

90. *De Trinitate*, 12, ch. 3-7 (*PL* 42: 999-1004). For the standard medieval interpretation of Augustine, refer to the text of Peter Lombard which all later commentators read, *Magistri Petri Lombardi Parisiensis episcopi Sententiae in IV libris distinctae*, 3rd ed., 2 vols. (Grottaferrata: Editiones Collegii S. Bonaventurae ad Claras Aquas, 1971-1981) 1:455-57.

91. "Whether it would be suitable for God to assume the female sex . . . I respond: it should be said that without doubt it is not suitable for God to assume the female sex in the unity of person, in the same way as the male.—And the reason for this is because the female sex is not of such dignity as that of the male." *Commentary on the Third Book of Sentences*, dist. 11, a. 3, q. 1, (*S. Bonaventure . . . Opera omnia*, 3: 270b).

92. "Indeed the male sex surpasses the female sex with respect to dignity of precedence and with respect to power of acting, and with respect to authority in presiding. With respect to dignity in precedence, because all, both men and women, were from one man, in whom the representation of the coming forth of things from one first and highest principle is expressed.—With respect to power of acting man similarly excels, for to act belongs to men and to be acted upon

belongs to women. Thus the male sex has more of an active power, and accordingly he is more robust both in fact and in name.—With respect to authority in presiding, similarly he excels by far, for following right order, a man has authority over women, not a woman over a man, just as the head is to the body, as the Apostle said." *Commentary on the Third Book of Sentences*, dist. 11, a. 3, q. 1, (*S. Bonaventure . . . Opera omnia*, 3:271a).

93. Bonaventure was quite aware of Aristotle's theory that a woman was physically a sort of "*vir occasionatus*," the unintended result of nature which ideally always sought the birth of a man. (cf. *De Generatione Animalium*, 2, ch. 3, 737a 25-30). In the objections he mentions Aristotle's argument himself, see *Sed contra*, a. In the body of the article, however, he bypasses all mention of Aristotle and simply refers to "the words of the Apostle," *viz.*, 1 Cor 11:3. (Editor's note: A recent English translation of this passage from Aristotle can be found in *Aristotle's De partibus animalium I and De generatione animalium I: (with passages from II. 1-3)*, trans. D.M. Balme [Oxford University Press: New York, 1992] 64-65.)

94. "Since therefore dignity of precedence, and power of acting, and authority in presiding were anticipated in the Word assuming human nature, it is here more appropriate that the male sex be assumed by the uncreated Word than the female because these three ought to be shared in a superior way in his assumed nature . . . " *Commentary on the Third Book of Sentences*, dist. 11, a. 3, q. 1, (*S. Bonaventure . . . Opera omnia*, 3: 271a).

95. See note 81.

96. "Order in the church is necessary for two reasons, *viz.*, on account of beauty and on account of rectitude. Since there is a great multitude in the church, clearly confusion would arise unless there were order . . . . Thus every wise person, by the very fact of being wise is a lover of beauty and would not produce a multitude without order . . . Furthermore, order is necessary for the sake of rectitude . . . . when a group is in a situation where it is able to go astray, it errs if it does not have a leader; therefore, when the church is in a situation where it is able to go astray, it requires a head and guidance." *Commentary on the Fourth Book of Sentences*, pt. 1, a. 2, q. 1 (*S. Bonaventure . . . Opera omnia*, 4: 614b). And in the subsequent question, Bonaventure adds, "So there will be an ordered distribution of the rituals (*sacramenta*), ministers ought to be ordered for this through the reception of some ritual (*sacramentum*), in which power is given so that the ministers of God be ordered for ministering and be ordered among themselves. For this reason 'orders (*ordo*)' is properly named." Ibid., pt. 1, a. 2, q.2 (Ibid., 4:616b).

97. ". . . the character of orders is an impressed mark, configuring us to the Lord Jesus Christ: but the Lord displayed all the orders . . . orders conform [us] for ministering or working . . . because all [orders] configure us more or less to Christ a character is imprinted, therefore, with each order." Ibid., dist. 24, pt. 2, a. 1, q. 1 (Ibid., 4:621b) While a character is impressed on the soul with each

order, the character differs with the different grades of order, or at the least this is the most probable opinion among theologians, at least as Bonaventure sees it.

In the following question, he says, ". . . in different orders different marks ought to be impressed as made clear to us by the diversity and continuity of the powers of ministry. Such a mark is character." (Ibid., dist. 24, pt. 2, a. 1, q. 2 (Ibid., 4:624a). And later talking about *sacred orders* he adds, "In another sense, strictly speaking 'sacred order (*sacer ordo*)' is so called because a person dispenses and in some sense handles the sacred thing itself by bringing and administering it to others, both a priest and deacon. In a third way [an order] is most properly called sacred because a person confects a sacred thing and this is appropriate to the highest order and for that reason he is called "priest (*sacerdotis*)." (Ibid., *dubia ad litteram*, n. 5 (Ibid., 4.638a).

98. "Furthermore, no one is able to receive orders unless one bears the image of God since in this ritual (*sacramentum*) a human being becomes God in some sense or the Lord when one becomes a participant in divine power. But the male is the image of God by reason of his sex as the First Letter to the Corinthians, chapter 11, says; therefore a women in no way is capable of being ordained." Ibid., dist. 25, a. 2, q. 1 (Ibid., 4:649a)

99. ". . . [orders] does not regard the soul alone, but the soul as it is conjoined to the flesh, and this by reason of signification which has to do with a visible sign, and because of this, of course, with the body, and the giving and use of the order considers this conjunction. For neither the significance of the order nor indeed the dispensation thus are suitable for women, as has been proved above." Ibid. (Ibid., 4:650a)

100. ". . . all orders prepare for the episcopacy if anyone is well conversant with this matter. But the bishop is the husband of the church, therefore, as a woman is not able to advance to the episcopacy but only a man. Moreover she could not be a husband of the church. Therefore the preceding orders are effected only in men." Ibid. (Ibid., 4:649a)

101. ". . . this position is the more probable and the one which can be proved by many authorities among the saints." Ibid. (Ibid., 4:650b)

102. For a discussion of the life of Thomas Aquinas which is both scholarly and accessible, see Weisheipl, *Friar Thomas d'Aquino.*

103. *S. Thomae Aquinatis, Scriptum supra quatuor libros Sententiarum, Commentary on the Fourth Book of Sentences*, dist., 25, q. 2, a. 1 [*Sancti Thomae Aquinatis . . . opera omnia*, (Parmae: P. Fiaccadori, 1852-1873) 25 vols., 7, 2:907]. This material can be read in any edition of the *Supplementum* which is included in most modern editions of the *Summa Theologiae*, Suppl., q. 39, a. 1 and ff. Thomas also discusses orders in the *Summa Contra Gentiles*, bk. 4, ch. 74-77, but does not touch directly on our question. It is fitting, he says, "that ministers of Christ to be human," (ch. 74) but this phrase is used only in the sense that ministers must be human beings, not angels, or of some other nature.

104. The reasons why Thomas ceased writing are canvassed by Weisheipl, *Friar Thomas d'Aquino* 21-23. Witnesses, such as his secretary, Reginald, and his

sister, noticed that Thomas' condition was changed after the Feast of St. Nicholas (Dec. 6). Thomas himself spoke of the change, saying, "I cannot write because what I have written now seems to me like straw," in terms which suggest that a mystical experience has been given to him beyond anything he had experienced before. A stroke or a physical breakdown has suggested itself to some critics. In any event, no more was written by him on the subject of orders.

105. Only one *quaestio* (q. 83) is set aside to discuss the Eucharist from a ritual point of view (i.e.. as *ritus*). Article 1 of the *quaestio* asks the important theological question, "Is Christ immolated in the celebration of this sacrament?" The answer is penetrating, but brief and raises points left unanswered. The remaining five articles move on to discuss trivial rubrical details, e.g., what time of day should Mass be celebrated; should sacred vessels be used; are minor ceremonies (like hand-washings) appropriate; etc.? After *quaestio* 83 the topic of the Eucharist is dropped and a discussion of Penance [Reconciliation] follows. The discussion of Penance is clearly incomplete, for the preface to *quaestio* 84 makes reference to projected *quaestiones* which Thomas never got around to writing up.

106. See n. 104.

107. "Next one asks about those ordained; and concerning this two things are asked; whether someone is prevented because of a defect in nature [and] whether someone is prevented because of circumstances of external fortune." Under the first article, he poses two lesser questions: "Whether the female sex prevents the reception of orders . . . Finally, it seems that boys and those who lack the use of reason are not able to take orders." *Commentary on the Fourth Book of Sentences*, dist., 25, q. 2, a. 1 (*Sancti Thomae Aquinatis . . . opera omnia* 7, 2:52b).

108. ". . . some things are required of the recipients of the ritual (*sacramentum*) as if of necessity, which, if lacking, no one is able to receive either the ritual (*sacramentum*) or the effect (*rem*) of the ritual; some things are required not out of the necessity of the ritual, but out of the necessity of the laws concerning the suitability of the ritual, and without such things anyone is able to receive the ritual, but not the effect of the ritual." Ibid. (Ibid.) Thomas makes his own the distinction of Peter Lombard between *sacramentum tantum* (the symbolism employed in the external rite of the sacrament), the *res* (the special grace offered by God in the sacrament), and *res et sacramentum* (the character, i.e., the element in the Divine gift which is given to the recipient irrespective of the individual's personal worthiness).

109. ". . . the male sex is required for the reception of orders not only according to the second mode, but likewise of the first. Hence, even if women underwent everything which is in [the ritual of] orders, they do not receive orders." Ibid. (Ibid.)

110. ". . . because with a ritual (*sacramentum*) there is a sign in which those things in the ritual are done, not only the effect (*res*) but also the significance of the effect is received, as is said about the last anointing, it is necessary that one be sick in order that the privation might be made known in the healing." Ibid. (Ibid.)

111. "As it is not possible for any degree of eminence to be signified by the female sex since a woman holds the status of subjection; she is, therefore not able to receive the ritual (*sacramentum*) of orders." Ibid. (Ibid., 7, 2:52b). The theme of subordination and preeminence is discussed in the recent work of Kari E. Borrensen, *Subordination and Equivalence* (University Press of America: Washington, DC, 1981), esp. 30-35, 170-79, 253-54, and 335-39. Borrensen compares Thomas' anthropology and theology with that of Augustine, who is frequently his source. The subordinate condition of women in Thomas is also investigated by A. Bernal-Palacios, "La condición de la mujer en Santo Tomas de Aquino," *Escritos del Vedat*, 4 (1974), 285-335.

112. Weisheipl *Friar Thomas d'Aquino*, 372-73. He notes that our present text of Thomas's commentaries on Paul "present many difficulties, and current editions are badly corrupted." Ibid. 247-49.

113. "Next one first indicates what is suitable to women; second what is not appropriate to them, as here, 'To teach, however, I do not permit to women'. Concerning the first, three things are appropriate to them, *viz.*, silence, discipline and subjection as these three proceed from one root, *viz.*, the defect of reason in them . . . . For the words of women are inflammatory. 'Conversation with them inflames like fire' (Sir 9:11); secondly, insofar as she is deficient: since to those who are deficient in reason it is proper to add to them . . . thirdly, this indicates subjection since it is natural that the body be dominated by the soul and reason inferior powers. And for that reason, as the Philosopher teaches, whenever any two mutually thus are constituted as soul to body . . . and the other is subject to the principal one . . . " *Epistola I ad Timotheum*, ch. 2, 1, 3 (*S. Thomas Aquinatis, Opera editio altera Veneta* [Venice, 1747] 7:307).

114. Over the passage in 1 Cor 11:14, "Does not nature itself teach you that any male is disgraced if he grows his hair," the *Reportatio* comments, "And he calls this same inclination natural that exists in women, but not in men, for the growing of hair which is a natural cover. Since any inclination is shown to be natural which is found in many." *I ad Corinthios*, ch. 11, 1, 3 (Ibid. 6:332a)

115. "Now he assigns a reason for this, saying 'For it is not permitted to them to speak,' of course by the authority of the church; but this is their role, that they should be subject to men. Therefore along with 'to teach,' he asserts prelacy and presidency; these are not suitable to those who are subjects. And indeed the reason why they are subject and not in command is because they are deficient in reason which is of the greatest necessity in presiding. And for that reason the Philosopher said in his *Politics* (book 4, chapter 11) 'that corruption of government exists when government falls to women.'" *In I Epistola ad Corinthios*, ch. 14, 1, 8 (Ibid., 6:390).

116. In the *Politics*, Aristotle frequently speaks about the inferiority of women and their incapacity for government, cf. bk. 1, chs. 5, 13; bk. 2, ch. 9; bk. 5, ch. 11; and bk. 6, ch. 4. (Editor's note: A recent English translation of these passages can be found in *The Politics*, trans. Carnes Lord [Chicago: University of Chicago Press, 1985] 40-41; 52-54; 73-78; 173-78; 186-88.)

117. Adam was not seduced in the sense that he accepted the devil's suggestion that he would become like God, as Eve had done. Adam was deceived, however, in this that he followed Eve's promptings so that he would not disappoint her (something he should not have done), and in believing that his sin would not be punished by God so severely and that he would be able to regain his original state.

118. " . . . it is said in Gen 2:18, 'It is not good for man [editor's note: the Latin here reads *hominem*, that is human, not specifically male] to be alone; we will make a helper similar to him.' I answer that it is stated that it was necessary for woman to be made, as scripture says as a helper for males." Not that a woman is a helpmate in everything, but "in helping in generation." Thomas adds in a somewhat misogynous spirit that a man with the help of another man can do almost anything else more conveniently than with the help of a woman. " . . . a man is able to be helped more conveniently in any other work by another man than by a women . . . " *Summa theologiae* (hereafter *ST*), I, q. 92, a. 1, something he would have found in Augustine.

119. " . . . in respect to her particular nature, woman is something defective and accidental. . . . But in comparison to universal nature, woman is not accidental, but is ordained for the work of generation by the intention of nature. The universal intention of nature depends on God who is the author of universal nature . . . " *ST*, I, q. 92, a. 1, ad 1.

120. " . . . subjugation is two fold. One is *servile*, according to which the leader uses the subject for his own use. . . .There is on the other hand, another subjugation . . . according to which a leader uses the subject for the use and good of the subject And thuswise a woman is naturally subject to a male from this subjugation, because the discretion of reason naturally abounds more in a human (*in homine*)" *ST*, I, q. 92, a. 1, ad 2.

121. "To the first objection it is said that the image of God is found in both male and in female as far as that in which the essence of the image principally consists, namely respecting the intellectual nature. Thus Gen 1 [27] when it said, 'in the image of God he created him,' i.e., as human. And there is added, 'male and female he created them' with 'them' said in the plural, as Augustine said, lest both sexes be understood to have been joined in one individual. But in a secondary sense the image of God is found in a male i.e., not found in a woman; for a male is the source of a woman and her end, as God is the source and end of all creatures. Thus when the Apostle had said that 'a male is the image and glory of God, while a woman is the glory of a male,' he showed why he had said this, adding [8, 9] 'a male was not created on account of a female, but a female on account of a male.'" *ST*, I, q. 92, a. 1, ad 1.

122. "I answer that it is said that someone is able to use 'by speaking' in two ways. In one way, conversing privately to one or a few. And as far as this is concerned, the charism of speaking can belong to women. In another way, publicly addressing the whole church. And this is not allowed to women." *ST*, II-II, q. 177, a. 2.

123. "But against this stands what the Apostle says, 1 Cor 14:34, 'Women are to be silent in churches,' and 1 Tim 2:12 'I do not permit women to teach.' Therefore the charism of speaking is not suitable to women principally on account of the condition of the feminine sex which ought to be subject to a male, as is evident in Gen 3:16. Indeed to teach and persuade publicly in the church does not pertain to subjects, but to the those in charge [*praelatos*; prelate]." Ibid.

124. "Secondly, lest the souls of human beings be aroused to lust. It says in Sir 9:11 'Conversation with them inflames like fire.' Thirdly, because women are not perfect in wisdom, as is commonly held, public doctrine is not appropriately entrusted to them." Ibid.

125. "Nevertheless men who are subjects, when commissioned, are more able to perform because they are not in such subjugation by nature of their sex, as are women, but from intervening circumstances." Ibid.

126. "In 1 Pet 4:10 it says that 'Everyone, as he or she has received a charism, administers it to one another.' But some women have received the charism of wisdom and knowledge, which they cannot use in ministering to others except through the charism of speaking. Therefore the charism of speaking is suitable for women . . . " Ibid. Thomas replies, " . . . it needs be said that those who have received a divinely given charism administer it in different ways according to their different conditions. Thus women, if they have the grace of wisdom or knowledge, are able to administer it in so far as private teaching is concerned, but not public teaching." Ibid., ad 3.

127. Raising the privileges of Mary, an objector uses a backhanded argument to suggest women might have a role to play. "God does nothing in vain . . .but Mary would have had those graces in vain as she could have never exercised their use: but we never read that she taught which is an act of wisdom." Therefore Mary must not have been endowed with special wisdom, grace, etc. To this Thomas replies, "To the third objection . . . there is no doubt that the Blessed Virgin received to a high degree the gift of wisdom and the gift of virtue and the gift of prophecy just as Christ had. Nevertheless, she did not receive them in such a way that she might make full use of them and of similar graces in the same way as Christ had, but according to that which fit her circumstances. She certainly made use of wisdom in contemplation according to Luke 2:19, 'Mary however kept all these words, pondering them in her heart.' On the other hand, she did not use wisdom as far as teaching goes; for that would not be fitting for the female sex, according to 1 Tim 2:12 'I do not permit women to teach.'" *ST*, III, q. 27, a. 5 ad 3.

128. "I respond having said that, granted the Son of God was able to assume from whatever matter he wished, nevertheless it was most fitting that he received flesh from woman. First because through this all of human nature was ennobled . . . Secondly, because through this the truth of the incarnation was manifested. . . . Thirdly because through this mode all the diversity of generations of humans is completed. For the first human was produced 'from the slime of the earth' without a male or a female; Eve was produced from a male without a female; truly

other humans were produced from a male and a female. Thus the fourth way was in some sense properly left to Christ as he was produced from a female without a male." Nonetheless, it was more appropriate for Christ to have been a man rather than a woman. "To the first objection therefore it is said that the male sex is nobler than the female: therefore he assumed human nature in the masculine sex. Lest the female sex be disparaged, however, it was fitting that he assumed flesh from a female." *ST*, III, q. 31, a. 4 and ad 1. In his earlier *Sentences*, he ties Christ's masculinity to his Messianic role. "Whether [Christ] ought to have assumed the female." " . . . it is said that we are not speaking here of the power of God because he is able to assume whatever body he wished. Speaking of the suitability however, because Christ came as a teacher and ruler and fighter for the human race for which women are not suitable . . . " *Commentary on the Third Book of Sentences*, dist., 12, q. 3, qla. 2.

129. *S. Thomae Aquinatis Scriptum Super Libros Magistri Sententiarum ad Hannibaldum Hannibaldensem Romanum, Episcopum Cardinalem* in *Opera Omnia* (Vivès: Paris, 1878), vol. 30.

130. H.-D. Simonin, "Les écrits de Pierre de Tarentaise," *Beatus Innocentius PP. V. (Petrus de Tarantasia, O.P.): Studia et documenta* (Ad S. Sabina: Rome, 1943), 334-35. Simonin calls attention to the genre of Franciscan-Dominican, Dominican-Franciscan theological literature of the time. A comparison of Bonaventure, Thomas, and Peter of Tarantaise immediately reveals the double dependency.

131. "I respond that certain things are required for sacraments (*sacramenta*) necessarily, without which a sacrament (*sacramentum*) does not exist; some things [are required] out of suitability, without which they are able to be set forward. The male sex is numbered among those things that are required out of necessity. Thus in no way are women able to be ordained, not only because of the obligations attached; e.g., doctrine is not suited to them, but because they ought not be preferred to a male in any ministry because a male is situated closer to God—a male is the image and glory of God; a woman, on the other hand, [is the image and glory] of a male, 1 Cor 11:14. Thus women ought to be led back to God through males and not the reverse." *Innocenti Quinti . . . qui antea Petrus de Tarantasia dicebatur, In IV Librum Sententiarum Commentaria* (A. Colomerius: Toulouse, 1649-52), 4 vols., *Commentary on the Fourth Book of Sentence*, dist. 25, q. 3, a. 1, 4:278b.

132. " . . . concerning a deaconess, I respond: a deaconess was so called, not from the character of orders, but from similar acts—that woman to whom it was allowed to read a homily at matins, not however to minister at Mass or to sing the Gospel . . . concerning a *presbytera* I respond: a *presbytera* was so called not from her own order, but from the order of the male priest to whom she was married." Ibid., 4:297a.

133. The objection reads, "Gal [3:28] In Jesus Christ there is no servant or free; nor male nor female; therefore there is no difference between male and female as far as the mysteries and rituals (*sacramenta*) of the new law." The

answer given is a brief, conventional notice " . . . before Christ there is no difference of persons in regard to *merit*, however there is in *office* . . . To the other objections he replies "Although order might reside in the soul, nevertheless its execution is through the mediation of the body . . . Although a good woman might be more worthy through merit, she still is not through nature or office . . . " And to the question of authority of a prelate, he says simply, "Prelature is granted to women over women on account of the danger of men and women living together." Ibid. A view we have already seen in Bonaventure, see n. 57.

134. Ulrich of Strasbourg was a Dominican philosopher and theologian who studied at Cologne under Albert the Great, 1248 to 1252. He would not have received a formal degree in theology, since the Cologne *studium* was not yet a university. He was Dominican Provincial of Germany from 1272 to 1277, and only then was sent on to the University of Paris. It is believed that he produced a commentary on the *Sentences,* but it is either lost or remains unidentified. He apparently died c. 1278, before completing his degree. The *Compendium Theologiae Veritatis* was written before that date, perhaps when he was lecturing in the Dominican convent in Strasbourg. See *NCE* 14:379b.

135. "There are five sacraments (*sacramenta*) of which it is said that they pertain to the common state of the person, but two of which it is said pertain to the common state of the church because orders pertains to spiritual birth and matrimony truly to carnal birth. There are six things concerning the substance of this sacrament: the first is the power of orders which requires that there be a bishop; the second is the matter, of course, anointing of a priest and the touch of those things which are to be touched by others; the third is the form of the words; the fourth is the male sex because a female does not receive the character of orders; the fifth is right intention; the sixth is that the one to be ordained is baptized." *Compendium Theologiae Veritatis,* bk. 6, ch. 36, in *Beati Alberti Magni Opera* (Clavdius Prost: Lyons, 1651), 12 vols., 12.2:131-32.

136. Henry of Ghent (1217-1293) was a lecturer at Paris from 1276. He was involved in 1277 in the celebrated condemnation of 219 suspect propositions by Tempier, Bishop of Paris, where he acted as a member of the Bishop's advisory commission. In theology, he is regarded as a member of the Augustinian school hostile to the inroads being made by Aristotelian ideas at the University. Indeed, his doctrine of the necessity of Divine illumination is essential for an understanding of his theology. His elevated notion of the role of the teacher, or the doctor, in communicating the faith makes what he has to say about women in this regard of special significance for his thinking. *NCE* 6:1035-1037.

137. "Concerning the second point, it is argued that a woman is able to be a teacher of this wisdom. First, as Prov 4:[3] says 'I was the only begotten before my mother and she taught me.' In fact that which was taught was this wisdom as is clear in this case, etc. Secondly as follows: it is not a lesser grace to prophesy than to teach, indeed to prophesy is to teach publicly those things that have been revealed to one, 1 Cor 14[12]. Whoever prophesied, spoke to humans for their edification; and women were allowed to prophesy, as were Mariam, sister of

Moses, Exod 14 [15:20]; Deborah, Judg [4:4]; Huldah 4 Kings 22 [2 Kings 22:14]; Anna Luke 1 [2:36] etc. Against this is that statement of the Apostle, 1 Tim 2:12 'I do not permit a woman to teach.'" a. 11, q. 2 (*Summae Quaestionum Ordinarium Theologi recepto praeconio Solemnis Henrici a Gandavo...* [In aedibus I. Badii: Ascensii, 1520; reprinted Franciscan Institute: St. Bonaventure, N.Y.,1953] 2 v., 1:77b).

138. "It is said that in order for someone to be able to teach *ex officio*, four things are required of him or her; two in respect to doctrine and two in respect of those things by which doctrine is dispensed. First is constancy of teaching, lest a teacher too easily be distracted from the known truth. Second is efficacy of performance, lest he or she cease from working because of illness. Third is the authority of the teacher, so that the hearers obey, believing him or her. The fourth is vivacity of words, so that gnawed by pity he or she urged on to the virtues. Therefore as far as this question is concerned it is said that the opposite of these four things is found in women because of which a woman is not able to teach *ex officio*; and therefore neither is she able to be a teacher of this wisdom. Concerning the first of two points, the end of the Gloss on Luke says: because the inferior sex does not have constancy of preaching; and is more infirm as to performance, the office of evangelizing is entrusted to males. A woman truly does not have the constancy for preaching and teaching and is easily seduced from the truth; and therefore after the Apostle in 1 Tim 2 said, 'I do not permit a woman to teach,' after a bit he added in some sense for this reason, 'Adam was not seduced; a woman was into a lie.' Secondly, a woman does not have efficacy in performing the office of teaching because the sex suffers frailty such that [her efficacy] is not sufficient to discuss and work in public. And therefore in the same place when he had said, 'I do not permit a woman to teach,' he added besides, 'but to be silent.' Thirdly, a woman is not able to have the authority of teaching on account of the condition of the sex which does not have freedom of performance since she ought to be under the power of another [according to] Gen 3 'You will be under the power of a male and he will rule you.' And therefore the office of teaching is forbidden to women, teaching, 'I do not permit a woman to teach,' immediately he added, 'nor to rule over a male . . .' Fourthly, a woman does not have the vivacity of words leading to mortification, but more provoking to sin; and therefore on that passage, 'I do not permit a woman to teach,' the Gloss says, 'if, in fact, she speaks, she incites more to wantonness and is enflamed; and therefore it is said in Ecclesiaticus 9 (Sir 9:11) 'Conversation with them inflames like fire.' Glossa, 'In corda auditorum.'" Ibid. (Ibid, 1:77b-78a).

139. "Furthermore, speaking of teaching for the support and fervor of charity, surely it is suitable for a woman to teach, as it would be for anyone else if they had sound doctrine; this privately and in silence, neither in public or in front of the church." Henry has already pointed out that this is not a question of whether a woman can, absolutely speaking, sometimes be capable of teaching and preaching, but whether she should assume that office in an official capacity. "It is said to this that this question and the following one differ from the preceding.

Indeed that question asked about the absolute power of doing something, who it is who has the ability to teach, whether God alone or in some way humans or angels. Truly these questions ask about the power of the law and authority; whether, of course, that status of a particular people allows that they have office of a teacher. Accordingly, it is answered to these questions in regard to the power of teaching not *de facto*, but by permission *de jure*. It is certainly clear that *de facto* any wise human whether male or female, whether old or young, whether in orders or secular, whether cleric or lay, whoever had knowledge is able to teach. Therefore it is said to this proposed question and similarly to others that any one is able to teach either *ex officio* or by permission." Ibid. (Ibid., 1:78a).

140. "It is said that prophecy was given to women not for public but private instruction, and if through it she taught males, this is a special grace that does not consider the distinction of sex, according to what is said in Col 3 [:10] 'Put on a new human who is renewed according to his image who created him' where there is neither male nor female. To the male, however, is given public instruction ... grace was granted to such women publicly to prophesy in the Old Testament as a reproach to males because they were made effeminate so as to cause public rule over men to be allowed to women; and similarly in the early church it was allowed to the women, Mary and Martha, to publicly preach and to the daughter of Philip to publicly prophesy because of the multitude of crops and the shortage of laborers, according to Acts 21 [:9]." Ibid. (Ibid.)

141. Whether Richard of Middleton (or Media Villa) (1249-1302) is English or French cannot be said with certainty since "Middle" town can refer equally to places in England or France. He gained his STM in 1284 and was Regent Master in Paris until 1287. While his ideas can be regarded as developing toward positions adopted by later scholastic authors, his texts were much admired and quoted by theologians of all schools well into the next century. See note 167. His general sacramental theory has been studied by Josef Lechner, *Sakramentenlehre des Richard von Mediavilla*, (J. Kösel & F. Pustet: Munich, 1925). Cf. also, *NCE* 12:48ln-b.

142. "I respond that the sex of a woman prevents reception of order *de jure* because she ought not be ordained, and *de facto* as well because even if all the exterior [rites] that are present to those who are ordained were present to a women, she would still not receive. The reason for this is [that] rituals (*sacramenta*) have strength from their institution; Christ in fact instituted this ritual (*sacramentum*) to confer on males only, not women. Twofold was the suitable reason for this institution." *Commentary on the Fourth Book of Sentences*, dist. 25, a. 5, q. 1; *Clarissimi Theologi Magistri Ricardi de Mediavilla . . . super Quatuor Libros Sententiarum . . . .*(R.P.F. Ludovico Silvestrio: Brixiae, 1591 [reprinted Frankfurt: Minerva, 1963]), 4 v., 4: 389a.

143. "The first [reason is] because the office of teaching is suitable for the ordained insofar as the entire order is ordained for the priesthood: now to teach publicly is not appropriate for women because of the weakness of [their] intellect and the fickleness of [their] emotions which defects women suffer more notably

than males as is commonly read: certainly it is fitting for a teacher to have a vivacious intellect for acquiring truth and stable emotions for persevering in their confession." Ibid. (Ibid.)

144. "The other reason is because orders constitute the ordained into some grade of eminence that in some way ought to be signified by the nature of the eminence of the one who is ordained; a woman truly has a subject status in respect to the state of a male that is furthermore in agreement with her nature because the sex of a women is naturally imperfect in respect to the sex of a male. We are able to extract these two reasons from the words of the Apostle in 1 Tim 2 [:11-12] saying, "A woman learns in silence with all obedience, I do not permit a woman to teach, nor to rule over a male.'" Ibid. (Ibid.)

145. The events in the life of Scotus (1266-1308) are summarized by Carlo Balic, "Duns Scotus, John." *NCE* 4:1002-06. Textual problems with the writings of Duns Scotus are notoriously difficult. During his lifetime, he continually revised his work, modifying and adding to his remarks as he went along. His early death left us with something of a work-in-progress rather than a definitive edition from his hand. Traces of these changes of mind, corrections and improvements can be found in the manuscripts and the early editions of his work. The critical edition now being prepared by the Scotistic Commission under Balic has done much to sort out the relations between the surviving texts. See *Ioannis Duns Scoti Opera Omnia, iussu et auctoritate Rmi. Pacifici M. Perantoni . . . edita praeside P. Carolo Balic* (Typis Polyglottis Vaticanis: Vatican City, 1950), 1:142-49 for a discussion of the Paris and Oxford versions and of the transmission of the fourth book.

146. *Ioannis Duns Scoti . . . Opera Omnia* (Vivès: Paris, 1895), vols. 19 and 24. Vol. 19 contains the *Opus Oxoniensis* text, dated 1304. Vol. 24 gives the *Reportata Parisiensis* text, dated 1303. [In Wadding's edition (Svmptibvs Lavrentii Durand: Laons, 1639) the Oxford is in vol. 9, the Paris text, vol. 11]. The edition of L. Wadding would appear to depend heavily upon the labors of Hugh Cavellus [MacCaughwell] (1571-1629); at least Cavellus' Venice, 1580, edition is identical with the *Reportata Parisiensis* text given in Wadding for the section of Book 4 we will be considering.

147. "I respond to the question, and I say that the exclusion of someone from reception of orders ought to be understood in two ways. One is either excluded from reception of orders in regard to the respectability and congruity of the mode of reception as when such an order is received in an orderly and respectable way with proper reverence. Or one is excluded from the reception of orders on account of necessity, and this can happen in two ways, either on account of the necessity of law or on account of the necessity of fact. In the first mode, I say that the state of childhood excludes from the reception of orders since children are not capable of receiving the sacrament (*sacramentum*) of orders with proper reverence, and therefore it is conferred and received disrespectfully. . . . Concerning the third mode, of course, of necessity of fact, I say the state of childhood does not exclude reception of any of the orders *de facto* received; truly it has been received and the

person is not to be reordained at another time." Thus reads the *Reportatio Parisiensis*, (*Opera Omnia* 24:369-370). The *Opus Oxoniensis* (1304) says substantially the same: "Here briefly I say that exclusion from an order or reception of orders, or the inability to receive orders, ought to be understood in three ways, of course, either inability in duty or in respectability; or inability licitly because it is against the law; or *de facto* which is not even possible, since if one pays attention to what occurs, nothing happens. In the first mode, a child, not having discretion, is not able to receive orders because he is not able to receive with due reverence such a status (*gradus*) as is conferred in orders. . . . oncerning the third mode of inability, I say that in this respect, whatever order, even sacred orders, is not found in a child, because the power of accomplishing some act, or status (*gradus*) by which someone is able to perform this act, must proceed in time that act, or the power related to that act." (*Opera Omnia* 19:137-38).

148. "But as far as sex is concerned, I say that the female sex simply impedes the reception of orders, and this as much from respectability as from necessity of law and fact . . . . They are excluded . . . by necessity of fact not by the Church and the precepts of the Apostles alone, because I do not believe that from the institution of the Church or by the precepts of the Apostles any status (*gradus*) useful for salvation was removed from any person, and much more so from an entire sex in life. If therefore the Apostles or the Church were not able justly to remove from any one person any status (*gradus*) useful for his or her salvation, except where Christ, who is head of them, instituted to withhold it, much more so from the entire sex of woman. Therefore Christ alone ordered this first of all who instituted this sacrament (*sacramentum*)." *Reportatio Parisiensis*, (*Opera Omnia* 24:369-70; and again in the *Opus Oxoniensis*, "This third mode of inability is in a women which is not held as if precisely through the determination of the Church, but this is had from Christ." (*Opera Omnia* 19:140).

149. "A twofold agreement is possible in this matter. One of which [states that] every order is received for succession to priesthood and teaching. It is appropriate in fact for the priesthood principally to teach as is had in *Adicimus* [*Decretum, Causa* 16, question 1, c. 19; see n. 30 above] and not appropriate for a deacon unless by commission where preaching or teaching is allowed for the reading of the gospel which it is appropriate for him to read. But this act is prohibited for women, 1 Tim 2 [11], 'Women learn in silence,' and 'I do not permit them to teach or to speak,' where the gloss [adds] 'not only I, but the Lord does not permit . . . " *Reportatio Parisiensis* (*Opera Omnia* 24:370). And in the Opus Oxoniensis, "And what the Apostles [says] in 1 Tim 2, [11] 'I do not permit a woman to teach,' understood of public teaching in church, it is not said to be only decreed by the Apostle, but 'I do not permit' because neither did Christ permit . . ." (*Opera Omnia* 19:1401).

150. " . . . and according to this weakness of intellect in them and fickleness of affection that they more commonly suffer than men. A teacher ought to have a vivacity of intellect in the recognition of truth and stability of affection in the

confirmation of it. Hence whatever is added by the decrees or the precepts of Paul concerning the exclusion of women from the reception of orders, they are nothing but completions or better expressions of the precepts of Christ about this. . . . " *Reportatio Parisiensis* (*Opera Omnia* 24:370). This particular aspect of the argument does not appear in the *Opus Oxoniensis*, however.

151. "The mother of Christ was most worthy and holiest, and yet he did not confer upon her power of this kind. And if you object that Magdalene was an apostle and as it were a preacher and protectress over all women sinners, I respond that she was a woman unique in this regard, uniquely accepted by Christ, and for that reason the privilege personally followed that person and ceased with that person . . . " *Reportatio Parisiensis* (*Opera Omnia* 24:370-71). And in the *Opus Oxoniensis*, "To which argument it is clearly observed that his mother, to whom no else ever was or ever will be equal in sanctity, was not placed into any grade of order in the church." (*Opera Omnia* 19:140).

152. "The second agreement might be this: order, as has been said above, is any grade of eminence over other people in the church and directed to any excellent act which in some way ought to be signified by excellence of status and grade in nature. A woman has a natural subjection in respect to men, therefore she ought to have no grade of eminence over any man because both by nature and by status and nobility [women] are baser than any man thus after sin the Lord subjected her to the lordship and power of men. But if she were able to accept some order in the church, she would be able to preside and dominate, and this is contrary to her condition. Therefore the bishop in conferring orders not only does badly because against the commands of Christ, but on the contrary he does nothing at all, nor does such a woman receive anything, because she is not a subject (*materia*) capable of receiving this sacrament (*sacramentum*) . . . .This is evident from the authority of the apostle in 1 Tim 2:11." *Reportatio Parisiensis* (*Opera Omnia* 24:370-71) while the *Opus Oxoniensis* adds citations from 1 Cor 14:34 and Gen 3:16 to prove the same point. "In fact, natural reason agrees with this saying which the apostle intimates in 1 Cor 14 [34]. For nature does not permit a woman, at least after the Fall, to hold the eminent grade in the human species, since indeed it was said to her for the punishment of her sins, Gen 3 'Under the power of men you will be.'" (*Opera Omnia* 19: 140).

153. "But on the contrary, it is objected thus: Where agent and recipient are of the same species, the effect is present, as the effect is not dependent on either one, nor the diversity from the diversity of either one of them (*Metaphysics* 12, text [18], [cf. 1070 a 25]), but the bishop conferring on a woman the sacrament (*sacramentum*) of orders is an agent of the same species as the recipient because sex does not change the determination of species. Therefore the proximate effect has the same determination in her as in a male so ordained. I say that the above is true of a natural agent, and when there is not an impediment on the part of the recipient. But if the principle agent was acting voluntarily, and the instrumental agent does not act except by the power of this one [the principle agent], then everything is determined for acting in a fashion determined by the superior agent,

as it is in the proposition of a bishop in respect to God . . . who imposed impediments because of the deformity of sex on the part of one of the recipients but not on the part of the other even if they were of the same nature. Thus it does not follow that if the same nature might undergo something, it might have the same effect on that nature. For if the bishop conferred orders on a woman, nothing would have happened as far as the ritual (*sacramentum*) is concerned, because he is not principally acting to imprint the character of orders, but only secondarily and instrumentally and therefore he imprints the character in that nature receiving the orders as determined by God, who principally imprints the character . . . " *Reportatio Parisiensis* (*Opera Omnia* 24:371). Cf. *Opus Oxoniensis* (*Opera Omnia* 19:140). This argument is to be found in abbreviated form in many of Scotus's followers.

154. Scotus has an objector ask, " . . . where the same thing both acting and acted upon [are] of the same species, here is the same effect. But a bishop is the same acting, and I propose that in the same way, he intends here and there, man and woman, and the soul of a man and a woman are the same species acted upon. Therefore if by the bishop doing something, the soul of man receives a character, it follows that doing the very same thing concerning a woman, her soul would receive the same thing. I respond that the major premises are true of acting affecting a form and acting in nature, but if he acts voluntarily and contingently, this is not true, . . ." The conclusion which should be drawn from the premises is, rather, " . . . this argument is good for proving that the minister makes no necessary act from which by necessity the effect of the ritual (*sacramentum*) follows, but only contingently, as in the majority of cases from divine agreement." *Opus Oxoniensis* (*Opera Omnia* 19:140). A discussion of the development of sacramental causality before Scotus can be found in *Dictionnaire de théologie catholique*, A. Vacant and others, eds., 15 vols. and indexes, (Paris, Letouzey, and Ané, 1930-67) (hereinafter *DTC*) 19:578-93.

155. Antonio Andaeas (1280-1320), so-called "Doctor Dulcifluus," was at the newly founded University of Lerida about 1315. He later became Franciscan Minister for the Province of Aragon, but beyond that little is known of him. Besides editions of his *Sentences,* which were frequently reprinted in the 15th and 16th centuries, he has left manuscripts for commentaries on the *Metaphyics,* a work on the three principles of nature and *quaestiones* over Gilbert de la Porree, suggesting an interest in arts and philosophy more than theology. *NCE* 1:647-48.

156. "I say, therefore, that no woman either *de facto* or by agreement or in any other way is able to receive any of the aforementioned sacred ecclesiastical orders. Nor is this believed to be from a prohibition of the church because the church by itself would not have excluded the whole female sex from the dignity without sin, and especially since these grades of the church are able to be of such a kind that in so far as in themselves they are for the perfection of the souls not only of other persons but even of the those having these grades. And for this reason I believe it was so instituted by Christ, as the apostle says to Timothy, "I do not permit a woman to teach in church." Since clearly Christ did not permit it,

and a sign [of this] was expressed since he did not institute in any such grade his own mother who exceeded in sanctity all pure creatures. The reason for this is strongly given when the apostle intimated in the First Letter to the Corinthians [14:34] that after the Fall God did not allow women to ascend to such grades of dignity because it was said to them in punishment in Genesis [3:16] 'you will be under the power of men.'" *Commentary on the Fourth Book of Sentences*, dist. 25, q. 1, a. 3, *Ant. Andreae Conventualis Franciscani ex Aragoniae Provinciae ac Joannis Scoti Doctoris Subtitis Discipuli Celeberrimi* (Venice, 1578), vol. 2, fol. 156 rb.

157. Little is known of the life of John of Bassolis. The date of birth, education, and even his country of origin is uncertain. He is thought to have been a teacher at Rheims in 1313. The *explicit* of the fourth book of his *Sentences* is dated 1313. If we identify him with an English Franciscan of this name, his death occurred in 1333; if he is identified with Juan de Basiols of Aragon, his date of death is 1347. M. Pasiecznik, who has made a study of Bassolis, leaves the question open. For Wadding, Bassolis was a faithful friend and careful disciple of Scotus, while K. Michalski and A. Callebaut see him as essentially a precursor of John of Mirecourt and a propagandist for Ockham. In our question, he follows the lead of Scotus. Cf, M. Pasiecznik, "John de Bassolis, OFM," *Franciscan Studies* 13.4 (1953) 59-77; 14.1 (1954) 49-80; also *Lexicon für Theologie und Kirche*, Michael Buchberger, ed., 10 vols. and indexes and supplements, (Freiburg: Herder, 1957-68) (hereinafter *LTK*) 5:1008.

158. "On distinction 25, I ask one question, naturally, whether canonical guilt and the state of childhood or the female sex impede one from the execution or ministration or reception of order . . . .On the fourth issue concerning the female sex, I say that simply and absolutely both *de facto* and *de jure*, it excludes from reception of any order. And I say that this is from the institution of Christ since it is not to be presumed that the church would deprive the whole sex of women from such a dignity unless because Christ thus clearly instituted males only *de facto* to be ordained in such a way. The sign of this is that since his mother, who was the most worthy woman, never wished to be ordained, nor to be preferred in the church. The apostle, however, was the promulgator of these laws writing to Timothy, 'Women, (he said) I do not permit to teach' doctrine (I say), which pertains to the ordained, publicly in church. And it is for this reason that a woman is taught to be subject according to the curse by God after the Fall (through her) of men and women in Genesis two [*recte* 3:16] 'you will be under the power of men.'" *Commentary on the Fourth Book of Sentences,* dist. 25, q. 1, *Opera de Joannis de Bassolis doctor subtilis Scoti . . . fidelis discipuli . . .* , (Paris, 1516-1517) vol. 2, fol. 106 va.

159. Durandus of Saint-Pourçain (c. 1275-1334) lectured on the *Sentences* at Paris as a Bachelor, 1307-1308. In the following year, the Dominican General Chapter reinforced earlier decrees requiring the brethren to teach and defend the doctrines of Thomas Aquinas. In 1310-1313, Durandus revised his commentary under the attacks of the Dominican Thomists, Harvey Nedellec and Peter de la

Palude, changing or removing offending passages. These modifications were apparently insufficient to placate his opponents, and attacks and replies continued. In 1317, Durandus was made Bishop of Limoux and later Le Puy en Velay, which effectively placed him beyond the control of the theologians of his Order. Between 1317 and 1327, he wrote the third and final version of his *Sentence* commentary. In the conclusion of this version (cf. *D. Durandi a Sancto Portiano . . . Petri Lombardi Sententias Theologicas Commentariorum, libri iiii* [Guerraea, Venice, 1571] vol. 2, 423 rb) he declared that it was the one edited and approved by him. As a theologian, Durandus enjoyed considerable influence, and his *Sentences* were frequently published in the 16th century, beginning with the Paris, 1508 edition. Cf. *NCE* 4:1114-16.

160. "Response. Something is able to impede the reception of orders either because it is in opposition to the requirement of the ritual (*sacramentum*) or to the requirement of the law, or to the appropriateness and deservedness of reception. In the first mode, the sex of a woman impedes reception of orders because the sex of a male is of the requirement of the ritual (*sacramentum*) of which the principle cause is the institution by Christ whose right it was to institute the rituals (*sacramenta*) both in regard to administers and in regard to recipients. Christ, however, did not ordain any but males at the Supper when he handed over the power of consecration to them, and after the Resurrection when he gave the Holy Spirit to them saying, 'whosoever sins you will remit, etc.' Nor did he promote his mother (even though she was the most holy of all women) to any grade of orders. The Apostle furthermore, who handed over to us what he had accepted from the Lord as 1 Cor. 11 holds, intimated that women ought not to be ordained nor to have the office of teaching in the church which is appropriate to the ordained as is touched upon in the argument." *D. Durandi a Sancto Portiano...Petri Lombardi Sententias, Commentary on the Fourth Book of Sentences,* dist. 25 q. 2 (Guerraea 2:364 va).

161. "Nor is it able to be said that this is from the legislation of the Apostle alone and not from the statute of Christ since it not possible to deprive anyone of a dignity useful for their salvation and allowed by Christ without prejudice since certainly this would be prejudice in temporal things. But the dignity of orders is useful for the promotion of salvation if used correctly, therefore if it would have been allowed by Christ that women would be able to be ordained, this would not be able to be deprived [them] without prejudice. It must be held then that women are not able to be ordained by the institution of Christ." Ibid. (Ibid.)

162. " . . . the reason furthermore is congruous, because through orders someone is placed in a grade of excellence above those not ordained. But such a grade is not allowed to women over men, but rather a state of subjugation because of the weakness of body, imperfections of their minds, etc. Therefore the sex of a woman thus impedes the reception of orders since this is opposed to the requirement of the symbol (*sacramentum*)." Ibid. (Ibid.)

163. Peter de la Palude (c. 1277-1342), the sixth son of the Lord Knight of Valembone, was a skilled diplomat and polemicist. He began his studies in the

Dominican Order at Toulouse, but was sent to Paris, becoming a Master of Theology there in 1314. The previous year, he had been appointed to a commission by the Dominican General Chapter to examine the works of Durandus. This commission drew up a list of 90 objectionable theses. He was appointed to a second investigatory commission in 1316-17, which again reported negatively on the theology of Durandus. Peter examined Books II and III of Durandus's *Sentences*. His criticisms there did not prevent Peter, however, from borrowing Durandus's text verbatim in his own commentary on the *Sentences*! Toward 1320, Peter composed a *Commentaria in Universa Biblia*. Between June, 1318, and September, 1320, he was again a member of a commission of theologians, this time established by the Pope John XXII, to examine the *Postilla supra librum Apocalipsis* of the Franciscan Spiritual Pierre Jean Olivi. This commission condemned 60 excerpts from Olivi's work (*Chartularium Universitatis parisiensis*, ed. H. Denifle and A. Chatelain [Paris: fratrus Delalain, 1889-1897] 4 v. (hereinafter *CUP*) 2:239). In 1329, John XXII made Peter the Patriarch of Jerusalem and sent him to the East to negotiate the return of the Holy Places. He was also called upon to examine the suspect views of John XXII on the question of the immediacy of the Beatific Vision after death. Peter was a vigorous defender of Thomas's theological doctrine and reputation, yet he was not always aware of its particular details. Cf. *NCE* 9:221.

164. "In the third place it is asked about the impediments to orders . . . . First about the impediment of nature . . . . As far as the first [question] concerning the impediment of nature there are three conclusions: first, that a woman is not able to be ordained either *de iure* nor *de facto*. Furthermore the matter of sacrament (*sacramentum*) is not able to be changed by dispensation of the Pope because he is not able to change the matter of a sacrament, although he would be able to give himself a crown because that is arbitrary." *Magistri Petri de la Palude Patriarci Herosolvmitani ordinis fratrum praedicatorum* . . . (Paris, 1514) , *Commentary on the Fourth Book of Sentences,* dist. 25 q. q. 3, a. 1, (Paris edition, fol. 133 rb).

165. " . . . every order is a sacrament (*sacramentum*) and not merely a sacramental. Hence if it were a true opinion to say that all orders outside of the priesthood were only sacramentally and proscriptively, not it would seem essentially associated with the sacrament, the Pope would able to change the form and the matter and the reception as he is able to in other sacramentals such as in the catechumenate and excorcism unless some one says that this is not similar since these sacred acts are instituted by God and not those." Ibid. (Paris edition, fol. 134 va).

166. "The sex of a male is a requirement for the ritual (*sacramentum*) of which the principle cause is the institution by Christ both in regard to administers and in regard to recipients. Christ, however, did not ordain any but males at the Supper when he handed over the power of consecration to them, and after the Resurrection when he gave the Holy Spirit to them saying, 'whosoever sins you will remit, etc.' Nor did he promote his mother (even though she was the most holy of all women) to any grade of orders. The Apostle furthermore, who handed

over to us what he had accepted from the Lord as 1 Cor. 11 holds, intimated that women ought not to be ordained nor to have the grade of doctrine in the church which is required of the ordained, saying 'I do not permit a woman to speak in church.' Nor is it able to be said that this is from the legislation of the Apostle alone and not from the statute of Christ since it not possible to deprive anyone of a dignity useful for their salvation and allowed by Christ without prejudice, especially in spiritual things. But the dignity of orders is useful for the promotion of salvation in such cases. But the dignity of orders is useful for the promotion of salvation if used correctly, therefore if it would have been allowed by Christ that women would be able to be ordained, this would not be able to be offered without prejudice . . . .The reason furthermore is consistent, because through orders someone is placed in a grade of excellence above those not ordained. But such a grade is not allowed to women over men, but rather a state of subjugation because of the weakness of body, imperfections of their minds, according to that passage in Genesis 3 [16] 'Under men you will be . . . ,' etc." Ibid. (Ibid.) Since the text from Genesis is well-known and was regularly employed, its addition here is not particularly indicative of any difference between them, and its omission in the earlier text can be explained as the fault of a copyist.

167. Bonaventure and Thomas Aquinas, for example, regarded all the four minor orders as grades of the one sacrament of Orders, and thought that each imparted a character upon the recipient. But this view was by no means universally shared, as they themselves recognized, cf., Bonaventure, *Commentary on the Fourth Book of Sentences,* dist. 24 pt. 2, a. 1, q. 1 and Thomas, *Supplement,* q. 35, a. 2.

168. "Nor does what is said in d. 27, q. 1, '*Dyaconissa*' and in d. 32, c. '*Presbytera*' [in the Decretum] oppose [this teaching] since the laws call a 'deaconess' not one in the order of the diaconate, but one who is allowed by a blessing to read a homily at matins; not however [to read] the gospel at Mass or to minister at the altar as is permitted to a deacon. The law calls truly a 'presbytera' a widow who has care of the church goods as it appears in the following law *Si mulieres*; or a 'presbytera' or 'presbyterissa' [is] the wife of a Greek priest; or the weekly chapter leader (ebdomodaria) who says prayers." *Commentary on the Fourth Book of Sentences,* dist. 25 q. 3, a. 1, (Paris edition, fol. 134 va).

169. " . . . a hermaphrodite ought not to be ordained as it would be a monster in nature and deformed in body, and is a disgrace as a cleric, and because of the danger since it is not known whether one is a man or women. It is appropriate however that there would the both together since in plants the masculine power and the feminine are perfectly joined, but never perfectly in animals, and most especially not in humans. If therefore the male sex prevails, he is a man and not a women and thus is able to be ordained, but ought not to be. If however it is the converse, then she is a woman and is not *de facto* able to be ordained." *Commentary on the Decretum,* causa 4, q. 3, cap. 3, par. 22 (Paris edition, fol. 133 ra) (For the text of the *Decretum,* see n. 47 above.)

170. William of Rubio (1290-?), from the Franciscan Province of Aragon, was a student at Paris between 1315 and 1325, possibly under Francis de la March. The Franciscan General Chapter of Assisi, meeting in 1334, examined and approved his commentary on the *Sentences*. No manuscript of his work survives, which is curious in light of its approval by the Chapter. We rely on an edition published at Paris in 1518. *F. Guilielmi de Rubione venerabilis admodum patris et theologi facile doctissimi, provincia Aragoniae quondam ministri Disputatorum in quatuor libros Magistri Sentetiarum*, 2 v. in 5, (Michaelis Conradi & Simonis Vincentii: Paris, 1518). Cf. *DTC* 6:1982; *LTK* 10:1148.

171. "In so far as the third issue is concerned, it is said that some are illegitimate and unfit for the reception of orders absolutely and simply; others, on the other hand, are [illegitimate and unfit] by aptness and by suitability in regard to the same reception and that by divine command. This is clear since every one who is absolutely illegitimate in regard to the reception of orders if he attempts to receive, nothing happens. One, on the other hand, who is illegitimate for reception by aptness although he is able to receive absolutely, not however without sin . . . " *Commentary on the Fourth Book of Sentences*, dist. 25, q. 3 (Paris edition, 2: fol. 196 rb).

172. " . . . it is clear that all those who are simply illegitimate by divine will are in no way able to receive any order since as the church is not able on its own authority simply and absolutely to make someone illegitimate, as was said above, consequently anyone simply and absolutely illegitimate as far as the reception of orders is concerned must be made illegitimate by God." Ibid. (Ibid.)

173. "But there are many i.e. absolutely impeded from receiving orders as every women. In fact the sex of a women in every case impedes the reception of orders which would not able to be, as has been shown, except through divine ordination." Ibid. (Ibid.)

174. "Certainly it seems unjust that the church would deprive the entire sex of women from that for which they are competent and which certainly would be for their salvation and utility. But it is evident that orders would be for the salvation and utility of women, thus as with men so they ought to be competent. Therefore the church most certainly would not be able to deprive a whole sex without some great sin. This is confirmed since either a woman is simply and absolutely illegitimate in regard to the reception of ordination according to divine providence and by law, or she is not. If then, as was first said, a woman would be able to receive orders absolutely without any law of the church obstructing to the contrary, which is false. If however, as was secondly said according to the proposition, indeed the absolute illegitimacy or incapability of women is not from the regulation of the church, but from the divine. In this way clearly they are said to be illegitimate, in fact absolutely. An act of ordination is impossible for all of them as it would be worthless." Ibid. (Ibid.)

175. Francis of Meyronnis (1285-1328) came from Digne in Provence and was at Paris from 1320 to 1321, taking his Master's degree there in 1323 (*CUP* 2:272). Several editions of his work exist from the early 16th century. They

present a text which is brief and compact, possibly at times abbreviating a longer work. The three early editions, which I have consulted, Bergamo, 1507; Venice, 1519 and Venice, 1520, are textually identical. Cf. *NCE* 6:32.

176. Cf. *Preclarissimum illuminati doctoris Francisci de Mayronis in quattuor Sententiarum libros scriptum* (Venice, 1519), *Commentary on the Fourth Book of Sentences,* dist. 25, q. 4, (Venice edition, fol. 221 vb). "Fourthly it is asked whether the sacrament (*sacramentum*) of orders can be conferred on any believer. I respond thus, since it is required of the matter of the sacrament (*sacramentum*). On the contrary it is evident that orders ought not be conferred on many even though they are believers. This question is initiated according to six uncertainties. The first if the state of childhood impedes . . . . The second if the sex of a woman impedes. It is simply stated as in accord with the teaching of the Apostle who did not permit them to teach in church." It would be interesting to know how Meyronnis might have answered the question, "Was the impediment of sex the result of the Apostle's teaching or did it stem from the will of Christ?" In the context of impediments to orders, Meyronnis frequently speaks about the Pope's absolute power to absolve all positive laws, leaving only natural law intact. (For example, a Pope, by his absolute power, could dispense someone's illegitimate birth so he could be ordained, inasmuch as that prohibition arises merely from positive law; whereas, by natural law, such people are capable of being ordained.) Was the impediment of sex something of first sort, or did it also arise by reason of natural law? Meyronnis argues against his predecessor Rubio (cf. n. 127) and says that the Church can impose illegitimating impediments against receiving the sacraments. She does so, for example, in the case of the sacrament of marriage. Meyronnis does not say if the impediment of sex is that kind of illegitimating factor or not. If it were, the Pope could, of course, dispense from the impediment of sex, and ordain women. Meyronnis does not carry the argument through one way or the other. "But what about suffering a deficiency in birth? (ie., illegitimacy?). It is said that it is possible to ordain by the absolute power of the Pope since this is solely prohibited by positive law. But from natural law he is capable [of being ordained], and if this is done, he is ordained *de facto....* But it seems doubtful that the church is capable of illegitimating any persons from the reception of orders. Thus if this were so, she would be able to do nothing; but she has instituted some illegitimacies for matrimony such as the consanguinity in the third degree. Here it seems difficult to see why it would not be able to be done *de facto* there as it is here. Whence it seems that [the church] is equally well able to illegitimate in the [above] proposition as [she is] here; nor does there appear to be any reason why not." Ibid. (Venice edition, fol. 221 vb).

177. Ibid. (Venice edition, fol. 221 vb).

178. The dates for the early life of William of Ockham (or Occam) are based upon the known date when he was first licensed to hear confessions by the Bishop of Lincoln, which was in 1318 (A. B. Emden, *A Biographical Register,* 2:1385). This suggests a date of birth about 1290, or perhaps a few years earlier. The place was probably the town of Ockham in Surrey. He entered the Franciscan Order and

was sent to study at Oxford, commenting on the *Sentences* probably between 1317 and 1319, but certainly before 1323. About the time he was to incept as Master, i.e., to complete his final academic exercises before taking the Master's degree in theology, his doctrine came under attack from the newly appointed Chancellor of Oxford, John Lutterel. Lutterel denounced 56 propositions extracted from the *Sentences* to Pope John XXII at Avignon. The Pope appointed a commission of six theologians to look at Ockham's doctrine and summoned Ockham to Avignon to defend himself. The work of the commission dragged on for four years, 1324 to 1328, with no result. The six commissioners divided themselves into three sections, the group that dealt with Book 4 of Ockham's *Sentences* reporting last and finding 16 suspect propositions. None of them, however, touch on the questions of orders. As a result of a dispute with the Pope on quite another matter, a matter dealing with the authority of the Pope over the Constitutions of the Orders, Ockham fled from Avignon with the Franciscan General, Michael of Cesena, in May of 1328. Ockham took refuge in the court of the Emperor, Ludwig of Bavaria, and spent the next ten years writing polemical tracts against papal authority in civil matters and in the Church. He was excommunicated for his unauthorized flight from Avignon and for his political tractates, but not for his philosophical and theological doctrines found in the *Sentences*. His movements after the Emperor's death are obscure. Evidence, which is sometimes presented, that he attempted to be reconciled with the papacy and return the seal of the Order to the Franciscan Minister General, is not well-founded. The date of his death is given as April 10, 1347, 1349, or 1350, the 1347 date being the most likely. (Cf. C. K. Brampton, "Traditions Relating to the Death of William of Ockham," *Archivum Franciscanum Historicum* 53 (1960), 442-49. Since William never received the degree of Master of Theology, but had only gone as far as incepting for it, his followers referred to him by his highest academic honor as the inaugurator of the *via moderna* because of his philosophic insights which led to the School of Nominalism, the title itself was not given to him with that in mind. For his life and doctrine, see G. Leff, *William of Ockham: The Metamorphosis of Scholastic Discourse* (Manchester: Manchester University Press, 1975), xv-xviii. For the dispute with Lutterel, C. K. Brampton, "Personalities at the Process Against Ockham at Avignon," *Franciscan Studies* 26 (1966) 4-25. An accessible edition of his *Sentences, Guillelmus de Occam, OFM, Opera Plurima* (Lyon, 1494-96; reprinted London: Gregg Press, 1962), 4 vols., *Super 4 Libros Sententiarum* is in vol. 4.

179. We possess the *Ordinatio* for Ockham's first book, revised by Ockham himself up to distinction 27, indicating his continuing interest in the subject matter in that book. Although Ockham did not return to edit the *Reportatio*, its contents are from hand of Ockham and it is complete. Leff, *William of Ockham*, xx.

180. The fourth book of the *Sentences* is divided by Ockham into fourteen questions, the first nine dealing with the sacraments. Questions 4 to 8 deal with Eucharist, but are almost exclusively concerned with explaining how it is

metaphysically possible for the body of Christ to be present under the form of bread.

181. With the exception of Biel's fifteenth-century work, the commentaries cover the century and come from all quarters of Europe. Information about the life and activity of some of the authors is hard to come by, although two, Holcot and Biel, are quite well-known. There was enough interest, nonetheless, for editions of these authors to be made in the fifteenth and sixteenth centuries.

For Adam Wodeham (c. 1295-1358), see *NCE* 1:118-19. (He is not to be confused with a certain Adam Godham, a sixteenth-century colleague of John Major.)

Robert Holcot (1290-1349) was Archbishop of Canterbury in the last years of his life. As well as his commentary on the *Sentences*, he wrote a much admired commentary on *Wisdom*. Few places him at Oxford in 1332 (*Medieval Studies* 2 [1949] 219). A revised and amplified version of his commentary, often with the commentary on *Wisdom*, went through several editions beginning with Lyon in 1497. *LTK* 8:1339.

Henry Totting von Oyta (1330-97) lectured at Prague, Erfurt, Paris (where he received his STM in 1378) and finally at Vienna at the time of its second founding, 1385. See A. Lang, "Heinrich Totting von Oyta," *Beiträge zur Geschichte der Philosophie und Theologie des Mittelalters* 33 (1937) 37-38.

Cardinal Peter d'Ailly (1350-1420) says nothing about our question in the works genuinely ascribed to him. His *Sentence* commentary breaks off with a discussion of the accidents in the Eucharist. For his life, see *NCE* 11:208-09.

Peter of Candia (Pope Alexander V of the "Pisan Line") (1340-1410) was Cretan by birth, but studied in England, doing a B.Th. at Oxford. His lectures on the *Sentences*, Paris, 1378-1381, are as yet unedited. I have consulted Oxford (Balliol MS 72) to find that Peter never gets to a discussion of orders. See Emden, *A Biographical Register* 1:345-46.

For Marsilius of Inghen (1330-1396), see *NCE* 9:297.

Gabriel Biel (1410-95), a late representative of the Nominalist School, also breaks off with the Eucharist. H. A. Oberman's study, *The Harvest of Medieval Theology: Gabriel Biel and late medieval nominalism* (Cambridge, Mass.: Harvard University Press, 1963) is valuable for relation to Reformation thought. See also *NCE* 2:552.

182. Thomas of Strasbourg, OSEA (c. 1275-1357), was at Paris in 1335. He followed Giles of Rome, an earlier Augustinian Master who was himself an enthusiastic Thomist. Thomas of Strasbourg was perhaps the first of his order to comment on all four books. He was Prior General of the Augustinians from 1345 to 1357. See *NCE* 14:122; *DTC* 15:780. His commentary was edited many times in the fifteenth and sixteenth centuries, including Strasbourg, 1490; Venice, 1564; and Venice, 1588.

183. "Some things are required by necessity and this in two ways since some things are required by the necessity of the sacrament, for example, that without which the one to be ordained does not receive the sacrament (*sacramentum*) of

orders especially in regard to the same extrinsic things done that ought to be done through the one ordaining in regard to the one to be ordained . . . .The conclusion is the second one, that the one to be ordained is to be of the masculine sex; this is of the necessity of the sacrament (*sacramentum*) since a female person, or that sex, is not capable of the sacrament (*sacramentum*) of orders whose ordination to teaching in the church is always prevented by the Apostle and was ordered to have her head covered in church when she prays. Such is the feminine sex; therefore it seems to be of the necessity of the sacrament (*sacramentum*) that the masculine sex ought to be ordained." *Thomae ab Argentina . . . Commentaria in IIII. Libros Sententiarum . . .* (Venice: I. Ziletti, 1564), 2 vols., *Commentary on the Fourth Book of Sentences,* dist. 25, a. 3 (Ziletti edition 2:142 rb; vb).

184. "The greater premise is clear: since ordination qualifies one to teach in church and this either by act, for example if one is a priest, or a deacon because of course a deacon is qualified to preach the Gospel; or by power if one is in certain orders below that of the diaconate. Certainly it is not suitable for any ordained person to always have his head covered in church when praying, as is evident in itself. The minor premise is able to be proved from the words of the Apostle since a woman ought to pray with her head covered, as the Apostle said in the First Letter to the Corinthians, 2 [34]. Nor ought she to teach since the Apostle said in First Timothy 2, 'I do not permit a woman to teach in church.'" Ibid. (Ziletti., 2:142 vb).

185. "Christ not confer the sacrament (*sacramentum*) of orders on his mother despite the fact that she was the most noble and holiest creature; therefore he wished that no woman be fit for a sacrament (*sacramentum*) of this kind. The preceding should be noted: since as is evident from what was said above, Christ conferred the sacrament (*sacramentum*) of orders only on men; the consequences certainly are clear: since Christ, as a good son who honored his mother before every other creature, and as a consequence, if a woman were suitable for this sacrament (*sacramentum*) according to divine regulation, Christ would have by no means withheld this grade of honor from his most revered and most beloved mother." Ibid. (Ziletti., 2:142 vb-143 ra).

186. " . . . Besides, if orders would be incompatible with the female sex, this would be above all for this, that the power of judging is not suitable for a woman. But this doesn't stand, since as is clear in Judges 4 [41]. Deborah judged the people of Israel, and presided over them for many years. Therefore according to sacred scripture orders is not incompatible with women." Ibid. (Ziletti., 2:142 vb). "To the second issue it is said that the power of judging is twofold: one form in temporal matters, another in spiritual matters. The first is not incompatible with women since there both were many women who had great temporal power and now do have in different parts of the world. Likewise such was power of Deborah. From this the argument follows. But spiritual power of judging is not suitable for any women, nor as a consequence, is orders whose power is simply spiritual." Ibid. (Ziletti., 2:143 ra).

187. The date assigned Denis the Cistercian's commentary comes from a chance remark in his own text. He speaks of his Master as a Franciscan, Francis of Paris, and as being contemporaneous with Henry of Hesse, a Dominican, Gombaldus and Facinus, along with several other authors of the last half of the 14th century. Their licensing occurred in 1376. *DTC* 11:2032. "According to the second uncertainty, 'whether a defect of sex or age impedes reception of any of the aforementioned orders'. . . the male sex is of necessity for whichever order for whichever recipient and is of necessity for the sacrament. Thus a woman neither *de facto* nor *de jure* is able to receive any of the aforementioned seven orders. This is proven because Christ instituted this sacrament (*sacramentum*) in men but not in women. Nor is it read that Christ conferred any order on any women, however holy, not even his mother, and therefore as baptism is not able to be done except in water, thus orders cannot be conferred except in the male sex." *Explicit quaestiones Dionisii Cisterciensi in quattuor libros Sententiarum . . . Parisiensis* s. 2, (c. 1511). *Commentary on the Fourth Book of Sentences,* dist. 24 (!), a. 3 (1511 edition, fol. 134 va).

188. The work is entitled *Petri Lombardi Parrhysiensis . . . Sententiarum textus . . . cuilibet distinctioni Henrici Gorchemii propositiones, Egidii de Roma elucibrationes, Henrici de Wurimaria, OSEA, additiones,* and it was published in Lyon in 1513. It is impossible to determine which passages refer to which authors, but the text is a good witness to common attitudes of their time. Henry of Gorkum (Gorichen) (1396-1431) is remembered as the author of the *Supplement* to the unfinished *Summa* of Thomas Aquinas. Henry filled out the plan of projected questions with material taken from Thomas's own commentary of the *Sentences.* Henry's *Supplement* became an habitual accompaniment to the *Summa* in later printed editions. Henry was also the author of *compilationes* helpful to students. While in the employ of the University of Cologne, he wrote against Hus and the Wyclifites. In the Albertist-Thomist debates at Cologne, he appears as a Thomist. Cf., A. Weiler, *Heinrich von Gorkum (d. 1431): seine Stellung in der Philosophie und der Theologie des Spätmittelalters* (Hilversum. P. Brand, 1962). Henry of Wulimaria (Urimaria) was also the author of the *Tractatus de quattuor instinctibus,* edited by R. Warnock and A. Zumkeller, *Der Traktat Heinrichs von Friemar über die Unterscheidung der Geister* (Wurzburg: Augustinus-Verlag, 1977). The text reads briefly: " Note that concerning the substance of orders there are six things. The first is the male sex in the one to be ordained, a woman in fact cannot receive the character." *Commentary on the Fourth Book of Sentences,* dist. 25, ch. 2, (Lyons edition, fol. 187 vb).

189. " . . . And since the ritual (*sacramentum*) is a sign of that what is done in the ritual (*sacramentum*), therefore not only the thing done (*res*) but also the signification of that which is done (*res*) is required. And a grade of a certain eminence is not able to be signified by the feminine sex since a woman has the status of subjugation. Therefore a woman is not able to receive the sacrament (*sacramentum*) of orders. Hence abbesses do not have any ordinary prelature, but

have it in some sense from a commission on account of the danger of the cohabit-ation of men and women . . . " Ibid. (Ibid.)

190. A short work, *Compendium breve et utile*, is edited among the *Omnia Opera* of Gerson, but, as the editor himself says, "but it does not appear to be his." This curious work, a *vademecum*, has also been attributed to Peter d'Ailly and William of Auvergne. It is one of the rare cases in which the sacrament of Orders was dealt with after confirmation and not after extreme unction. It says, "There are some things that impede the reception of orders, and some only impede the execution of orders and not the reception. The first that impedes reception of the orders simply is the feminine sex." *R. G. Gulielmi Parisiensis episcopi de Septem Sacramentis Libellus* (Lyon, 1587), fol. 19 r. Also, *Joannis Gersonii doctoris et cancellarii parisiensis Opera*, (Paris, [s.n.], 1606) 4 v., 2:103. In the edited text, Thomas is referred to as a saint, and Peter of Tarentaise is not listed as a Pope, suggesting a mid-thirteenth-century date for a long lived, popular work.

191. A discussion of the work of John Wyclif (? - 1384), and the extent of his influence on the Lollards, is beyond the scope of this article. H. B. Workman, *John Wyclif, A Study of the English Medieval Church* (Oxford: Clarendon Press, 1926), 2 vols., gives an account of the life and writings, as well as the research up to the 1920s. This can be supplemented by K. B. McFarlane, *John Wycliffe and the Beginning of English Non-conformity* (London: English Universities Press, 1952); J. H. F. Thomson, *The Later Lollards 1414-1520* (Oxford: Oxford University Press, 1965); and "Lollard Doctrines and Beliefs," in John Adam Robson, *Wyclif and the Oxford Schools: The Relation of the "Summa de Ente" to Scholastic Debates at Oxford in the Later Fourteenth Century,* (Cambridge, Cambridge University Press, 1961) 239-51. Wyclif's anti-clericalism is well-known. He certainly left the impression that evil-living priests should not presume to offer the Eucharist or to preach, and that much in the way of ministry could be done by good layfolk. It is possible that Wyclif's admirers garbled his remarks and drew conclusions from his premises which were less guarded than his own. Accusations would be made after his death that Lollards favored having women preachers and allowed them to celebrate the sacraments. Their activity is recorded in McFarlane, *John Wycliffe and the Beginning of English Non-Conformity*, 135-38, on the examination of Walter Brut (Brit), who said women have the power of the keys and to preach; C. Cross, "Great Reasoners in Scripture: The Activities of Women Lollards 1380-1530," in *Medieval Women*, D. Baker, ed. (Oxford: Basil Blackwell, 1978), 359-80; M. Ashton, "Lollard Women Priests?" *Journal of Ecclesiastical History* 31.4 (1980), 441-61, esp. 445-8. Catto gives an important caution in all this: "The debate over women's powers is an academic one, as there is no evidence for women actually doing such things as preach, or confect the Eucharist." J. I. Catto, *William Woodford, OFM (c. 1330-1397)* (Oxford D. Phil. Dissertation, 1969), 447. Interest among the Lollards seems to have been to narrow the gap between layfolk and the clergy, rather than to raise the position of women. Women did not perform clerical functions among the Lollards in Shahar's opinion, *The Fourth Estate: A History of Women*, 267.

192. " . . . right at the beginning of this tract, a pair of questions prepared a snare for the feet of the Wyclifites who are alarming the Catholics. The first concerns the reception of orders. The second concerns those to be ordained. The first is occasioned by sex; if the masculine is required by necessity. Wyclif himself was not embarrassed to labor frequently on behalf of the feminine in his book, *On the Power of the Pope* so that [a woman] might be a suitable priest of the church, or bishop or even Pope. . . . thus Wyclif clearly teaches in his book, *On the Power of the Pope*, chapter nine. Those clever concerning the absolute power of God say that as God is able to communicate not only to laity, but to females and to irrational animals the power to confect and administer whatever sacrament (*sacramentum*) . . . " *Doctrinale Antiquitatum Fidei Catholicae Ecclesiae*, tit. 7, ch. 58, (Venice: Antonius Bassanesius, 1757-59) 3 vols., 3:371. Later on, in chapter 59, he says, "To the argument of Wyclif proving that females can be priests since [the objections to this] do not arise from the law of God concerning the priesthood itself . . . .But this is used in a somewhat careless manner. Wyclif on behalf of a feminine priesthood in response to certain aforementioned argument in chapter nine of *On the Power of the Pope*: It is reasonable, he says, for Christ and his apostles and indeed devote people all to be sacramental priests. It follows from that which the Apostle Peter said, 'A holy people and a royal priesthood.' [2 Pet 2:9] And Chrysostom said the same. From these it is clear in the first place that females are priests." Later in the same chapter, Netter says of Wyclif, "You say that Augustine witnessed that devote people are included in the sacramental priesthood from which you exclaim that it is clear from this that females are priests . . . in that place, namely, *The City of God*, [bk. 20, chapt. 10] . . . .So Augustine had written 'They were priests of God, and of Christ, and reigned with him for a thousand years. And not only of bishops and priests alone is this thus said, but of all Christians we say according to the mystical chrism: so are all priests for they are members of one priesthood.' Of which the Apostle Peter: 'A people,' he said, 'a royal priesthood.' Is this the authority whereby you say 'females are priests?'" *Doctrinale*, tit. 7, ch. 59, (Bassanesius 3:376-77). For a concise discussion of *potentia dei absoluta* and *potentia dei ordinata*, cf., Oberman, *The Harvest of Medieval Theology*, 376-77.

Thomas Netter of Walden (c. 1370-1430) studied at Oxford, where he learned of the doctrines of Wyclif at close hand. An initial interest turned to implacable hostility when he became convinced that Wyclif was interpreting the Scriptures in an arbitrary fashion to favor his own point of view. Netter's work, the *Doctrinale Antiquitatum Fidei Catholicae Ecclesiae*, edited in three parts, was written to refute Wyclif and his followers. Parts II and III of the *Doctrinale* are entitled *De Sacramentis* and *De Sacramentalibus*, and cover much of the same material, one in a more professional, the other in a more polemical fashion. Netter was ordained in 1396, and, although he is described as an Oxford Master of Theology by B. Blanciotti, he does not seem to have pursued an academic career for any length of time (see *Doctrinale* [Bassanesius 3:14]). In his works against Wyclifites, Netter appears to address an audience of educated clerics and layfolk, employing numerous quotations from the Fathers marshaled in a polemic manner and using virtually no quotations from the professional theologians of the schools. Netter was close to the government of Henry V, appearing as the King's Orator at the Council of Pisa, and as a delegate of his Order at Constance. He doubtless found the anti-Hussite and anti-Wyclifite spirit at Constance congenial to his own way of thinking. In 1414, he became the Carmelite Provincial of England. In 1419, he was sent by Henry V to Lithuania to mediate between the Teutonic Knights and Vladislaw, King of Poland. As we have said, Netter was asked to write the *Doctrinale* by Henry V in 1421, but that King did not live to see its completion. Between 1425 and 1428, Netter appears to have produced the two treatments of the sacraments found in Books II and III, and dedicated both of them to Martin V. He preached the funeral oration for Henry V, and became the confessor to the young King, Henry VI. Netter fell ill at Rouen while traveling with the King dying there in 1430. In addition to Robson, and Blanciotti's Life in the *Doctrinale* see Emden, *A Biographical Register*, 2:1343-4; *DNB* 15:231-3; and *NCE* 10:363b.

193. For the state of the Lollards twenty years after Wyclif's death, see J.A.F. Thomson, *The Later Lollards (1414-1320)*, (London: Oxford University Press, 1965).

194. "Wyclif himself was not embarrassed to labor frequently on behalf of the feminine in his book, *On the Power of the Pope*, so that [a woman] might be a suitable priest of the church, or bishop or even Pope. It is a shameful that something is said by Christian man which once known will be mockery to the Jews and a scandal to the Saracens. But on the other hand, I fear to hide an abyss of such foulness. Most especially when I suspect that based on this position his follows have assumed the authority to have ordained female priests, celebrators of masses and other sacraments (*sacramenta*), as readers of scripture and preachers in the Lollard assemblies." *Doctrinale*, tit. 7, ch. 59, (Bassanesius 3:371).

195. " . . . Extraordinary thing that Christ, the first pontiff was thus pharisaically lead astray, that when considering a sign visibly instituted for humanity, he would never chose his own mother, predestined and a virgin, for the priesthood, but rather chose Judas, a married male, lost in such monstrous sins and known beforehand to be so. Extraordinary again that the plenary synod of apostles instituted no females when it ordained seven males as deacons. In respect to the same issue, the glorious Paul labored against this ordination of all females when he limited indispensably all those to be ordained to the male sex: 'A bishop ought to be,' he said, 'beyond reproach, a man of a single wife.' He did not say 'a wife of a single man' but 'a man, temperate, accomplished, virtuous,' and deacons should be 'men of a single wife' as in the exposition of Ambrose on Romans 16:13 [*Commentaria in Epistolam ad Romanos*, ch. 16, (*PL* 17:1801)] 'I greet Rufus chosen in the Lord, and his mother, and ours.' He had put him ahead of his mother according to his election to the administration of grace, in which his mother had no place. He clearly had been chosen, that is, promoted by the Lord

to those things of His that needed to be done. He held his mother, however, to be so holy that the Apostle called her also his own mother. Observe how the mother of Rufus, because she was a woman, had no place in the administration of a priest, as however she was so very holy that the Apostle adopted her as mother." *Doctrinale*, tit. 7, ch. 59, (Bassanesius 3:372-3).

196. Ibid. (Bassanesius 3:372-4). Netter also points out the ineptness of women for the office of preaching, and the dangers inherent in conversations with them, in the first part of the *Doctrinale*, where he talks about the members of Christ's Church and their offices. "You may conclude, then, two points from these experts. The first is from a generic baseness against the laws of order and nature. The second is from her unsuitability for teaching correctly and her facility for seduction that the first man had not turned against to take precautions by the most sincere discourse in natural reason. The alluring voice truly entices and the species of woman inveigles and in the end the intellect is spun around in a net of sweet words. As in the words of Haimo [of Halberstadt *PL* 117:790-1; citation is unclear] on the place in Timothy, 'On that account, it is not permitted to her teach because she is a weaker sex than a male. And one should be warned lest as seduced through the serpent she brought about the death of the world, so likewise easily falling into error herself, she would lead astray others to the same error.' And Anselm [says] the same in the *Annotations*. 'If she speaks, she more inflames and is inflamed.' Thus Anselm." Ibid. (Bassanesius 1:638).

197. Netter rhetorically asks Wyclif why he does not hear Augustine out when he talks about the "priests who will reign with Christ for a thousand years." (see n. 192) "But why do you not hear ' . . . not as bishops or priests who now in the church are properly called priests . . . . ' how other improperly with people [i.e., the common priesthood of all of the faithful, the "royal priesthood"]? But if there are feminine priests by that common law since then there would be according to the prophecy of John, 'priests of God and of Christ' (see n. 192) By this same law would not all lay men and children be priests? No, he said 'unless they were ordained'" Ibid. (Bassancsius 2:377-78). That women were not to be properly priests was an attitude even in the Old Law, one which has been carried into the New, Netter adds. "And yet under the Law the priesthood or sacrifice for sin or to eat of any offering was forbidden to the feminine itself because of sex; and it was not allowed to females what then was allowed to their husbands, 'Every offering and sacrifice for sin and for crimes have been returned to me and fall in the holy of holies; it will be yours and your sons. In the sanctuary you eat it; husbands only eat from that which is consecrated.' [Num. 18:9] From that fourth homily of Origen on Leviticus [Origen, *Fourth Homily on Leviticus*, ch. 8, (*PG* 12:443-4)] 'This he wished to be observed so that only males eat from it, females touch nothing.' Thus Origen. As therefore the feminine has been assigned by her sex, then, unfit for the priesthood since she was not able to eat of the sacrifice as the masculine is; so too in the New Testament since she is not able to speak in church but to remain silent." Ibid. (Ibid.). Netter acidly concludes that what members of the common or popular priesthood are commissioned to do, which is

common to men and women, is to offer a sacrifice of praise, not to offer sacred things as public officers of the Church. "Now you see the priesthood of the people and the office of them. Life will pertain to the priesthood of this popular form, not the offering given to another. 'To offer,' he said, 'you give to God the offering of praise, the offering of prayer, the offering of mercy, the offering of chastity.' This is the priesthood of the people and of men and the feminine. Under which in no way ought you still to seek what is not conceded, as Wyclif incited you in the aforementioned chapter nine. It is clear according to what has been said that as all holy men and women as members of Christ are priests since they offer holy things. Thus Wyclif. These are thus priests as members, but not offering holy things through the public office of the church, designated properly to priests." Ibid. (Bassanesius 3:378).

198. "Chrysostom [cf. Commentary on the First Letter to Timothy, ch. 2, 11; Homily 9 (*Patrologiae cursus completus . . . series graeca*, ed. J. P. Migne, 161 vols. [Paris: J. P. Migne, 1857-66] 62:545)] stated the mind of the Apostle well concerning the silence of women that it was ordered commonly because of their sex, and at the same time their subjugation. 'On account of which,' he said, 'God subjugated her since she acted wrongly by the equality of honor, not by pre-eminence.' And he judges this to be the punishment of her sex according to those words of the Apostle. 'the woman was deceived' and he disputes here what remains of nature. The feminine has received this punishment in her sex, as Adam according to his species infected all nature. Nevertheless, it is granted to women to procure their salvation through physical birth and the education of their sons, just as spiritually to bear male sons through the gift of the priesthood. What is forbidden simply in the first female, is forbidden to all females because of their sex according to the law of Paul [1 Cor 14:34]." Ibid. (Bassanesius 3:381).

199. The John Hus of the *Sentences* is the Hus who recently completed his theological studies. Born about 1369, he received a Bachelor's in Theology from the University of Prague in 1404. He was already a famous reform preacher, having been appointed to Bethlehem Chapel in 1402, a chapel established to give sermons in the Czech language. Hus, as a reformer, was influenced by Wyclif's ideas, which had made an impact in Bohemia toward 1400. While Hus openly admired Wyclif, he did not make use of his thought in an uncritical manner. In Hus' hands, Wyclif's ideas received a more "Catholic inflection." (*NCE* 8:271) In any event, none of Wyclif's ideas inclining to the ordination of women appear in Hus' article in his *Sentences*. For a brief discussion of the relation of Wyclif to Hus, cf., introduction to Hus' *Tractatus de Ecclesia*, ed. S. H. Thomson (Boulder: University of Colorado Press, 1956).

200. " . . . the male sex is of the necessity of the sacrament, by which the feminine sex or that of women is not fit for the sacrament (*sacramentum*) of orders as neither in the old law nor in the new the Lord showed that this sex accepted orders." *Magistri Joannis Hus Opera Omnia*, ed., W. Flajshans and M. Komínoková (Prague, 1905-1908; reprinted Osnabrück: Biblio-Verlag, 1966), 3

vols., *Commentary on the Fourth Book of Sentences,* dist. 24 (!), q. 5 (Flajshans and Komínoková, 2, fasc. 2: 635).

201. "This is held by certain remote causes: first since is it not fitting for women to pray with their heads uncovered, 1 Cor 11:2 and because a woman ought not preach, 1 Tim 2. But these conditions or causes would not have been sufficient since other causes would not have been sufficient before the prohibition by Paul. For the same reasons, it is again asked why women are not able to preach and not to pray with their heads uncovered.—The answer. Therefore to the first cause, evidently God since He did not express this or model it, and since afterwards Paul prohibited the act of sacred orders to women, therefore women are not able to be ordained . . . why in fact this is so, He alone knows." Ibid. (Ibid.)

202. Hus mentions this in connection with his answer to the traditional objection raised by the canon, *presbiter* (*Decretum,* dist. 32, c. 18; for text see n. 37 above). "A *presbytera* is instructed how she ought to manage her gift, therefore it seems that the presbyteral order is suitable for women." Hus answers, "But according to this, blessed would be the Lord Christ who did not confer orders on the most holy virgin, but rather on Judas, the man of Iscariot, whom he damned." Ibid. (Ibid.)

203. Denis the Carthusian (1402-1471), the *Doctor Ecstaticus,* is remembered for his mystical theology and not for his systematic writings, which were also considerable. The *Rule* of his Order discouraged active and pastoral life, and true to that *Rule* Denis emerged from the cloister only three times in his life, and then only for brief periods. One of them was to accompany Nicholas of Cusa, the German Cardinal, on his legatine visitation of the Rhineland and the Low Countries, 1451-1452. The chronology of Denis' writings has yet to be worked out, but it seems that his *Sentences* were written while he was completing his theological studies toward 1425, or shortly thereafter. A. Stoelin has worked out an incomplete chronology, see *Sacris Eruditi* 5 (1953): 361-401, and has also discussed his mystical theology in "Denys le Chartreux," *Dictionnaire de spiritualité ascétique et mystique,* Marcel Viller, and others, eds., 17 vols., (Paris: Beauchesne, 1937-1995, 3:434-43. See also *Dictionnaire d'histoire et de géographie ecclésiastique,* Alfred Baudrillart and others, eds., 25 vols. to 1995, (Paris: Letouzey and Ané, 1912-) 14:256-60; *NCE* 4:764-5.

204. He received an M.A. degree from the University of Cologne in 1424, but I find no record of any theological degree. Denis remained-faithful to a Thomistic orientation in theology all his life. Statements that he later became an "Albertist" are to be discounted. See A. Stoelin, "Denys the Carthusian," *Month* 26 (1961):218-30. Denis' voluminous writing has been edited in 36 volumes, *Doctoris Ecstatici D. Dionysii Cartusiani Opera Omnia.* The edition is known as the Montreuil-Turin-Parkminster edition because it was published in those three cities from 1896 to 1913.

205. " . . . some women both from natural disposition and from the gift of grace are more disposed for elevation to God than many males; are wiser, more

virtuous in all devotion. Therefore ahead of many males they are likewise more suitable and worthy of holy orders. And if it is said that the feminine sex is the sex of subjugation; it may be objected that the are many feminine leaders, and one of them has been constituted lady or queen of the whole world, the mother of God incarnate, the most holy and most transcendent virgin Mary. . . . " *Commentary on the Fourth Book of Sentences,* dist. 25, q. 4 (Montreuil, Turin, Parkminster: Typis Cartusiae S.M. de Pratis, 1896-1913), 44 vols., vol. 20 (Turin, 1913), 54a.

206. "To this St. Thomas responds in the first place to the first issue: some things are required for the reception of the ritual (*sacramentum*) as it were out of the necessity of the sacrament, some from the necessity of the laws. If the first is missing, a person is not fit for the ritual (*sacramentum*), nor of the thing [signified], that is to say, of the grace nor of the character of the sacrament (*sacramentum*). Without the other, a person is truly able to receive the ritual (*sacramentum*), but not the thing signified by the ritual (*sacramentum*) nor the grace. The sex of a male, in fact, is of the necessity of the sacrament (*sacramentum*) in the first way. Therefore whatever might be done in the presence of a woman, she does not receive sacrament (*sacramentum*) of orders just as some one does not receive extreme unction who is not truly sick. Without doubt as a ritual (*sacramentum*) is a sign of something which is accomplished in the ritual (*sacramentum*), not only the thing signified, but also the signification of the thing is required . . . " Ibid. (Ibid.)

207. "And as any eminent grade is unable to be signified by the feminine sex, since a woman has the status of a subject, she is not suitable for sacramental orders." Ibid. (Ibid., 25:55). Denis brings this out in more detail when commenting on Paul's first letter to the Corinthians, ch. 11. Over the passage, "Christ is the head of all males; while the head of a woman is a male," he says, " . . . Christ is the head of all the elect according to either nature, even of the angels since as God, he is creator of all . . . but as human [Christ] is said to be head of all males, in likeness to a natural head. The first reason being his perfection...the fullness of all graces was in Christ . . . the second by reason of eminence, since as head is eminent over the other members, so Christ is to the elect . . . the third by reason of influence. Whatever way indeed the head influences the life and natural motion of the members, thus Christ influences . . . fourth, by reason of connaturality. As indeed the head is connatural to the members, thus Christ is to humans whose nature he assumed. Furthermore, when it is said that Christ is the head of males and a male the head of women, it should not be understood that Christ is not the head of women (he is indeed head in both ways of women as well as males) but this should be understood though a certain joining together and conformity, since a male conforms more with Christ than a woman." Moreover, when Paul says, "Every male praying or prophesying with his head covered disfigures his head," Denis remarks, "This should be understood of public and solemn prayer and prophesy, not of private or secret. As when some one prays in the person of the Church . . . Although the Apostle certainly does not permit a woman to teach . . . namely publicly and solemnly in front of all the multitudes, he does not,

however, prohibit women to teach in their communities . . . the reason for the veiling of women is because they are subject to males and because males mediate between Christ and them." And later on he notes, "And thus a male is the imitative image of God since the divine perfection reflects from him in the mode of a certain eminence." *Enarrationes in Omnes Beati Pauli Epistolas*, 1 Cor 11:3 (*Opera Omnia*, [Montreuil, 1901] 13:175-76).

208. 1 Tim. 3:2; Titus 1:6.

209. "Moreover Bonaventure adds truly concerning the impediment of bigamy [in asking whether] the sacrament of Orders is richer than any other sacrament by reason of signification since not only that which is shown outwardly to the one receiving signifies something, but indeed the one receiving himself is a sign. For the bishop ordaining, as well as the priest ordained, signify Christ. This two-fold signification is suitable likewise to marriage since the male signifies Christ, the wife the Church. Since therefore it is of the primary signification of orders that the ordained might signify Christ and the spouse of the Church, a bigamist who has a widowed wife or two wives, cannot validly signify since the Church has only one spouse and Christ only one spouse. A bigamist ought not be admitted to orders, most strongly not sacred orders, in which a person expressly represents Christ. For that reason one is never allowed to be dispensed from these laws nor ought they be dispensed." Ibid. (Ibid., 25:56-57). Denis was not equipped, of course, as an historian to decide whether or not dispensations had ever been granted to individuals who were already twice married. He was also aware that failure to carry through the symbolism in the case of bigamy did not hinder the validity of the ordination. " . . . not that a bigamist would not be *de facto* ordained if they went forward, but because the perfection of the symbol (*sacramentum*) would be lacking in him since for no reason would this be able to be complemented or recompensed by a human." Ibid. (Ibid.)

210. "In the Book of Judges [4:41] Deborah the prophetess is read to have presided. This was in temporal things, not in the sacerdotal things since even now some women preside in a temporal way." Ibid. (Ibid., 25:566).

211. William of Vorrillon (Ruillonis, or perhaps de Valle) (c. 1390-1463) commented on books one through three of the *Sentences* while at Paris (1427-1430). He was listed as a Bachelor in 1429. His whereabouts between 1430 and 1448 are unknown, although it is possible he was lecturing at Poitiers, where scholars loyal to Charles VII resided during the English occupation of Paris. In 1448, when he returned to Paris to be licensed (*CUP* 4:677-78), his *Sentences* presumably were completed. The commentary on Book Four of the *Sentences*, then, can be dated before 1448. William treats of the sacrament of Orders along with the sacrament of extreme unction in a single question, distinction 25 of Book Four. Today, this would be regarded as a startling bit of economy. The two sacraments have little in common (except perhaps the fact that they are listed one after the other in lists of the seven sacraments), and both would seem to deserve a separate treatment, especially since his treatment of matrimony is quite long. In the course of a brief answer, William mentions the ordination of women in an

aside and in textbook fashion. " . . . The third conclusion is this: concerning the law canonical penalties for bishops who promote children to orders; by no means women . . . the third part it is clear, etc. Christ, in thus beginning orders, placed his mother into no order." *Viri celeberrimi . . . . magistri Guillermi de Vorrillon . . . opus super quatuor libros Sententiarum feliciter consummatum est . . .* (Lyon, 1489), Nva. See I. Brady, *Mediaeval Studies* 10 (1948), 225-27.

212. "The third difficulty [difficulties 1 and 2 deal with Extreme Unction and the Tonsure] . . . who is that 'presbytera' which [*Decretum*] distinction 32, c. 18 [for text see n. 37 above] contains? The subtle doctor responds in three ways in question one, distinction 25, solving principally the second

213. Nicolas of Orbellis (?-1472/5) probably received his Master's degree about 1464-1471, since he makes reference to a new privilege given by Paul II at the end of his *Sentence* commentary, (*Commentary on the Fourth Book,* distinction 45, question 3). He was a member of the Observant, or reform branch, of his Order. He is reported to have taught at Angers in the second half of the fifteenth-century. *DTC* 11:625-7. Although little is know about him, his work was popular and went through several editions by the early 16th century (Paris, 1488, 1499; Lyons, 1503; Venice, 1507; Paris, 1509, 1511, 1515, 1517, and 1520). Gui of Brianson (?-1485) received his STM at Paris in 1450 and was teaching at Toulouse in 1487-1488. See *DTC* 6:833; *LTK* 4:1288; and *Franciscan Studies* 29 (1942), 156.

214. For Orbellis's work, I have consulted Bodley *incunabulum*; Don f. 37 [R], which survives without title page or colophon. "I respond that the sex of women impedes reception of orders *de jure* since they ought not to be ordained and likewise *de facto* since if the exterior acts were done for a woman as they are done for those who are ordained, she would not have received orders since Christ instituted this sacrament (*sacramentum*) to be conferred only on the masculine sex. . . . Two reasons are assigned for this, one since the office of orders qualifies one for doctrine in so far as every order is ordained to the presbyterate to which the office of preaching chiefly is appropriate. It is appropriate certainly to the order of the diaconate [as it is stated in the law] *In sancta* [*Decretum*, dist. 92, c. 1; Friedberg, 1:317]. In fact, to teach publicly is not appropriate to women due to the weakness of their understanding and fickleness of their emotions from which defects women suffer more noticeably than men according to common law. Another reason is assigned since the order established the ordained into some grade of eminence. A women truly has the status of subjugation in respect to a male. These two reasons are able to be elicited from the words of the Apostle, 1 Tim 2 'I do not permit a woman to teach nor to dominate a male.'" *Commentary on the Fourth Book of Sentences*, dist. 25, q. 3 (Don f. 37 [R], fol. 00, iii, rb). And Brianson says, " . . . to this doubt I say that the sex of women is not suitable for the reception of orders since all the sacraments (*sacramenta*) are had from the institution of Christ. Christ in fact instituted this sacrament (*sacramentum*) of orders to give to males only and not to women. Of which institution, a two-fold reason was fitting. One since ordination requires the office of doctrine in so far as

every order is ordained to the presbyterate to which the office of doctrine is appropriate as [the law] *Adicimus* [states] [*Decretum, causa* 16, question 1, c. 19; see n. 30 above for the text]. What is furthermore appropriate to the order of the diaconate [is stated in the law] *Per lectis* [*Decretum*, dist. 25, c. 1; Friedberg, 1:90. Thus what ought to be understood is that the priest hold principally the office and deacons are by delegation, or what the *Glossa ordinaria* [on the *Decretum*] on [the law] *In sancta* [*Decretum* dist. 92, c. 1; Friedberg, 1:317] calls preaching and reading the Gospel. Indeed to teach publicly is not appropriate for women due to the weakness of their understanding and fickleness of their emotions from which defects women suffer more noticeably than men according to common law. One has to have a lively intellect in recognition of the truth to teach doctrine, and stable emotions in the delivery. Another reason is assigned since the order establishes the ordained into some grade of eminence. A women truly has the status of subjugation in respect to a male. This is indeed consonant with nature since the sex of women is naturally imperfect as she is according to the Philosopher, a 'defective male' (*vir occasionatus*), that is, imperfect [for references to this text in Aristotle, see n. 93 above]. For this reason, the Apostle says in 1 Tim 2, "A woman should learn in silence with all subjugation. I do not permit a woman to teach, nor to dominate a male." *Expl. Quartum Collectarii Super Sententias Magistri Guidonis Brihansonis* . . . (Paris, 1512), *Commentary on the Fourth Book of the Sentences*, dist. 25 (Paris edition, fol. 193 ra).

215. "Thus he not did place his blessed mother, who has never been or never will be equaled in sanctity, in any grade of orders in the church." Orbellis, *Commentary on the Fourth Book of Sentences*, dist. 25, q. 3 (Don f. 37 [R], fol. 00, iii, rb).

216. Antoninus Pierozzi (1389-1459) was born in Florence and entered a Dominican House at Fiesole, a friary of strict observance, in 1405. The Schism of 1378 was already nearly 30 years old, and the education pattern of the Order was disrupted. The reforming Cardinal, John Dominici, advised him to study within his own convent, and, as a result, Antoninus did not pursue a theology course at a university. Throughout his life, he held a series of administrative posts and superiorships in his Order, working always for the cause of religious reform and regular observance of the *Constitutions*. In 1431, he was made Auditor General of the *Rota* by Eugenius IV, and observed the Council of Florence when it sat in that city in 1439. Eugenius IV appointed him Archbishop of Florence in 1446 to the general satisfaction of all of the factions in the city. Although his career was not an academic one, he produced one of the most significant theological treatises of his time, the *Summa Theologiae Moralis*, a systematic theological statement of all aspects of Christian morality. His deep acquaintance with the practical side of human nature, with classical theology and with church law, combined to produce a text which profoundly influenced later theologians. For his life and influence, see R. Morçay *Saint Antonin, fondateur du Convent de Saint-Mark, Archeveque de Florence, 1389-1459* (Tours: A. Mame; Paris: Gabalda, 1914). For an edition of his *Summa*, see *Sancti Antonini, Archiepiscopi*

Florentini, Ordinis Praedicatorum, Summa theologica . . . (Verona: Augustinus Carattonius, 1740; reprinted Graz: Akademische Druck, 1959) 4 vols.

217. In a kind of waste-basket category entitled, "some other irregularities [excluding from Orders]," he notes: "An hermaphrodite is irregular and one is called so in this manner who participates in both sexes, that is masculine and feminine. He is here rejected from promotion on account of deformity and monstrosity, as is argued in distinction 36, *Illitteratos* [c. 1], [of the *Decretum*; Friedberg, 1:131]. If such a person tends more towards the masculine sex than the feminine, although one ought not be ordained nor to minister having been ordained, nevertheless one receive the character. But if such a person tends more towards the feminine sex than the masculine, or even if one participates equally in both, one has not received the character. According to William *a fortiori*, then 'even more the feminine is not receptive of orders'" *Summa Theologica, Pars Tertia, Titulus* 23, ch. 6, para. 6 (Verona edition, 3:1468). He immediately adds, "If on the other hand, a woman is called '*presbytera*' as in *distinction 32, Presbyer* [of the *Decretum*, for the text and reference see n. 37 above] this is not because she had the order of priesthood but because she was the wife of a priest and a deaconess since she says the homely on the Gospel . . . "

218. John Major (or Mair) (1469-1549/50) was a Scotsman who divided his time between Paris and the Scottish universities. He took his STM at Paris in 1505, well before the outbreak of the new reforming spirit in Germany. He taught at Paris until 1518, when he returned to Scotland to teach at the University of Glasgow and later at St. Andrews (1522). In 1525, he was again in Paris, at the College of the Montaigu, where he built his reputation as the "prince of the theologians." In 1531, he went back to Scotland to St. Andrews, this time to stay. His commentary on the *Sentences*, which appears in four revisions, included a vast amount of scholastic lore served up in a somewhat eclectic fashion. In philosophy and theology, he followed the thought of Ockham and was the leading Terminist (Nominalist) at Paris. Major had no sympathy for the new reform, and the preface of the last edition of his *Sentences* (1530) reflects his disappointment at the success of "the new and detestable calamity of Martin Luther." The Reformation served to undermine the influence which a voluminous work like his might have had, for neither Protestant nor Catholic reformers were interested in pursuing the late fifteenth-century scholastic debates which were enshrined in its pages. His work in political theory is, of course, quite another matter, and in this area his influence was lasting. *DNB* 12:830-32; *DTC* 9:1661-2. Mackay's sketch of Major's life in *A History of Greater Britain . . . by John Major*, A. Constable and A. J. Mackay, trans. Scottish Historical Society 10 (Edinburgh: Edinburgh University Press, 1892), is still the best, but should be read in conjunction with J. Durkan, "John Major: After 400 Years," *Innes Review* 1.2 (1950), 83-100. A recent bibliography is by S. Durkan, "The School of John Major: Bibliography," *Innes Review* 1.2 (1950), 140-57. For his political influence, J. H. Burns, "The Conciliarist Tradition in Scotland," *The Scottish Historical Review* 42.2 (1963), 10, and my *Doctrinal Authority in the Church on the Eve of the Reformation*

(UCLA Doctoral Dissertation, Ann Arbor, Mich., 1978), 467-83, can be consulted. F. Stegmuller, *Repertorium Commentariorum in Sententias Petri Lombardi*, (Würzburg: Schöning, 1947) lists four separate editions of Book Four of Major's *Sentences* (1509, 1512, 1516, and 1521), all of which precede his acquaintance with the work of Luther. I have consulted the editions of 1509 and 1516.

219. "Again a women is not able to be ordained as a priest and if one would attempt it, nothing would happen. But the divine law is the sole cause, even though there are many supporting reasons . . ." *Quartus Sententiarum Johannis Maioris*. (Paris: Poncetus le Preux 1509) *Commentary on the Fourth Book of Sentences*, dist. 24, q. 1 (fol. 131 va).

220. "It should be pointed out that many things are held by divine law that are not expressly contained in divine law nor are they evidently able to be deduced from this; take for example the preceding question concerning a woman not able to be ordained to the priesthood and concerning the institution of each of the orders. This was proved by the ancients with few suitable reasons . . . .Similarly in the New Testament we read the supreme pontificate was given to the successors of Peter by Christ . . . " *Joannis Maioris Doctoris theologi in Quartum Sententiarum* . . . (Paris: Lodoco Badius, 1519), *Commentary on the Fourth Book of Sentences*, dist. 24, q. 2, (fol. 211 rb). Although published in 1519, the book was actually completed in 1516 at Montis Acuti Collegium.

221. "Concerning this issue, I raised some small doubts about the understanding of it . . . the third to be doubted is who is able to be ordained? . . . To the third doubt, it is said that any person is not able to be ordained inasmuch as they are feminine or not baptized . . . at this is from divine institution. Indeed if any bishop should attempt to ordain any of these, nothing would happen. The argument for this is that the Christ-bearing virgin did not have any office since that is unsuitable for the sex of women. Therefore the Apostle says truly in the First Letter to Timothy, chapter two, 'I do not permit a women to preach, nor to dominate over a male.'" *Commentary on the Fourth Book of Sentences*, dist. 24, q. 1, (fol. 210 rb).

222. "There are imprudent and garrulous women who regularly chatter ineptly about this office, complaining because they are prohibited to hear confessions. Some honest women approached the Roman Pontiff. He gave to them a pix to guard all night in which a bird was hidden, prohibiting them most strictly lest they open it. It is customary to say of a woman that she is always perverse concerning that thing which is prohibited to her. One of them opened the pix and the Pontiff's bird escaped. In the morning, asking whether they had opened the pix, and them denying it, he concluded in the end that they would not know how to hold secret the sins heard in confession. It would be disgraceful for them to wander through the countryside and gather news in the city but to remain quietly at home, that is, with household duties (*economicorum*)." *Commentary on the Fourth Book of Sentences*, dist. 24, q. 1 dist. 24, q. 1, (fol. 131 va).

223. Luther, "An dem Christlichen Adel deutcher Nation," *D. Martin Luther's Werke; kritische Gesammtausgabe* (Weimar: H. Böhlau, 1883-)6 (1888):407.

Bibliography

Primary Sources

Abbo of Fleury. *A Defence to Hugh and Robert, Kings of France.* Vol. 139: 461B-72A in *Patrologiae cursus completus . . . Series latina,* edited by Jacques Paul Migne. (Paris: Garnier Fratres and J.P. Migne,1878-90). (hereafter cited as *PL*)

Abelard, Peter. *Letter.8: The Insititution or Rule for Holy Women.*153-224 in *Petri Abailardi Opera . . .*, edited by Victor Cousin. (Paris: Apud Aug. Durand, 1849).

Alan of Lille. *Four Books of the Catholic Faith Against the Heretics. PL* 210:305A-430A.

Albert the Great. *On the Sacraments.* Vol. 26 in *Sancti doctoris ecclesiae Alberti Magni Ordinis Fratrum Praedicatorum Opera Omnia,* edited by Bernhard Geyer. (Cologne: Ashendorff, 1951).

Alexander of Hales. *Commentary on the Sentences of Peter the Lombard. Magistri Alexandri de Hales Glossa in Quatuor Libros Sententiarum Petri Lombardi.* (Florence: Collegium S. Bonaventurae, 1957).

Ambrosiaster (Pseudo-Ambrose). *Commentary on the Letters of Paul. Ambrosiastri qui dicitur Commentarius in Epistulas Paulinas,* Henry Joseph Vogels, ed. (Hoelder-Pichler: Vienna, 1966-1969).

Annales Altahenses. W. de Giesebrecht and E. von Oefele, eds., Monumenta germaniae historiae, Scriptores rerum Germanicarum in usum scholarum ex Monumentis Germaniae historicis recusi, 1. (Hannover: Bibliopolii Hahniani, 1891).

Annales Camaldulensis ordinis Sancti Benedicti . . . Giovanni Mittarelli and Anselmo Costadoni, eds. (Venice: Apud Jo. Baptistam Pasquali, 1755).

Antoninus Pierozzi of Florence. *Summa of Moral Theology. Summa Theologiae Moralis, Sancti Antonini, Archiepiscopi Florentini, Ordinis Praedicatorum, Summa theologica . . .* (Verona: Augustinus Carattonius, 1740; reprinted Graz: Akademische Druck, 1959).

Antonio Andaeas. *Commentary on the Sentences of Peter the Lombard. Ant. Andreae Conventualis Franciscani ex Aragoniae Provinciae ac Joannis Scoti Doctoris Subtitis Discipuli Celeberrimi.* (Venice, 1578).

Anonymous. *Manual on the Sacraments.* (University of Oxford, Bodleian Library, Bodley Ms. Laud 2).

_____. *A Brief and Useful Compendium. R. G. Gulielmi Parisiensis episcopi de Septem Sacramentis Libellus.* Lyon, 1587 and vol. 2 in *Joannis Gersonii doctoris et cancellarii parisiensis Opera.* (Paris, [s.n.], 1606).

Aristotle. *On the Parts of Animals and On the Generation of Animals. Aristotle's De partibus animalium I and De generatione animalium I: (with passages from II. 1-3).* D.M. Balme, trans. (Oxford University Press: New York, 1992).

_____. *The Politics.* Carnes Lord, trans. (Chicago: University of Chicago Press, 1985).

Atto of Vercelli. *Letter to Ambrose the Priest. PL* 134:113D-15D.

Aurelian of Arles. *Rule for Virgins. PL* 68:399A-406D.

Burchard of Worms. *Twenty Books of Decrees. PL* 140:537A-1058C.

Bonaventure. *Commentary on the Sentences of Peter the Lombard.* Vols. 1-4 in *Doctoris Seraphici S. Bonaventure . . . Opera omnia.* (Quaracchi: Collegium S. Bonaventurae, 1882-1902).

Calixtus II. *The Bulls of Pope Calixtus II. Bullaire du Pape Calixtus II, 1119-1124: Essai de Restitution,* Ulysse Robert. ed. 2 vols. (Paris: Imprimerie nationale, 1891 and *PL* 163:1093A-1338A).

Codex diplomatico padovanno dal secolo sesto a tuto l'undecimo. Andrea Gloria, ed., Monumenti storici publicati dalla deputazione Veneta de storia patria, 2, Serie prima documenti, 2. *(*Venice: A spese della Società, 1877).

Corpus Iuris Canonici. E. Friedberg, ed. Graz: Akademische Druck- u. (Verlagsanstalt, 1959).

Decretales Pseudo-Isidoriana. Paul Hinschius, ed. (Leipzig: B. Tauchnitz, 1863; reprinted Aalen: Scientia Verlag, 1963).

Denis the Carthusian. *Commentary on the Sentences of Peter the Lombard. Doctoris Ecstatici D. Dionysii Cartusiani Opera Omnia.* (Montreuil, Turin, Parkminster: Typis Cartusiae S.M. de Pratis, 1896-1913).

_____, *Expostion of all of the Letters of the Blessed Paul. Doctoris Ecstatici D. Dionysii Cartusiani Opera Omnia.* (Montreuil, Turin, Parkminster: Typis Cartusiae S.M. de Pratis, 1896-1913).

Denis the Cistercian. *Questions on the Sentences of Peter the Lombard. Explicit quaestiones Dionisii Cisterciensi in quattuor libros Sententiarum . . . Parisiensis* s. 2. N.p., 1511.

Diplomata regum et imperatorum Germaniae. *Ottonis II diplomata*, Th. Sickel, ed., Monumenta Germaniae historica inde ab anno Christi quingentesimo usque ad annum millesimum et quingentesimum. (Hannover: Hansche Buchhandlung, 1888).

Donatus of Besançon. *Rule for Virgins. PL* 87:273A-297B.

Durandus of Saint-Pourçain. *Commentary on the Sentences of Peter the Lombard. D. Durandi a Sancto Portiano . . . Petri Lombardi Sententias Theologicas Commentariorum, libri iiii.* (Guerraea: Venice, 1571).

Francis of Meyronnis. *Commentary on the Sentences of Peter the Lombard. Preclarissimum illuminati doctoris Francisci de Mayronis in quattuor Sententiarum libros scriptum.* (Venice, 1519).

Gilbert of Limerick. *On the Customs of the Church. PL* 159:997A-1004A.

Gui of Brianson. *Commentary on the Sentences of Peter the Lombard. Expl. Quartum Collectarii Super Sententias Magistri Guidonis Brihansonis . . .* (Paris, 1512).

Guidonis Orchellus. *Tract on the Sacraments. Tractatus de Sacramentis ex eius Summa de Sacramentis et Officiis. Ecclesiae*, Damian and Odulph Van den Eynde, eds. Franciscan Institute Publications, text series, 4. (St. Bonaventure, N.Y.: Franciscan Institute, 1953).

Hanibald of Hanibaldis. *Commentary on the Sentences of Peter the Lombard. S. Thomae Aquinatis Scriptum Super Libros Magistri Sententiarum ad Hannibaldum Hannibaldensem Romanum, Episcopum Cardinalem* in *S. Thomae Aquinatis ... Opera Omnia.* Vol. 30. (Vivès: Paris, 1878).

Henry of Ghent. *Theological Summa. Summae Quaestionum Ordinarium Theologi recepto praeconio Solemnis Henrici a Gandavo . . .* In aedibus I. (Badii: Ascensii, 1520; reprinted Franciscan Institute: St. Bonaventure, New York, 1953).

Henry of Gorkum, et al. *Commentary on the Sentences of Peter the Lombard. Petri Lombardi Parrhysiensis . . . Sententiarum textus. . . cuilibet distinctioni Henrici Gorchemii propositiones, Egidii de Roma elucibrationes, Henrici de Wurimaria, OSEA, additiones.* (Lyon, 1513).

Honorius Augustodunensis. *Jewel of the Soul. PL* 172: 541-738B.

Hugh de St. Cher. *Commentary on the Sentences of Peter the Lombard.* (University of Oxford, Bodliean Library, Bodley Ms. Can. Pat. Lat. 208).

_____. *Commentary on all the Letters of St. Paul. Hugonis de Sancto Charo... in epistolas omnes D. Pauli . . .* (Lyon, 1669).

Hugh of St. Victor. *On the Sacraments of the Christian Faith. PL* 176:173-618B.

Huguccio (Hugh of Pisa). *Commentary on the Decretum.* Admont Ms 7.

Innocent III. *Letter to the Bishop of Burgos and Abbot of Morimundo. Decretales* l. 5, t. 38, c. 10 in *Corpus Iuris Canonici,* E. Friedberg, ed. Graz: Akademische Druck- u. (Verlagsanstalt, 1959).

Ivo of Chartres. *Decretum. PL* 161:48-1022D.

_____. *Panormia. PL* 161:1045-1344D.

John of Bassolis. *Commentary on the Sentences of Peter the Lombard. Opera de Joannis de Bassolis doctor subtilis Scoti . . . fidelis discipuli . . .* (Paris, 1516-1517).

John Duns Scotus. *Commentary on the Sentences of Peter the Lombard. Opus Oxoniense. Ioannis Duns Scoti . . . Opera Omnia.* Vol. 19. (Vivès: Paris, 1895).

_____. *Commentary on the Sentences of Peter the Lombard. Reportata Paristensis. Ioannis Duns Scoti . . . Opera Omnia.* Vol. 24. (Vivès: Paris, 1895).

John Hus. *Commentary on the Sentences of Peter the Lombard. Magistri Joannis Hus Opera Omnia,* W. Flajshans and M. Komínoková, eds. (Prague, 1905-1908; reprinted Osnabrück: Biblio-Verlag, 1966).

John Major. *Commentary on the Sentences of Peter the Lombard. Quartus Sententiarum Johannis Maioris.* (Paris: Poncetus le Preux 1509).

_____. *A History of Greater Britain . . . by John Major,* trans. by A. Constable and A. J. Mackay. Scottish Historical Society 10. (Edinburgh: Edinburgh University Press, 1892).

John Teutonicus and Bartholomew of Brescia. *The Standard Commentary on the Decretum. Glossa ordinaria, Decretvm Gratiani emendatvm et notationibvs illvstratvm: vna cum glossa . . .* (Venice: Apud

Magnam Societatem vna cum Georgio Ferrario & Hieronymo Franzino, 1584).

Le Liber ordinum en usage dans l'église Wisigothique et mozarabe d'espagne du ciquième au onzieme siècle. Marius Férotin, ed. Reprint of the 1904 edition edited by Anthony Ward and Cuthbert Johnson. Bibliotheca «Ephemeredes liturgicae» subsidia 83. Instrumenta liturgica Quarreriensia 6. (Rome: C.L.V. Edizioni liturgiche, 1996).

Leo the Great. *Letter to Theodoret of Cyrrhus.* PL 54:1046B-1055A.

Luther, Martin. "An dem Christlichen Adel deutcher Nation," *D. Martin Luther's Werke; kritische Gesammtausgabe.* Vol. 6. (Weimar: H. Böhlau, 1883-?).

Nicolas of Orbellis. *Commentary on the Sentences of Peter the Lombard.* University of Oxford, Bodleian Library, Bodley *incunabulum*; Don f. 37 [R].

Les Ordines Romani du Haut Moyen Age. Michel Andrieu, ed., Spicilegium sacrum Lovaniense, Études et documents 28. (Louvain: Spicilegium sacrum Lovaniense, 1956).

Die Ordines für die Weihe und Krönung des Kaisers und der Kaiseren. Reinhard Elze, ed., Monumenta Germaniae historica, Fontes juris Germanici antiqui in usum scholarum separatim editi, 9. (Hannover: Hansche Buchhandlung, 1960; reprinted Hannover: Hansche Buchhandlung, 1995).

Peter the Lombard. *The Four Books of Sentences. Magistri Petri Lombardi Sententiae in IV Libris Distinctae,* 3rd ed. Spicilegium Bonaventurianum; 4, 5. (Grottaferrata: Editiones Collegii S. Bonaventurae ad Claras Aquas, 1971-1981).

Peter de la Palude. *Commentary on the Sentences of Peter the Lombard. Magistri Petri de la Palude Patriarci Herosolvmitani ordinis fratrum praedicatorum* . . . (Paris, 1514).

_____, *Commentary on the Decretum. Magistri Petri de la Palude Patriarci Herosolvmitani ordinis fratrum praedicatorum* . . . (Paris, 1514).

Peter of Poitiers. *Five Books of Sentences.* PL 211:789-1280D.

Peter of Tarentaise. *Commentary on the Sentences of Peter the Lombard. Innocenti Quinti . . . qui antea Petrus de Tarantasia dicebatur, In IV*

Librum Sententiarum Commentaria. (A. Colomerius: Toulouse, 1649-52).

Richard Fishacre. *Commentary on the Sentences of Peter the Lombard.* University of Oxford, Balliol College, Balliol Ms. 57 and University of Oxford, Oriel College, Oriel Ms 43.

Richard of Middleton. *Commentary on the Sentences of Peter the Lombard. Clarissimi Theologi Magistri Ricardi de Mediavilla . . . super Quatuor Libros Sententiarum . . .* (R.P.F. Ludovico Silvestrio: Brixiae, 1591; reprinted Frankfurt, Minerva, 1963).

Robert of Arbrissel. *Precepts for Right Living. PL* 162:1081D-1086C.

The Rule of St. Benedict in Latin and English with Notes. Timothy Fry, ed. (Collegeville, Minn.: The Liturgical Press, 1981).

Rupert of Deutz. *On the Divine Office.* Rhaban Haacke, ed., *Ruperti Tjuitiensis Liber de divinis officiis,* Corpus christianorum, Continuatio medievalis, 7. (Turnhout: Brepols, 1967).

Sacrorum conciliorum nova et amplissima collectio. John Dominic Mansi and others, eds. (Paris: H. Welter, 1901-1927).

Simon of Hinton. *Summa.* University of Oxford, Bodleian Library, Bodley Ms. Laud 2.

Les Statuta Ecclesiae Antiqua. Les Statuta Ecclesiae Antiqua, Edition etudes critiques Charles Munier, ed., Bibliotheque de l'institut de droit canonique de l'université de Strasbourg 5. (Paris: Presses universitaires de France, 1960).

Thietmar of Merseburg. *Chronicle. Die Chronik des Bischofs Thietmar von Merseburg und ihre Korveier Überarbeitung.* Robert Holtmann, ed. Monumenta Germaniae historicae, Scriptores rerum germanicarum, 9. (Berlin: Werdmannsche Bundhandlung, 1935).

Thomas Aquinas. *Commentary on the Sentences of Peter the Lombard. S. Thomae Aquinatis, Scriptum supra quatuor libros Sententiarum. Sancti Thomae Aquinatis . . . opera omnia.* (Parmae: P. Fiaccadori, 1852-1873).

_____. *Notes by Reginald of Piperno on Thomas Aquinas' Lectures on the first Letter to Timothy. Opera editio altera Veneta.* (Venice, 1747).

_____. *Notes by Reginald of Piperno on Thomas Aquinas' Lectures on the First Letter to the Corinthians. S. Thomas Aquinatis, Opera editio altera Veneta.* (Venice, 1747).

Thomas Netter. *On the Ancient Teaching of the Faith of the Universal Church.* (Venice: Antonius Bassanesius, 1757-1759).

Thomas of Strasbourg. *Commentary on the Sentences of Peter the Lombard. Thomae ab Argentina . . . Commentaria in IIII. Libros Sententiarum . . .* (Venice: I. Ziletti, 1564).

Ulrich of Strasbourg. *Compendium of the Truth of Theology. Compendium Theologiae Veritatis Beati Alberti Magni Opera.* (Clavdius Prost: Lyons, 1651).

Urban II. *Letter to Rainold, archbishop of Rheims. PL* 151:309D-311D.

Waldebert. *Rule for Virgins. PL* 88:1053A-1070C.

William of Auxerre. *The Golden Summa. Summa Aurea in Quattuor Libros Sententiarum . . .* (Paris, 1500, reprinted Frankfurt/Main: Minerva, 1964).

William of Ockham. *Commentary on the Sentences of Peter the Lombard. Guillelmus de Occam, OFM, Opera Plurima.* (Lyon, 1494-1496; reprinted Gregg Press: London, 1962).

William of Rothwell. *Commentary on the Sentences of Peter the Lombard.* British National Library, Harley Ms. 3211.

William of Rubio. *Commentary on the Sentences of Peter the Lombard. F. Guilielmi de Rubione venerabilis admodum patris et theologi facile doctissimi, provincia Aragoniae quondam ministri Disputatorum in quatuor libros Magistri Sentetiarum.* (Michaelis Conradi & Simonis Vincentii: Paris, 1518).

William of Vorrillon. *Commentary on the Sentences of Peter the Lombard. Viri celeberrimi . . . magistri Guillermi de Vorrillon . . . opus super quatuor libros Sententiarum feliciter consummatum est . . .* Lyon, 1489.

Secondary Sources

Ashton, M. "Lollard Women Priests?" *Journal of Ecclesiastical History,* 31 (1980): 441-61.

Beneden, Pierre van. *Aux origines d'une terminologie sacramentelle: ordo, ordinare, ordinatio dans la littérature chrétienne avant 313.* (Louvain : Spicilegium sacrum Lovaniense, 1974).

Bériou, Nicoles. "The Right of Women to Give Religious Instruction in the Thirteenth Century." 134-45 in *Women Preachers and Prophets through Two Millennia of Christianity*, edited by Beverly Wayne Kienzle and Pamela J. Walker. (Berkeley: University of California Press, 1998).

Bernal-Palacios, A. "La condición de la mujer en Santo Tomas de Aquino." *Escritos del Vedat* 4 (1974): 285-335.

Borrensen, Kari E. *Subordination and Equivalence.* (University Press of America: Washington, DC, 1981).

Bougerol, Jacques Guy, ed. *Bibliographia Bonaventuriana (c. 1850-1973).* (Grottaferrata: Collegium S. Bonaventura).

_____. *Introduction a l'étude de Saint Bonaventure.* Bibliothèque de théologie. série 1. Théologie dogmatique, vol 2. (Tournai : Desclée, 1961).

Bradshaw, Paul F. "Medieval Ordination." 377-78 in *The Study of Liturgy*, edited by C. Jones, G. Wainwright, and others. (New York: Oxford University Press, 1992).

Brampton, C.K. "Personalities at the Process Against Ockham at Avignon." *Franciscan Studies* 26 (1966): 4-25.

_____. "Traditions Relating to the Death of William of Ockham." *Archivum Franciscanum Historicum* 53 (1960): 442-49.

Brundage, James. *Medieval Canon Law.* (London and New York: Longman, 1995).

Burns, J. H. "The Conciliarist Tradition in Scotland." *The Scottish Historical Reveiw* 42.2 (1963):10.

Catto, J. *William Woodford, OFM (1330-97).* Thesis for Doctor of Philosophy. (University of Oxford, 1969).

Chadwick, Henry. *The Early Church.* (London: Penguin Books, 1967).

Congar, Yves. "Church History as a Branch of Theology." 85-96 in *Church History in Future Perspective* edited by Roger Aubert. *Concilium*, 57. (New York: Herder and Herder, 1970).

_____. *Lay People in the Church: A Study for a Theology of the Laity.* 2nd rev. ed. Donald Attwater, transl. (Westminster, MD: The Newman Press, 1967).

_____. "My Path-findings in the Theology of Laity and Ministries." *The Jurist* 32 (1977): 169-88.

_____. "Note sur une valeur des termes «ordinare, ordinatio»."*Revue des sciences religieuses* 58 (1984): 7-14.

_____. "Ordination invitus, coactus de l'église antique au canon 214." *Revue des sciences philosophiques et théologiques* 50 (1966): 169-97.

Cross, C. "Great Reasoners in Scripture: The Activities of Women Lollards 1380-1530." 359-80 in *Medieval Women,* edited by D. Baker. (Oxford: Basil Blackwell, 1978).

Devic, Cl. and J. Vaissete. *Histoire générale de Languedoc avec des notes et les pièces justificatives,* eds. (Toulouse: E. Privat, 1872-92).

Dondaine, A. "La Somme de 'Simon de Hinton." *Recherches de théologie ancienne et médiévale* 9 (1937): 5-22; 205-18.

Duchesne, L. *Le Liber Pontificalis.* 2nd ed. (Paris: E. de Boccard, 1955-57).

Durkan, J. "John Major: After 400 Years." *Innes Review* 1.2 (1950): 83-100.

_____. "The School of John Major: Bibliography." *Innis Review* 1.2 (1950): 140-57.

Eisen, Ute. *Women Officeholders in Early Christianity: Epigraphical and Literary Studies.* (Collegeville, Minn.: The Liturgical Press, 2000).

Espín, Orlando. "Toward the Construction of an Intercultural Theology of Tradition." *Journal of Hispanic/Latino Theology* (forthcoming).

Ferrante, Joan M. *Woman As Image in Medieval Literature From the Twelfth Century to Dante.* (New York: Columbia University Press, 1975).

Fiorenza, Elisabeth Schüssler. *In Memory of Her: A Feminist Theological Reconstruction of Christian Origins.* (New York: Crossroad, 1983).

Fransen, Gerard. "La tradition des canoniste du moyen âge." 257-75 in *Etudes sur le sacrement de l'ordre.* Lex orandi, 22. (Paris: Éditions du Cerf, 1957).

Fuhrmann, Horst. *Einfluß und Verbreitung der pseudoisidorischen Fälschungen.* 2 vols. Schriften der Monumenta Germaniae historica, 24. (Stuttgart: Hiersemann, 1972).

Gräf, Hermann. "Ad monachum faciendum: Die Mönchsprofess nach einem Fest-Sacramentar von Venedig aus dem 11. Jh." *Ephemerides liturgicae* 88 (1974): 353-69.

Graham, Rose. *S. Gilbert of Sempringham and the Gilbertines; a History of the Only English Monastic Order.* (London: Elliot Stock, 1903).

Gryson, Roger. *The Ministry Of Women In The Early Church.* Jean Laporte and Mary Louise Hall, transl. (Collegeville, Minn.: Liturgical Press, 1976).

Gy, Pierre Marie. "Les anciennes prières d'ordination." *Maison-Dieu* 138 (1979): 93-122.

Healy, Emma T. *Woman According to Saint Bonaventure.* (Erie, PA: Villa Maria College, 1956).

Hochstetler, Donald. *A Conflict of Traditions: Women in Religion in the Early Middle Ages: 500-840.* (Lanham, New York, London: University Press of America, 1992).

Hughes, Kathleen. *Early Christian Ireland: Introduction to the Sources.* (London: Hodder and Stoughton, 1972).

Jansen, Katherine Ludwig. "Maria Magdalena: *Apostolorum Apostola.*" 57-96 in *Women Preachers and Prophets through Two Millennia of Christianity,* edited by Beverly Wayne Kienzle and Pamela J. Walker. (Berkeley: University of California Press, 1998).

Kraemer, Ross Shepard and Mary Rose D'Angelo, eds. *Essays in Women and Christian Origins.* (New York and Oxford: Oxford University Press, 1999).

Kilmartin, Edward. *The Eucharist in the West: History and Theology.* Robert Daly, ed. (Collegeville, Minn.: Liturgical Press, 1998).

Labontaine, Paul Henri. *Les conditions positives de l'accession aux ordres dans la première législation ecclésiastique (300-492).* (Ottawa, Éditions de l'Université d'Ottawa, 1963).

La Fontaine, Paul-Henri. "Le sex masculin, condition de l'accession aux ordres, aux IVe et Ve siecles." *Revue de l'universite d'Ottawa,* 31.1 (1961): 137*-82*.

Le Bras, G., Ch. Lefebvre, J. Rambaud, eds. *L'âge classique : 1140-1378: sources et théorie du droit.* Histoire du droit et des institutions de l'Église en Occident, 7. (Paris: Sirey, 1965).

Lechner, Josef. *Sakramentenlehre des Richard von Mediavilla*. J. Kösel & F. (Pustet: Munich, 1925).

Leclercq, Jean. "Eucharistic Celebrations Without Priests in the Middle Ages." *Worship* 55 (1981):160-68.

_____. "Prières médiévales pour recevoir l'eucharistie pour saluer et pour bénir la croix." *Ephemerides liturgicae* 97 (1965): 329-31.

Leff, Gordon. *Paris and Oxford Universities in the Thirteenth and Fourteenth Centuries: An Institutional and Intellectual History*. (New York: Wiley, 1968).

_____. *William of Ockham: The Metamorphosis of Scholastic Discourse*. (Manchester Univ. Press: Manchester, 1975).

Lynch, K. F. "Some 'Fontes' of Alexander of Hales." *Franciscan Studies* 13 (1953):119-46.

Macy, Gary. "The Eucharist and Popular Devotion." 41-2 in *Proceedings of the Fifty-second Annual Convention of the Catholic Theological Society of America*, vol. 52, edited by Judith A. Dwyer. Catholic Theological Society of America, 1997. Reprinted in Gary Macy. *Treasures from the Storehouse: Essays on the Medieval Eucharist*. (Collegeville, Minn.: Liturgical Press of America, 1999).

_____. "The Ordination of Women in the Early Middle Ages." *Theological Studies* 61 (2000): 481-507.

_____. ed. *Theology and the New Histories*. Proceedings of the Annual Convention of the College Theology Society, 1998. (Maryknoll, NY: Orbis Press, 1999).

_____. *Theologies of the Eucharist in the Early Scholastic Period*. (Oxford: Clarendon Press, 1984).

Martin, John Hilary. *Doctrinal Authority in the Church on the Eve of the Reformation*. Doctoral Dissertation at the University of California, Los Angeles, 1978.

_____. "The Ordination of Women and the Theologians in the Middle Ages." *Escritos del Vedat*, 16 (1986): 115-77 and 18 (1988): 87-143.

Mayeski, Marie Anne. "Excluded by the Logic of Control: Women in Medieval Society and Scholastic Theology." 70-95 in *Equal at the Creation: Sexism, Society, and Christian Thought*, edited by Joseph Martos and Pierre Hégy. (Toronto: University of Toronto Press, 1998).

McFarlane, K. B. *John Wycliffe and the Beginning of English Nonconformity*. (London: English Universities Press, 1952).

McNamara, Jo Ann and John E. Halborg, eds. *Sainted Women of the Dark Ages*. (Durham and London: Duke University Press, 1992).

Metz, René. "Benedictio sive consecratio virginum." *Ephemerides liturgicae* 80 (1966): 263-93.

Mitchell, Nathan. *Mission and Ministry: History and Theology in the Sacrament of Order*. (Wilmington, Delaware: Michael Glazier, Inc., 1982).

Morçay, R. *Saint Antonin, fondateur du Convent de Saint-Mark, Archeveque de Florence, 1389-1459*. (Tours: A. Mame; Paris: Gabalda, 1914).

Morris, Joan. *The Lady was a Bishop: The Hidden History of Women with Clerical Ordination and the Jurisdiction of Bishops*. (Cambridge: Cambridge University Press, 1978).

Muessig, Carol. "Prophecy and Song: Teaching and Preaching by Medieval Women." 146-50 in *Women Preachers and Prophets through Two Millennia of Christianity*, edited by Beverly Wayne Kienzle and Pamela J. Walker. (Berkeley: University of California Press, 1998).

Nelson, Janet. "Les femmes et l'évangélisation au ixe siècle." *Revue du Nord* 69 (1986): 471-83.

O'Meara, Thomas F. "Emergence and Decline of Popular Voice in the Selection of Bishops." 21-32 in *The Choosing of Bishops*, edited by William W. Bassett. (Hartford, Connecticut: The Canon Law Society of America, 1971).

Pasiecznik, M. "John de Bassolis, OFM." *Franciscan Studies* 13.4 (1953): 59-77; 14.1 (1954): 49-80.

Principe, Walter. "The History of Theology: Fortress or Launching Pad." 19-40 in *The Proceedings of the Catholic Theological Society of America*, 43, edited by John P. Boyle and George Kilcourse. (Macon, Georgia: Mercer University Press, 1988).

Pryds, Darleen. "Proclaiming Sanctity through Proscribed Acts: the Case of Rose of Viterbo." 159-72 in *Women Preachers and Prophets through Two Millennia of Christianity*, edited by Beverly Wayne Kienzle and Pamela J. Walker. (Berkeley: University of California Press, 1998).

Raming, Ida. *The Exclusion of Women from the Priesthood: Divine Law or Sex Discrimination?* Norman R. Davis, transl. (Metuchen, N.J.: The Scarecrow Press, 1976). (A new edition of this work in English translation is due to appear from Scarecrow Press in 2003).

Rand, L. "Ordination of Women to the Diaconate." *Communio* 8 (1981): 370-83.

Rezette, J. "Miscellanea." *Antonianum* 51 (1976): 522.

Rigali, Norbert. "On the Humanae Vitae Process: Ethics of Teaching Morality." *Louvain Studies* 23 (1998): 3-21.

Ross, Susan. Extravagant Affections: A Feminist Sacramental Theology. (New York: Continuum, 1998).

Rusconi, Roberto. "Women's Sermons at the End of the Middle Ages: Texts from the Blessed and Images of the Saints." 173-95 in *Women Preachers and Prophets through Two Millennia of Christianity*, edited by Beverly Wayne Kienzle and Pamela J. Walker. (Berkeley: University of California Press, 1998).

Schillebeeckx, E. *Ministry, Leadership in the Community of Jesus Christ.* John Bowden, transl. (New York: Crossroad, 1981).

Shahar, Shulamith. *The Fourth Estate, A History of Women in the Middle Ages.* Chaya Galai, transl. (London: Methuen, 1983).

Smalley, Beryl. *The Study of the Bible in the Middle Ages.* 3rd ed. (Oxford: Blackwell, 1983).

Stegmuller, F. *Repertorium commentariorum in Sententias Petri Lombardi.* (Würzburg: Schöning, 1947).

Stenton, M. *Anglo-Saxon England.* 3rd ed. (Oxford: Clarendon Press, 1971).

Stoelin, A. "Denys the Carthusian." *Month* 26 (1961): 218-30.

Sweeney, Garret. "The Wound in the Right Foot: 'Unhealed'." 207-34 in *Bishops and Writers: Aspects of the Evolution of Modern English Catholicism*, edited by Adrian Hastings (Wheathampstead, Hertforshire: Anthony Clark, 1977).

Tellenback, Gerd. *Church State and Christian Society at the Time of the Investiture Contest.* R. F. Bennett, transl. (Oxford: Basil Blackwell, 1966).

Thomson, J. H. F. *The Later Lollards 1414-1520.* (Oxford: Oxford University Press, 1965).

_____. "Lollard Doctrines and Beliefs." 239-51 in *Wyclif and the Oxford schools: the relation of the "Summa de ente" to scholastic debates at Oxford in the later fourteenth century,* edited by John Adam Robson. (Cambridge, Cambridge University Press, 1961).

Thurston, Bonnie Bowman. *The Widows: A Women's Ministry in the Early Church.* (Minneapolis, Minn.: Fortress Press, 1989).

Tilley, Terrence. "Practicing History, Practicing Theology." 1-20 in *Theology and the New Histories* edited by Gary Macy. (Maryknoll, NY: Orbis Press, 1999).

_____. *Inventing Catholic Tradition.* (Maryknoll, N.Y.: Orbis Books, 2000).

Torjesen, Karen Jo. *When Women Were Priests.* (San Francisco: HarperSanFrancisco, 1993).

Van der Meer, Haye. *Women Priests in the Catholic Church? A Theological-Historical Investigation.* Arlene and Leonard Swidler, transl. (Philadelphia, Temple University Press, 1973).

Walz, P. A. "The *Exceptiones* from the Summa of Simon of Hinton." *Angelicum* 13 (1936): 282-368.

Weiler, A. *Heinrich von Gorkum (d. 1431): seine Stellung in der Philosophie und der Theologie des Spätmittelalters.* (Hilversum: P. Brand, 1962).

Weisheipl, James A. *Friar Thomas d'Aquino: His Life, Thought, and Work.* (Garden City, N.Y., Doubleday, 1974).

Wemple, Suzanne Fonay. "Women from the Fifth Century to the Tenth Century." 169-210 in *A History of Women in the West,* edited by George Duby and Michelle Perrot. (Cambridge, Mass. and London: Harvard University Press, 1992).

_____. *Women in Frankish Society: Marriage and the Cloister 500 to 900.* (Philadelphia: University of Pennsylvania Press, 1981).

Witherington, Ben. *Women in the Earliest Churches.* Society for New Testament Studies, Monograph Series, 59. (Cambridge: Cambridge University Press, 1988).

Workman, H. B. *John Wyclif, a Study of the English Medieval Church.* (Oxford: Clarendon Press, 1926).

Zerfaß, Rolf. *Der Streit zum die Laienpredigt. Eine pastoral-geschichtliche Untersuchung zum Verständnis des Predigtamtes und zuer sienen Entwicklung im 12. und 13. (Jahrhundert.* Frieberg, Basel, Wien: Herder, 1974).

Index

abbess, xi, 1, 2, 3, 4, 6, 8, 9,
11, 12, 13, 14, 15, 19, 20,
21, 24, 25, 27, 28, 29, 49,
50, 51, 52, 92, 101, 117,
118, 119, 147, 155

Abbo of Fleury, 22, 161

abbot, xi, 4, 5, 11, 25, 117

Abelard, Peter 12, 13, 161

Adam, 44, 50, 59, 60, 61, 62,
68, 69, 71, 72, 78, 90, 95,
128, 132, 152,

Alan of Lille, 36, 161

Albert the Great, 38, 74, 131,
161

Alexander of Hales, 37, 38,
110, 161, 172

Ambrosiaster, 45, 115, 161

Annales Altahenses, 5, 23, 161

Annales Camaldulensis, 20,
161

Antoninus Pierozzi of
Florence, 101-2, 157-8, 161

Antonio Andaeas, 83-4, 137,
161

Aquinas, Thomas 33, 64-73,
75, 83, 89, 93, 98, 99, 107,
112, 113, 125, 139, 141,
147, 166

Aristotle, 68, 69, 71, 77, 82,
106, 124, 127, 157, 163

Ashton, M. 148, 167

Atto of Vercelli, 7, 20, 29, 162

Augustine, 60, 61, 77, 94, 95,
115, 123, 127, 128, 149, 151

Aurelian of Arles, 27, 162

baptize, 8, 11, 24, 31, 37, 43,
48, 75, 93, 102, 104, 112,
113, 131, 159

Bartholomew of Brescia, 41,
164

Beleth, John 13

Beneden, P. van, 4, 168

Bériou, N., 27, 168

Bernal-Palacios, A., 128, 168

Bonaventure, 33, 56-65, 66,
71, 72, 73, 74, 77, 83, 97,
99, 106, 110, 117, 118, 121,
122, 123, 124, 125, 130,
131, 132, 141, 155, 162,
163, 168, 170

Borrensen, K., 127, 168

Bougerol, J-G., 121, 168

Bradshaw, P. 21, 168

Brampton, C.K., 144, 168

Brianson, Gui , 101, 158, 163

Brigid of Kildare, 49, 117

Brundage, J., 22, 168

Burchard of Worms, 40, 162

Burns, J.H., 158, 168

Calixtus II, 2, 19, 162

canonesses, 1, 6, 9-10, 25, 26,
118

canonists, xi, 4, 5, 7, 8, 11-14,
39, 40- 52, 55, 75, 93, 104,
105, 111

Carthage, Councils of, 40, 43,
113

Cataphrygians, 45, 46, 54, 58,
95, 115, 119, 122

Catto, J., 148, 168

Chadwick, H., 5, 168

Chalcedon, Council of, 28, 40,

44, 45, 46, 114, 116, 120
confession, 2, 3, 11, 26, 103,
    118, 134, 143, 159
Congar, Y., ix, 4, 5, 6, 21, 22,
    23, 29, 30, 168
Cross, C., 26, 60, 71, 148, 169

deacon, xi, 8, 9, 10, 39, 43, 45,
    109, 113, 115, 119, 122, 125
    135, 141, 146, 150, 157 See
    also diaconate
deaconess, xi, 1, 2, 3, 6, 7, 8-9,
    10, 11, 12, 14, 15, 19, 24,
    25, 26, 28, 44, 45, 46, 47,
    53, 58, 74, 86, 91, 104, 114,
    115, 116, 119, 120, 122,
    130, 141, 158 See also
    diaconate
Debora, 91, 100, 111
Decretales Pseudo-Isidoriana,
    24, 25, 162
Denis the Carthusian, 92-100,
    153, 154, 155, 162
Denis the Cistercian, 94, 163
diaconate, vii, xi, 3, 11, 15, 25,
    28, 42, 46, 47, 86, 95, 116,
    141, 146, 156, 157
Donatus of Besançon, 26, 27,
    163
Dondaine, A., 121, 169
double monastery, 48, 49, 50,
    74, 117, 118
Duchesne, L., 112, 169
Durandus of Saint-Pourçain,
    84-5, 138, 139, 163
Durkan, J., 158, 169

Eisen, U., 7, 23, 24, 25, 169
Episcopae, 6, 7, 8, 24

Espín, O., 29, 169
Eucharist, viii, ix, 13, 14, 26,
    29, 31, 35, 36, 42, 63, 65,
    84, 87, 90, 104, 105, 110,
    126, 144, 145, 172, 173, 179
Eve, 44, 50, 59, 60, 61, 68, 69,
    71, 72, 95, 106, 111, 128,
    129, 158,

Fabian, 47, 109
Ferrante, J., 123, 169
Fiorenza, E. Schüssler, 23, 169
Fishacre, Richard, 52-5, 57,
    119, 120, 168
Francis of Meyronnis, 88-89,
    142, 163
Fransen, G., 5, 25, 169
Fuhrmann, H., 24, 169

Genesis, 44, 59, 61, 68, 69, 70,
    81, 84, 85, 106, 138, 141
Gilbert of Limerick, 2, 163
Glossa ordinaria (on the
    Decretum) 41-5, 47, 52, 53,
    54, 58, 68, 71, 113, 114,
    115, 157
Glossa ordinaria (on
    Scripture) 71, 81, 132-4
Gospels, 43, 46, 58, 67
Gräf, H., 170
Graham, R., 119, 170
Gratian, 12, 13, 24, 40, 41, 42,
    44, 45, 46, 47, 48, 52, 57,
    109, 112, 114
Grosseteste, Robert, 52
Gryson, R., 111, 114, 170
Guidonis Orchellus, 110, 163
Gy, P-M., 4, 170

Hanibald of Hanibaldis, 73, 163
Healy, E.T., 123, 170
Henry of Ghent, 76-8, 79, 133, 163
Henry of Gorkum, 65, 147, 163
heretic, 13, 35, 104, 110
hermaphrodite, 46, 47, 86, 102, 115, 141, 157
Hochstetler, D., 24, 26, 27, 170
Honorius Augustodunensis, 13, 29, 164
Hugh de St. Cher, 38, 111, 164
Hugh of St. Victor, 36, 164
Hughes, K., 117, 170
Huguccio, 12, 46, 47, 52, 115, 116, 164
Hus, John, 96-7, 152, 153, 164

impediment, 37, 45, 52, 54, 58, 79, 84, 87, 88, 97, 98, 99, 102, 116, 119, 136, 140, 143, 154
Innocent III, 4, 11, 54, 107, 120, 164
Innocent IV, 52
Ivo of Chartres, 110, 164

Jansen, K. Ludwig, 27, 170
John Duns Scotus, see Scotus, John Duns
John of Bassolis, 83, 138, 164
John Teutonicus, 41, 45, 46, 53, 58, 115, 164
jurisdiction, 24, 50, 51, 80, 117, 118, 119

Kilmartin, E. 29, 170

Labontaine, P.H., 114, 115, 170
La Fontaine, P.-H., 112, 170
Laodicea, Council of, 7, 8, 40, 44, 114
Le Bras, G., 111, 170
Lechner, J., 133, 171
Leclercq, 10, 26, 171
Leff, G., 110, 144, 145, 171
Leo I, 5-6, 43, 112, 165
Luther, Martin, 104, 160, 165
Lynch, K.F., 111, 171

Macy, G., xi, xii, 1, 26, 29, 30, 171, 174, 181
Major, John, 102-4, 145, 158, 164, 169
Martha, 76, 133
Martin, J.H., xi, xii, 2, 29, 31, 97, 104, 150, 164, 171, 181-2
Mary, mother of Jesus, 28, 54, 70, 71, 81, 91, 96, 98, 103, 107, 119, 120, 129, 153
Mary Magdalene, 81, 136
Mary and Martha, 76, 132
Matins, 46, 53, 86
Mayeski, M.A., 19, 22, 26, 171
McFarlane, K.B., 148, 171
McNamara, J.A., 20, 172
Metz, R., 15-6, 19, 172
Mitchell, N., 3, 172
Morçay, R., 172
Morris, J., 1, 26, 118, 172
Muessig, C., 27, 172

Nelson, J., 27, 172
Netter, Thomas, 94-6, 149,
    150, 151, 167
Nominalism, 88, 89, 90, 101,
    102, 107, 144, 157
nuns, 1, 2, 3, 6, 7, 11, 12, 15,
    19, 20, 21, 42, 49, 53, 101,
    111, 119, 120, 121, 156

O'Meara, T., 171
Orbellis, Nicolas, 101, 156,
    165

Pasiecznik, M., 138, 172
Paul, Letters of, 31-2, 38, 43,
    45-6, 67-9, 70-1, 74, 76, 78,
    80, 81, 83, 91, 94, 95, 96,
    101, 105, 106, 109, 111,
    113, 114, 115, 116, 127,
    135, 150, 152, 154, 161,
    162, 164
        1 Corinthians, 32, 38,
    68, 69, 70, 71, 74, 84, 85,
    96, 103, 105, 111, 113, 115,
    125, 138, 146, 154
        1 Timothy, 25, 32, 38,
    45, 68, 69, 70, 71, 72, 76,
    78, 80, 91, 94, 95, 99, 100,
    103, 105, 115, 137, 138,
    146, 151, 152, 159
Peter Abelard, see Abelard,
    Peter
penance, 2, 3, 11, 14, 24, 27,
    65
Peter de la Palude, 83, 85, 138,
    139, 165
Peter of Poitiers, 36, 39, 110,
    111, 165
Peter of Tarentaise, 73, 121,

148, 165
Peter the Lombard, 14, 32, 33,
    34, 35, 36, 37, 38, 39, 52,
    79, 88, 93, 109, 110, 123,
    126, 163, 164, 165, 166,
    167, 168, 169, 175
preach, 11, 14, 15, 27, 32, 36,
    38, 43, 48, 52, 70, 76, 77,
    78, 83, 88, 91, 94, 95, 96,
    101, 104, 109, 111, 112,
    113, 118, 119, 133, 146,
    148, 152,
presbyterae, 6, 7, 8, 9, 12, 24,
    25, 44, 45, 74, 88, 114, 120
presbyterate, vii, xi, 3, 11, 15,
    24, 156
Principe, W., 30, 172
prophetess, 112, 155
Pryds, D., 27, 172

queen, xi, 4, 5, , 23, 98, 153

Raming, I., 11, 12, 24, 25, 27,
    28, 112, 175
Rand, L., 114, 173
Reginald of Piperno, 67, 166
Rezette, J., 123, 173
Richard of Middleton, 77-9,
    80-1, 132, 133, 166
Rigali, N., 30, 173
Robert of Arbrissel, 118, 166
Ross, S., 23, 30, 170, 173
Rule of St. Benedict, 22, 166
Rupert of Deutz, 13, 166
Rusconi, R., 27, 173

Schillebeeckx, E., 119, 173
Scotus, John Duns, 78, 79-83,
    87, 88, 89, 91, 97, 101, 107,

134, 137, 138, 164
Shahar, S., 109, 173
Simon of Hinton, 54-5, 121,
    166, 174
Smalley, B., 111, 173
Soter, 42, 52, 112, 119
Stegmuller, F., 158, 173
Stenton, M., 116, 117, 173
Stoelin, A., 153, 156, 173
subdiaconate, xi, 109
Sweeney, G., 30, 173

Tellenback, G., 111, 173
Thietmar of Merseburg, 166
Thomas Aquinas, see Aquinas,
    Thomas
Thomas of Strasbourg, 91-2,
    145, 167
Thomson, J.H., 148, 150, 173,
    173
Thurston, B., 23, 174
Tilley, T., 15, 29, 30, 174
Torjesen, K.J., 23, 24, 174
tradition, vii, 8, 15, 17, 22, 25,
    29, 30, 72, 81, 99, 100, 102,
    105, 106, 169

Ulrich of Strasbourg, 74-5,
    131, 167
Urban II, 5, 167

Van der Meer, H., 118, 174
virgin, 1, 12, 15, 22, 23, 116

Waldebert, 2, 21, 26, 27, 167
Walz, P.A., 121, 174
Weiler, A., 147, 174
Weisheipl, J.A., 32, 68, 174
Wemple, S. Fonay, 23, 24, 25,

26, 28, 174
widows, 1, 7, 15, 22, 23, 25,
    45, 53, 57, 114, 117, 120,
    121
William of Auxerre, 36, 38,
    110, 167
William of Ockham, 33, 75,
    89, 90, 97, 107, 143, 144,
    167, 168, 171
William of Rothwell, 55, 121,
    167
William of Rubio, 87, 141, 167
William of Vorrillon, 101,
    155, 167
Witherington, B., 23, 174
Workman, H.B., 148, 174
Wyclif, John, 93, 94, 95, 96,
    148, 149, 150, 151, 152, 174
Wyclifites, 94, 147, 148, 149

Zerfaß, R., 27, 174

About the Authors and Editors

Bernard Cooke, Ph.D. is a prominent U.S. theologian who has served as president of both the College Theology Society and the Catholic Theological Society of America and received from the latter its John Courtney Murray award. Following doctoral studies at the Institut catholique de Paris, where he abtained the doctorate in 1956, he has taught theology at Marquette, Boston College, Loyola of New Orleans, Santa Clara, Holy Cross (Worcester), Gonzaga, Incarnate Word (San Antonio), and San Diego Universities in the U.S. and the Universities of Windsor and Calgary in Canada. He has lectured widely in the U.S. and abroad. He is the author of more than twenty books and numerous articles, many of them dealing with sacramental ritual.

Gary Macy, Ph.D. is currently a professor in the Department of Theology and Religious Studies at the University of San Diego. He received both his bachelor's and his master's degrees from Marquette University where he specialized in historical and sacramental theology. He earned his doctoral degree in Divinity from Cambridge University in 1978. In 1991-1992 Dr. Macy was an Herodotus Fellow at the Institute for Advanced Studies at Princeton. Dr. Macy has published three books on the history of the Eucharist, *Theologies of the Eucharist in the Early Scholastic Period, The Banquet's Wisdom: A Short History of the Theologies of the Lord's Supper,* and most recently, *Treasures from the Storeroom: Essays on Medieval Religion and the Eucharist.* He has published and lectured extensively on medieval theology and religious practice and has received four national awards for his books and articles.

John Hilary Martin, O.P. completed his bachelor's, M. Div., and Lectorate in Theology degrees at the Dominican School of Philosophy and Theology in Berkeley. After Ordination he studied in England with the Dominican community of Blackfriars and received a M. Litt degree from the University of Oxford in 1960. After graduation he returned to Berkeley joining the faculty of the Dominican School which was soon to take part in the formation of the Graduate Theological Union, a consortium of six Protestant and three Roman Catholic theological schools. The 1960's was an exciting time to be engaged in ecumenical ventures with the interreligious dialogue just around the corner. In 1970, with this in mind, he went to study at UCLA and completed his Ph.D. there in 1978, specializing in history and the history of religions. From 1982 to the present Fr. Martin has spent a portion of his time living with aboriginal communities in Outback Australia on many occasions, especially with the aboriginal community at Wadeye (Port Keats), the same group which W.E.H. Stanner studied in 1935 and in the 1950's. Fr. Martin has been a Visiting Professor from time to time at the Yarra Theological Union in Melbourne and with the Australian Catholic University. His appointment remains with the doctoral faculty of the Graduate Theological Union at the Dominican School of Philosophy and Theology in Berkeley, California.